Meeting Shakespeare at the Bar

Reading the Bard Through the Lens of the Law

Len Niehoff

ABA
AMERICAN BAR ASSOCIATION
Litigation Section

Cover design by Jill Tedhams/ABA Design; Shakespeare image: eri/PIXTA; bottles and glasses image: Adobe Stock / liliya shlapak

Printed in the United States of America.

30 29 28 27 26 5 4 3 2 1

ISBN 978-1-63905-755-9

Library of Congress Cataloging-in-Publication Data
Names: Niehoff, Leonard M. author
Title: Meeting Shakespeare at the bar : reading the bard through the lens of the law / Len Niehoff.
Description: 1. | Chicago : American Bar Association, 2026. | Includes bibliographical references. | Summary: "A look at literature through the lens of the law using Shakespeare's works"--Provided by publisher.
Identifiers: LCCN 2025053315 (print) | LCCN 2025053316 (ebook) | ISBN 9781639057559 paperback | ISBN 9781639057566 epub
Subjects: LCSH: Shakespeare, William, 1564-1616--Knowledge--Law | Law in literature | Justice in literature | Trials in literature
Classification: LCC K240 .N54 2026 (print) | LCC K240 (ebook)
LC record available at https://lccn.loc.gov/2025053315
LC ebook record available at https://lccn.loc.gov/2025053316

For my wife, Lisa, and our son, Jordan

Contents

About the Author

Len Niehoff serves as Professor from Practice at the University of Michigan Law School, where he teaches courses in Civil Procedure, Evidence, First Amendment, Law & Theology, Legal Ethics, Media Law, and Shakespeare & the Law. He is the author of multiple books, more than 100 articles, and dozens of editorial columns. A practicing litigator for over forty years, he has been quoted as a legal expert by numerous major media outlets, including the *New York Times, Washington Post, Wall Street Journal*, and NPR. He holds degrees in law and English Literature from the University of Michigan.

Preface

Shakespeare really knew how to start a play. To take a familiar example, he opened *Hamlet* with the words "Who's there?," the perfect overture to an extended exploration of questions of identity. On the theme that beginnings matter, permit me to offer some background on the origins of this book.

The story begins with a Civil Procedure course that I have for many years taught to first-year first-term students at the University of Michigan Law School. That course addresses how civil lawsuits work, and it covers material that is both highly technical and mercilessly complicated. Ask a practicing lawyer what their hardest and least favorite class was in law school and many of them will without hesitation say: "Civil Procedure."

I know because they say it to me all the time.

After years of teaching the course, I realized that toward the end of October my students typically fell into a deep slump. They were no longer buoyed by the adrenaline that comes with starting law school, and they were not yet energized by the terror of imminent final examinations. That roomful of bright lights that I'd met on the first day of class had dimmed a little. I concluded that they needed a break from the rigors of legal doctrine and an opportunity to get refreshed and restarted.

To liven things up and rescue them from their creeping lethargy, I decided to throw them a Halloween party during our October 31 class session. I served cider and donuts and I invited students to wear costumes that had some connection with the material we'd addressed in the course.

Almost all of the students took me up on the invitation, with hilarious results. One year, several students, dressed as various players in a case we had studied, recreated with great poignancy the death of a cow on a railroad track. Another year, a diminutive student in nondescript clothing identified herself as the "short plain statement" required by the rule that governs complaints.

For the Halloween class, I also had my students read Arthur Miller's play *The Crucible*, a work whose subject—the Salem Witch Trials—felt appropriate to the season. I assumed that most of the students would have encountered the play before, as undergraduates or in high school. And I was right: almost all of them had read it on some previous occasion or had seen it performed. A couple of them had even acted in productions of it.

What I hoped they would discover was that now, with just a few months of legal education behind them, they experienced the play differently. I hoped they would see things in it that hadn't previously caught their attention, like concerns about the failure of due process, bias on the part of judges and juries, the blending of church and state, and the absence of effective rules of evidence. And see them they did, beyond my wildest expectations.

It's not unusual to think about the law through the lens of literature. For example, to varying degrees, and with varying levels of success, legal scholars and Supreme Court justices regularly draw on the conventions of literary interpretation to help us understand legal texts. But what I wanted my Civil Procedure students to do—and what they successfully did—was to reverse that process and to look at literature through the lens of the law.

I wanted them to read *The Crucible* as lawyers—or, at least, as future lawyers. To belabor the metaphor for a moment, I wanted them to understand that the law gives us a multifunctional lens that can zoom in, telescope out, bring things into focus, and capture the wide-angle perspective. In short, I wanted them to see that looking at *The Crucible* through the lens of the law brought them a fresh and important perspective to the play. It also gave them some equally fresh and important insights into the law. That's more than just an incidental benefit; I do, after all, teach at a law school.

After a few years of teaching *The Crucible* this way, I decided to try bringing the same approach to some of the plays of Shakespeare. At a personal level, the move was a natural one because I have been a dedicated student of Shakespeare's work my entire adult life. My passion for it set in many years ago, before I began my undergraduate studies, when I briefly served as an apprentice in a Shakespearean acting company—an engagement that was cut short by my realization that no sensible person would pay money to see me perform.

The move was also a natural one because of a close affinity that exists between Shakespeare's work and the nature of legal study. One of the challenges that law students (especially new ones) face is becoming comfortable with ambiguity and uncertainty. Life has taught them that right answers exist, but in law school we routinely engage with questions that don't have any.

So does Shakespeare.

Furthermore, a great deal of legal education consists in identifying the issues presented and laboring to properly frame the questions that those issues raise. In many instances, the asking isn't just something we do; it's the main thing we do. The asking is the point.

Again, the same holds true for Shakespeare.

Shakespeare biographer Jonathan Bate quotes Anton Chekhov as saying that "the task of the writer is not to solve the problem but to state the problem correctly," and Shakespeare's work is thick with this sensibility. For instance, Shakespeare could have written a play in which he makes unmistakably clear that Brutus should, or should not, have conspired to assassinate Julius Caesar; but it would not have been nearly as interesting, engaging, and morally provocative as the play that he wrote. And it would be no fun to teach.

I started my law school experiments with Shakespeare by conducting an abbreviated two-session mini-seminar in which we discussed *Measure for Measure* and *The Merchant of Venice*, plays with legal proceedings front and center in their plots. It went so well that I asked permission to expand the mini-seminar to a full course. My long-suffering and indulgent bosses generously granted the request, and a class on Shakespeare & the Law became part of my regular teaching rotation.

The conversations that my students and I have shared in our two-hour weekly meetings of that course inspired me to write the book you have in your hands.

My students come from diverse backgrounds, so those conversations ranged widely across worldviews, philosophies, and disciplines, and I've tried to carry that expansive spirit forward here. I've done so not just out of faithfulness to the depth, breadth, and variety of our classroom discussions, but out of the conviction that taking on big ideas is, well, very Shakespearean. An enterprise worthy of his name seems to me to try, in some humble sense, to tap into the greatness of soul and grandness of curiosity that characterize his work.

I can't recreate the excitement and the epiphanies that come with talking these things through in a roomful of inquisitive, inspired, and intellectually supercharged law students. But I hope you will experience this book as the next best thing: as a conversation of sorts. A conversation about what we see in Shakespeare's plays when we look at them through the lens of the law. A conversation about what such an approach helps us discover within the law—and within ourselves.

To write a book about Shakespeare is to engage in an extended exercise in humility. I have needed lots of help, I have gotten it, and I have many institutions and individuals to thank: the Litigation Section of the American Bar Association for approving and supporting this project; my wonderful liaison with the ABA, Michelle Oberts, for her invaluable counsel along the way; my candid and careful editor Edna Epstein, for her efforts with texts that arrived to her in various stages of disrepair; the University of Michigan Law School, for providing summer writing stipends; my law school colleague, Dorothy Kryskowski, for aid with the text; the students in my Shakespeare & the Law mini-seminar and seminars, for their boundless curiosity and goodwill; and, above all others, my wife and best friend Lisa Rudgers, for enthusiastically engaging with each chapter to make sure it would interest inquisitive non-lawyers as well as members of the legal profession.

As Will writes in *Twelfth Night*: "I can no other answer make but thanks, and thanks, and ever thanks."

With all that said, the fault for any errors or omissions lies with me and me alone. I wish that I had, like Will, an authorship controversy to hide behind so I could blame others for whatever fumbles may have found their way into the text. But, alas, what you have here is mine.

Because, like all writers, I am needful of grace, and out of respect for Will's gift for beginnings, I therefore start where he starts *Henry V*:

"Your humble patience I pray . . . gently to hear, kindly to judge."

Introduction

An Invitation to Roistering

In the summer of 2012, Martha Carlin, a history professor at the University of Wisconsin–Milwaukee, happened upon an obscure document in the Edinburgh University Library. It consisted of twenty-seven pages of notes, written by an anonymous author near the middle of the seventeenth century, and looked like nothing more than a messy old bundle of papers. Fortunately, digging into messy old bundles of papers is what historians do.

On closer inspection, Professor Carlin discovered that the document contained a treasure. A portion of it provided a rare glimpse into the personal life of perhaps the most famous person about whom we can confidently say the least: William Shakespeare. The passage described how Shakespeare and his "roystering associates," including fellow playwright Ben Johnson and actor Richard Burbage, gathered to meet at the Tabard Inn to talk, drink, and carve their names into the wooden panels of the inn's "large room."

Long before Shakespeare's merry band landed there, the Tabard Inn had serious literary cred. In the fifteenth century, Geoffrey Chaucer's *Canterbury Tales* made the inn famous as the site where his pilgrims began their legendary journey. Located in the relatively lawless Southwark suburb of London, the Tabard hosted not only religious seekers but also drunkards, criminals, and prostitutes. Think of it as part dive bar and part station of the cross.

An anecdote that places Shakespeare at the Tabard Inn takes some of its appeal from its historic resonance. Will and his artistic crew probably chose the venue precisely because of its connection with Chaucer and his masterpiece. They may have gathered there as a tip of the hat to literary tradition, just as today's writers stay at the Algonquin Hotel as a nod to its famous roundtable of wits.

But the story is also intriguing because it makes the towering, almost abstract, figure of William Shakespeare feel a bit more human, familiar, and accessible. The casual mischief of the tale brings those stodgy portraits of him to life. We can imagine him sitting at the Tabard, and we can imagine sitting there with him, laughing and telling tales, hoisting a tankard or three, and passing a bare bodkin for a little friendly vandalism on the tavern walls.

It helps foster the fantasy to remember that, in Shakespeare's time, the Tabard's regular patrons probably included lawyers. The inn sat opposite a courthouse, making it a convenient watering hole for thirsty ministers of justice. As long as there have been trials, there have been reasons for lawyers to gather after the proceedings to celebrate, lament, continue an argument, or share a war story—"with advantages," as Henry V says. The Tabard Inn seems like a promising destination for well-lubricated postmortems.

Perhaps, while Will and Ben and Dick exchanged barbs and talked about their triumphs and flops at one table, a coterie of lawyers did their own version of the same thing at another. Given the setting, it seems unlikely that those conversations took place in splendid isolation. And so maybe, just maybe, from time to time some lucky counselor found himself at Shakespeare's table, talking about justice and injustice, comparing the dramas of the stage and of the courtroom, ruminating over things legal and things not so much.

This book pursues the fantasy and invites you to that table. It brings you into the company of history's greatest master of perspective and best student of human nature and human institutions. It welcomes you into an extended dialogue with a mind and soul of unmatched clarity, depth, and empathic capacity. It ushers you into a bit of thoughtful and enjoyable roistering over some of the most magnificent plays ever written.

So, pull up a chair. Have a seat. And join our conversation about law, lawyers, life, and all things litigious. Mr. William Shakespeare has some thoughts. I'm sure you'll have some, too.

❂ ❂ ❂ ❂ ❂

An introduction to a book, like an opening statement at a trial, tells you what to expect. So, let me say a few words about what this book is and isn't.

In brief, this book is an effort to look at Shakespeare's plays through the interpretive and analytic lens that the law gives to us. I know from teaching my law school seminar on the subject that reading his plays this way leads us in lots of fascinating directions—more than "are dreamt of in our philosophy." But a commitment to this approach also means that there are some things this book isn't.

This isn't a book about the law of Elizabethan or Jacobean England. Although I may sometimes refer to legal principles that were in place at

Shakespeare's time, that's not our focus. We're out to see what we can learn about Shakespeare's plays by looking at them through the lens of *our* law, not *his*.

This also isn't a book about formal rhetoric. Shakespeare biographers agree that during his school years young Will would likely have been exposed *ad nauseum* to the technicalities and conventions of classical argument. I'll have occasion to refer to that training but, again, our focus lies elsewhere.

Finally, this isn't a book just for lawyers. Given the publisher and the subject matter it seems likely that many of my readers will have some connection with the legal profession. But, then, many of the attendees at Shakespeare's plays were lawyers, too, and, to say the least, he managed to write for a broader audience. I have tried to follow his example.

So, if you're not a member of the legal profession, please keep reading. And, if you are, please bear with me when I occasionally explain for the uninitiated a term or principle or fragment of legal doctrine that you already know. We want as many different kinds of people around the table as we can fit. Will was all about filling seats.

Reading Shakespeare from the perspective offered here takes us in some predictable directions. As we might expect, it provides insights into how Shakespeare viewed the institution of the law itself, not only as a vehicle for achieving an equitable and ordered society, but as a cudgel that is subject to manipulation and abuse. In these plays, the absence of law generally signals serious trouble, but its presence doesn't necessarily make things better, and its strict enforcement often leads to disaster.

As we also might expect, reading these plays in this way offers insights into how Shakespeare thought about trials and the various participants in them—lawyers, judges, witnesses, and parties. Shakespeare lived in a litigious time and was no stranger to lawsuits himself. Consistent with his approach to pretty much everything, Shakespeare painted a complex portrait of these proceedings and their players, a portrait made still richer when viewed from the perspective of current litigation practice.

But reading Shakespeare through the lens of the law draws us into some less obvious territory as well. Shakespeare was interested in the connection between mental health, competency, and moral responsibility—so is the law. Shakespeare was interested in marginalized people and the stigmas and prejudices that burden them—so is the law. Shakespeare was interested in evidence and in what counts as proof of a fact—so is the law. Shakespeare was interested in the problem of role morality, where behavior we would otherwise think ethically obnoxious finds its justification in the role someone holds within a society. The law is interested in that, too, as are the people who write the ethics rules that govern lawyers.

At times, so spacious an undertaking may seem to conflate two very different worlds: the world of Elizabethan and Jacobean England, on the one hand, and our modern world, on the other. When we explore issues like the antisemitism in *The Merchant of Venice*, or the brutal sexual violence of *Titus Andronicus*, or the racism of *Othello*, we may wonder whether we're fairly judging the playwright and the play or have unfairly imported contemporary sensibilities into our analysis.

I cordially invite you to put the concern aside. In doing so, it may help to remember that Shakespeare himself was quite comfortable with anachronisms and occasionally used them to connect an ancient setting with a contemporary dilemma. I've used them just as freely, and with the same goal of keeping these wonderful plays as familiar and relevant as possible.

Treating these plays as precious things fixed in amber would do a terrible kind of violence to them. We serve them best by approaching them as living things with an evergreen capacity to surprise us. And surprise us they do: As one prominent theatrical director of Shakespeare has observed, wherever we go in our thinking we are likely to find Will already there waiting for us.

I mentioned earlier that you don't need a law degree to read and enjoy this book. By the same token, you don't need to be a Shakespeare expert. In my seminar, I've had to develop a pedagogical approach that accounts for the fact that my students bring into the classroom a wide range of familiarity with Shakespeare's plays. Mindful of the potential variety of readers of this book, I've adopted a similar approach here.

We'll take one play at a time. Before reading each chapter, you may wish to read (or re-read) the play under discussion, or to view one of the film versions of it offered on a streaming service, or to breeze through a summary of its plot. (The Folger Shakespeare Library website contains excellent, very brief synopses of every play.) But you don't need to do any of that if you don't want to. I've tried to write each chapter so that you can follow its main points even if you don't know the play or haven't read it in a while.

I start each discussion with a section called "Backdrop." It tells you a little about when Shakespeare wrote the play (we think), what he was up to when he wrote it (to the extent we know), what he used (or probably used) as sources, what some critics have said about it, and why that particular play is a good candidate to view through the lens of the law.

Each chapter then goes on to look at two different law-related themes that the play under discussion explores. For example, in Chapter 1 we use *Titus Andronicus* to look at the problem of revenge and at the challenges presented by making violence—especially sexual violence—the subject of entertainment. As I suggested above, these exercises will send us off in all sorts of interesting directions, but don't blame me for the crazy diversity of subjects. Blame Shakespeare. He thought about pretty much everything, as does the law. So we will have to do so, too.

Before we plunge bravely ahead, however, I need to say a few things about Shakespeare's life, particularly the years leading up to the first play that we'll consider, *Titus Andronicus.* It's the kind of information you'll want to know before joining him over drinks. And, because we're going to spend a lot of time together, and get to know him passably well, from this point on I'm mostly going to address our mutual friend as "Will."

It's how I've come to think of him. I hope you'll come to think of him that way, too.

Will was born in April of 1564. We don't know the precise date of his birth, but church records indicate he was baptized on the 26th. Based on a variety of assumptions, by tradition we celebrate his birth on April 23rd. We mark his death on that same date in 1616.

Will was born in Stratford, a market town about 100 miles from London with a population of around 2,000. Stratford was a rural community, surrounded by fields, pastures, and woods. You might say that Will grew up a country boy, but his father's various activities also exposed him to the spheres of politics and commerce. As we'll see, that exposure wouldn't always have left a positive impression.

Infant mortality was high at the time; indeed, Will's parents had earlier lost two children. Shortly after his birth, an outbreak of plague struck England, and plague would come and go throughout Will's life, sometimes closing the theaters on which his livelihood depended. But for the plague, we might not have some of Shakespeare's greatest poetry, his lifelong Plan B when the stage shut down.

Will was born into an ostensibly Protestant country, where Catholics were condemned and persecuted. But he came from Catholic stock, and he spent his formative years in a part of Warwickshire that the government viewed as stubbornly, if surreptitiously, Catholic. Some scholars think that his father remained a dedicated Catholic, despite the prohibition and potential risks, but the matter has been widely debated.

In many ways England flourished under Queen Elizabeth, who occupied the throne at the time of Will's birth and would do so until his career was well established. But there was a constant drumbeat of plots against her throughout her reign, and it was a time of profound political danger and instability. Because she never married or bore a child, the worrisome question of succession hung over her rule.

Physical danger and horrific violence were common in the England that Will knew. In London, especially the parts Will haunted later in his life, street crime was by our standards rampant. Shakespeare biographer Michael Wood notes that when Will achieved adulthood he probably carried a sword, and not just for show.

Gruesome violence was a matter of official policy and everyday entertainment. Executions were fairly routine events, the methods used could be unspeakably brutal, and the heads of the dispatched were frequently displayed on pikes near the city's entrance. Cockfighting and bearbaiting were wildly popular. And audiences flocked to see blood-soaked plays, a point clearly not lost on the blossoming playwright.

Will's father, John, came from a line of farmers, as did many people in Stratford. John initially worked as a glover, a skilled trade, but moved into government service and held a series of increasingly important municipal positions. Eventually he became High Bailiff, the functional equivalent of Mayor, acquired real estate, and applied for a coat of arms.

Will's mother, Mary Arden, came from a well-regarded family and could claim ancestors who fought in famous battles. Her father was a man of standing within Stratford and from him she inherited some money and land. We don't know for certain, but it seems likely that both of Shakespeare's parents were literate. For much of Will's early life, his parents exhibited all the signs of genteel respectability and financial promise—but then something went wrong.

We know that John abruptly left office in 1576 and that by 1578 the family was selling off land and other property. We don't know exactly why, but the evidence suggests that John had become embroiled in two lucrative, but forbidden and highly risky, activities: dealing in wool without a license and loaning money at interest. The wool trade collapsed in 1576–77 and it appears that John's fortunes went with it. The Shakespeare family did not lose everything, but clearly these events cast them into substantial distress. The coat of arms would have to wait.

We have no record of Will's formal education, but as the son of the High Bailiff he would have been entitled to attend the town's free school, and there is no reason to think his parents would have forgone the opportunity to send him there. Such schooling typically began at age 7 and consisted largely in relentless drilling on classical languages (especially Latin), formal rhetoric, and English history. Under ordinary circumstances, this education ended at around 15 or 16, which many students probably thought none too soon, but Will may have left school earlier because of the family's money troubles.

What Will did with himself from 1578 to 1582, our first set of lost years, is anyone's guess, and just about everyone has guessed at it. All we know for sure is that he resurfaces for us again in 1582, at age 18, when he applies for a marriage license. His betrothed was Anne Hathaway, who at 26 was older than Will and pregnant. Will and Anne went on to have three children, Susanna (born in 1583) and Hamnet and Judith (born in 1585).

After the arrival of Judith and Hamnet, our record of Will's activities again goes dark. Theories abound as to what he did from 1585 to 1592, our second set of lost years. My favorite invention comes from the eighteenth-century critic Samuel Johnson, who concocted a theory that Will started his London career by tending to people's horses when they arrived at the theater and then worked his way up from there. Shakespeare scholar Stephen Greenblatt dismisses the theory as a charming but utterly implausible fantasy that casts Will as the "patron saint of parking attendants."

In any event, in 1592 a remarkable thing happened: Shakespeare's name started appearing in reviews as a young London dramatist who was attracting attention. It's in this year that the figure we know as William Shakespeare steps out of the shadows and into the light. And scholars concur that one of his earliest plays was *Titus Andronicus*, the first play we'll look at through the lens of the law.

It's a tough and haunting piece of theater and we have our work cut out for us. But, come, lean into the conversation. There's a lot to explore here.

And we are in the company of one of the stage's greatest explorers.

1

"A Wilderness of Tigers"

Titus Andronicus

Backdrop

As we'll discuss in future chapters, Shakespeare based some of his works on a single identifiable source, like a historical chronicle or an earlier play. *Titus Andronicus*, in contrast, reflects lots of scattered influences: the "theatre of cruelty" of the Roman playwright Seneca, the Elizabethan revenge plays that were popular at the time, and a mishmash of classical myths and medieval folktales. In *Titus Andronicus*, Will brought all these influences together in a hot and pungent stew—perhaps an unfortunate metaphor, given that the play ends with a mother cannibalizing her two sons.

Brace yourself. Even through our jaundiced twenty-first-century eyes, *Titus Andronicus* is a stunningly violent play. Michael Wood calls it "the Elizabethan equivalent of a Quentin Tarantino movie," and I think that understates matters. Earlier generations of critics found the work so repellent that they doubted Will wrote it. The evidence suggests that his audiences loved the play, perhaps because of all the bloodshed rather than in spite of it.

Modern scholars generally accept the play's authorship but their critical assessments vary wildly. Harold Bloom held the view that *Titus* amounted to nothing more than Shakespeare's effort to prove he could dream up a more outrageously violent play than his rivals. Bloom could "concede no intrinsic value" to the work and confessed that, having seen it performed once, he didn't plan ever to see it again.

Marjorie Garber, on the other hand, has described the play as "undervalued or misunderstood." Yes, she acknowledges, *Titus* is an early effort, but she believes that it shows Shakespeare already "very much in command of both his theater and his plot." Her assessment: "In many ways," such as its "unrelenting pileup of horrors, *Titus* is the most modern play of Shakespeare's that we have." With all due respect to Harold Bloom, whose analyses I always find thought-provoking, I'm with Marjorie Garber on this one.

Like Garber, I view *Titus* as a powerful and disquietingly modern piece of work that gives us lots of food for thought—as it were. But it's also unrelentingly hard and gruesome, and definitely not for everyone, and we need to approach it with our eyes wide open and our loins girded. I'm a fan of the play, but as Samuel Johnson said of John Milton's epic poem *Paradise Lost*, "None ever wished it longer than it is."

At first glance, *Titus Andronicus* may not appear to have much to do with the law. To the contrary, it may seem like an utterly lawless play, where everyone kills anyone they want based on whatever whim or malice moves them at the moment. Sure, consequences to all this villainy follow, and they uniformly are not good, but they don't come from the law. When Titus exclaims in Act IV that Justice has fled the earth, the observation seems spot on.

Nevertheless, I believe that *Titus Andronicus* has a lot to do with the law. It provides intriguing insights into two issues of keen and persistent interest to legal scholars and others who think about how our legal system functions. The first of those issues is the problem of revenge, which remains more with us today than we like to admit. And the second is the problem of using graphic violence—especially sexual violence—as entertainment. Like revenge, we've continued to make that part of our lives as well, our claims to qualifying as civilized people notwithstanding.

Let's sit down with Will and listen closely to what he has to say.

We can even share some stories of our own.

With your indulgence, I'll start us off.

Revenge and the Law

Over my forty-plus years of practicing law, I've represented lots of clients. I know from experience that if you ask clients what they want out of litigation, most of them will say something like "fair compensation" or "justice" or "my day in court" or "for the truth to be known." But what a lot of them really want is revenge—in the case of plaintiffs, for what was done to them, in the case of defendants, for the insult of having been hauled into court.

When in the Bible the Lord said that vengeance was His, He clearly hadn't checked first with the average client.

I've never had a client use the word "revenge" in describing the outcome they were after. I suspect that the language sounds too archaic or overreaching or, well, Shakespearean. But, when clients talk honestly about what they hope to achieve in a lawsuit, it's not unusual for them to slip into territory that—in tone or substance—at least hints at revenge. And I get the message, even if they don't expressly mention dancing on the graves of the opposing party's ancestors.

To be honest, sometimes lawyers want revenge, too. Years ago, an attorney who I held in less than stellar regard brought a frivolous lawsuit against one of my clients. When I threatened to seek sanctions against him—that is, to have the judge order him to pay me my attorney fees—he dropped the case. Then, after a brief pause for refreshment, he brought an almost identical case against my client in a different court. When I threatened sanctions again, he sent me the nastiest and most unprofessional letter I have ever received.

I will confess to wanting revenge.

And, eighty thousand dollars in sanctions against him later, I got it.

We often think of revenge in simple terms, if we think about it all, which we may studiously avoid if we fancy ourselves decent human beings with modern sensibilities. But it turns out that the matter of revenge is complicated and that it has interesting and important connections with the law—including *our* law. No one has thought about those connections more deeply or provocatively than William Ian ("Bill") Miller, one of my colleagues at the University of Michigan Law School. Bill is an Olympic-level polymath who has published wonderful books on everything from courage to disgust to humiliation to getting older. But he is perhaps best known for his writings on Icelandic blood-feud literature and on the idea of revenge.

Those writings include a highly engaging 1999 essay in which Bill argues, as he puts it, "in defense of revenge." He begins the piece by acknowledging that "Officially revenge is a bad thing." It has become "vulgar and unfashionable, a source of embarrassment to the refined."

In our current thinking, Bill argues, we like to distinguish revenge from the rule of law. That distinction depends, however, on us viewing revenge in a certain way. For the contrast to hold up, we have to imagine revenge as reflecting a culture of anarchy in which anything goes and everyone grants themselves the unilateral authority to respond as they like to injuries both real and imagined. The rule of law differs from this concept of revenge in many ways, including in that it has rules. And law.

But Bill argues that this understanding of revenge is historically inaccurate and ignores the close relationship that has often existed (and may still exist) between revenge and law. He cites as an example the legal order represented in the ancient Icelandic sagas. Parts of that social structure do indeed look a lot like revenge; but other parts set limitations on who could do what and to whom they could do it—and those parts look like law.

Here's an example. Say that you're an Icelandic Viking, as you have perhaps always wanted to be. And say that someone has killed a member of your family. May you sue them? Yes. If you win, what's the penalty? They will be made an outlaw. May you kill them? Yes; in fact, you are obligated to do so if you can. May someone else kill them? Yes. May you kill another member of the perpetrator's family? No; that's outside the rules. Bill writes: "Law can go a long way toward countenancing revenge and still remain law."

Indeed it can. After the 1995 bombing of the Alfred P. Murrah Federal Building in Oklahoma City, I found myself in a frank conversation with a friend who had been a lifelong opponent of capital punishment. He'd closely followed the news coverage of the event and had wept over the photographs of the carnage, especially the famous one of the fireman holding the dead infant from the building's childcare center.

My friend told me that he wanted to see Timothy McVeigh executed. I asked why, in light of all the arguments I'd heard him make over the years against the death penalty. He said one word: "Revenge." A lot of people may have felt the same way. But we would be hard pressed to argue that the judgment condemning McVeigh to death didn't "remain law" just the same.

To get at the complexity of our contemporary relationship with revenge, Bill directs our attention to popular films where an avenging figure has a key role. The vengeance film, he notes, follows a particular formula: Someone commits a terrible wrong against the protagonist. The wrong creates a kind of debt on which the protagonist has a legitimate claim to collect. The protagonist wants payback, and they get it, and we cheer them on as they do. We find the whole thing deeply satisfying. I recently watched with bemused interest while one of the kindest people I know leapt to her feet and cheered at a movie when a sadistic Nazi character took a bullet between the eyebrows.

A common theme in these movies, Bill points out, is the inadequacy of the law. The wrongdoer evades punishment as the result of a legal technicality or other failure within the system. For justice to get done, our protagonist must take matters into their own hands. We root the avenger along because they have moral (if extralegal) grounds for doing what they do. It's a simple equation, Bill writes: "Dirty Harry knows you will be outraged by the wrongdoer, hate him for what he has done and who he is, and experience the satisfaction of justice done when Harry makes your day by blowing him away."

A maxim of La Rochefoucauld holds that hypocrisy is the tribute that vice pays to virtue. As Bill Miller says, our official position is that revenge is bad. But, in the right context, it feels awfully good. And oh how we delight in watching it happen. Now *that's* entertainment.

❂ ❂ ❂ ❂ ❂

Titus Andronicus toys with everything we think we know about revenge, about law, and about the relationship between them. And it does so starting right in the very first scene of the very first act, when the formidable Roman general Titus Andronicus kills the son of Tamora, queen of the Goths, with whom he has been at war. This incident gets the play going by challenging one of the assumptions we may make about how revenge operates—or, at least, should operate.

The assumption I'm talking about is that revenge, when properly executed, has a kind of proportionality to it. That proportionality helps justify the action and removes it from the realm of uncontrolled self-indulgent mayhem. To use Bill Miller's metaphor, the avenger has the right to collect on the debt owed, but nothing more. We imagine a "mathematics of revenge" by which the debt is discharged, a score is settled, and justice is done.

The Icelandic laws that Bill Miller describes reflect such a spirit of proportionality. Under this system, if one man kills another man's brother, then the surviving brother can kill the murderer and stay within the boundaries of justice. But the surviving brother would breach those boundaries by killing anyone else, like multiple members of the murderer's family. That's the sort of thing done by a petulant Mafia boss who wants to send a message, not by a righteous avenger who wants to settle a debt so society can go on about its business.

Shakespeare begins *Titus Andronicus* by showing us that the messiness of human interactions undermines any sensible notion of a mathematics of revenge. Violence doesn't yield a clear retributive calculation, especially in war. So, we learn almost immediately that Titus has lost twenty-one sons to the Goths, suggesting he that he is entitled to revenge. But is he? Surely, he has killed more than that number of Goths along the way. How do we determine who is really ahead in the body count? And which bodies matter for these purposes?

Let's assume that we could make such a calculation and confirm that Titus is down by twenty-one. What is a proportional response? Killing twenty-one Goths, some or all of whom may be blameless in these events, seems excessive. At the same time, killing just one of Tamora's sons seems paltry and random. Is there a formula that tells us the answer?

As the play unfolds, any idea of a meaningful mathematics of revenge vaporizes. Titus has taken his vengeance, but Tamora believes that his execution of her son entitles her to strike back. With the help of her lover Aaron and her sons, she exacts a fearsome price: two of Titus's sons are killed; Titus gives up his hand in an effort to save them; and Tamora's sons rape and disfigure Titus's daughter Lavinia, robbing her of her honor, dignity, virginity, bodily autonomy and integrity, limbs, and tongue. This seems like a wildly disproportionate response, but at what point does it become so?

And then there's this: Do Tamora's excesses entitle Titus to another round of revenge? Alas, Tamora had only two more sons for Titus to take. But was it permissible for Titus to make up in cruelty what he lacked in quantity by murdering her sons, baking them into a pie, and serving them to her on a plate? How do we factor cruelty into the calculation?

Titus Andronicus shows us that the mathematics of revenge is an illusion. The inherent disorder of human interactions, and the deeply personal level at which a wronged person experiences their suffering, precludes anything like a reliable estimate of when enough is enough. We see this play out in courtrooms, where bitter feuds drag on so long that they deplete the very resources the fight concerns, like the case of *Jarndyce v. Jarndyce* in Charles Dickens's novel *Bleak House*. And we see it play out on the international stage, where peace is deferred over and over again because there's always a new wrong to avenge.

We wait in sad perpetuity for things finally to be deemed "even." They never are. They never can be.

It doesn't work that way in the real world.

When I teach *Titus Andronicus* to law students, I ask them whether the various acts of revenge that occur in the play—particularly toward the end—leave us with the sort of satisfaction that Bill Miller finds in contemporary vengeance films. To a person, they say no. Indeed, it's hard to imagine anyone leaping out of their seat and cheering as the vengeance of this play reaches its climax at the banquet. I think there are a couple reasons this is so.

One relates to our revulsion at the filial cannibalism. The banquet scene is hard to read and harder to watch. Marjorie Garber says that she found its portrayal in Julie Taymor's film *Titus* so repugnant that it converted her to vegetarianism. Revulsion does some work here, perhaps, but I find a different explanation more persuasive.

The contemporary films that Bill describes satisfy us because they imagine—and then honor—a mathematics of revenge that *Titus* rejects as a fantasy. In those movies, the hero's response to the wrong feels proportional, even if it is not mathematically precise, leaving us with a sense that justice has been done. We root for the protagonist because the villain gets what they deserve.

In contrast, no one deserves to have their children cooked up and served to them as a main course—not even Tamora, although she might at least qualify as a contender. But *Titus Andronicus* tells us that this place—the excessively punitive place that no one deserves—is exactly where you end up if you follow your imagined mathematics of revenge to its inevitable conclusion. The only certainty about the mathematics of revenge is that it will not play out mathematically.

Will's grim depiction of the ineluctable consequences of revenge might prompt us to think of the law as the sound and civilized alternative. But Will saw the complexity in everything, and the law is no exception. So, alas, when the law enters the story in *Titus Andronicus*, which it does only rarely, things don't go much better.

The closest thing we have to a legal proceeding in the play comes in the third scene of Act II. Aaron concocts a plan, which he shares with Tamora, to kill Bassianus, the brother of king Saturninus, and to frame Titus's sons for the murder. He hides a bag of gold in a pit. Tamora's sons stab Bassianus to death and place his body near the treasure. Aaron leads Titus's sons to the pit, where both fall in.

At this point, Saturninus enters the scene and finds his brother murdered and Titus's sons beside the body. Tamora produces a convenient piece of evidence—a letter that reflects a plot to kill Bassianus—and Saturninus promptly concludes that Titus's sons slew his brother for the treasure. Saturninus orders them dragged to prison, to languish there until he has "devised some never-heard-of torturing pain for them." Given the brutality of the *heard-of* torturing pains known to Will's audience (such as hanging, drawing, and quartering), that command must have drawn a shudder.

Titus pleads for his sons, but without success. Saturninus declares that "the guilt is plain." Case closed. Off with their heads.

So much for the law.

Granted, we have law here, in the sense that no one denies Saturninus's authority to adjudicate the guilt or innocence of Titus's sons. But this law comes without due process, without a presumption of innocence, without an opportunity to be heard, without cross-examination or counterargument, and without representation. In short, this law comes without any of the things that make an adjudication fair and just. This law looks a lot like revenge.

To my mind, it is this keen skepticism about human institutions—even more than the play's raw violence—that makes *Titus Andronicus* so palpably modern. The play tells us that the mathematics of revenge is illusory. It tells us that, by its very nature, vengeance will yield disproportionate consequences. It tells us that we cannot hope for justice while also leaving the matter of adjudication to the wronged person—the one least likely to be able to recognize and maintain proportionality.

But the play goes further. It also warns us against believing that law will come to the rescue—particularly if we define law solely by reference to its authority. It tells us that, in the end, the only difference between law and revenge may be who does the chopping.

In this sense, *Titus* invites a question that we usually frame today by reference to Nazi rule. If a morally corrupt and unjust regime creates a terrible law, is it still law? Do we still have some obligation to honor it? Why or why not? Stay tuned: We will meet this theme over and over again in Shakespeare's plays. Just as we sometimes meet it in the morning news.

Titus Andronicus remains powerful and relevant, especially for those of us who are interested in the law, precisely because we have not put the problems it describes to rest. The dilemmas of law, revenge, and proportionality that the play explores are as present now as ever. To paraphrase William Faulkner, that past is not dead.

It is not even past.

Violence as Entertainment

As I noted earlier, Harold Bloom dismissed *Titus Andronicus* as Shakespeare's sophomoric effort to write a play that bested his rivals in its gory brutality. If that's right, then Will had some formidable competition. Plays like Christopher Marlowe's *Tamburlaine* and Thomas Kyd's *Spanish Tragedy* drew heavily on the traditions of Seneca's "theatre of cruelty." Bloom imagines young Will saying "Here, hold my ale" and setting out to show everybody else how it's done.

Bloom views the violence of *Titus* as so extreme as to become grimly comic, better fodder for Mel Brooks than Kenneth Branagh, and I see what he means. In a notorious episode in Act III, for example, Titus finds himself with an awkward problem: He needs to depart the scene with the heads of his two sons and his severed hand, more than he can carry in his present state. He takes one head, his brother takes another, and this leaves the matter of the hand, which Lavinia cannot carry because she has no hands of her own. So, Titus asks her to take the amputated appendage in her mouth, which she does, and off they go. This over-the-top episode can prompt the sort of nervous, defensive laughter that we sometimes hear in movie theaters in response to a particularly grisly scene in a slasher horror film.

I hesitate to argue with so revered a critic as Harold Bloom, but arguing is what I do for a living, and I don't take *Titus Andronicus* to be a juvenile exercise in violence for its own sake or an extended exhibition of the playwright's ability to make us feel revolted. Rather, I see *Titus* as calling a very important and perpetually relevant question, although it does so indirectly and implicitly. In short, I think that the extreme nature of the play's violence compels anyone in the audience who has even a shred of decency to ask why they have come to a play like this for—of all things—entertainment. Those people who walk out of the theater midway through a performance of *Titus Andronicus*, as they sometimes do, have presumably found the question unanswerable.

❖ ❖ ❖ ❖ ❖

From time to time, our country's laws have struggled with this issue, exploring whether we should censor graphically violent texts and images produced for "entertainment" purposes. We can roll our eyes at some of these efforts, like the mid-twentieth-century movement to keep comic books out of the hands of children to ensure they didn't have any fun. But worries about our society's culture of violence, and particularly about the desensitization of children to acts of brutality, have persisted into our own time, and not without reason.

Consider, for example, the 2011 Supreme Court case of *Brown v. Entertainment Merchants Association.* That case involved a California law that restricted the sale or rental of violent video games to minors. One might think that such a regulation would appeal to a legally and socially conservative jurist like Antonin Scalia. But he wrote the majority opinion holding the statute unconstitutional.

The California legislature's impulse to try to keep these games out of the hands of minors is understandable. In an opinion concurring in the result, but not in the Court's reasoning, Justice Alito offered an unsettling description of what the games had to offer:

> In some of these games, the violence is astounding. Victims by the dozens are killed with every imaginable implement, including machineguns, shotguns, clubs, hammers, axes, swords, and chainsaws. Victims are dismembered, decapitated, disemboweled, set on fire, and chopped into little pieces. They cry out in agony and beg for mercy. Blood gushes, splatters, and pools. Severed body parts and gobs of human remains are graphically shown. In some games, points are awarded based, not only on the number of victims killed, but on the killing technique employed.
>
> It also appears that there is no antisocial theme too base for some in the video-game industry to exploit. There are games in which a player can take on the identity and reenact the killings carried out by the perpetrators of the murders at Columbine High School and Virginia Tech. The objective of one game is to rape a mother and her daughters; in another, the goal is to rape Native American women. There is a game in which players engage in "ethnic cleansing" and can choose to gun down African-Americans, Latinos, or Jews. In still another game, players attempt to fire a rifle shot into the head of President Kennedy as his motorcade passes by the Texas School Book Depository.

Justice Alito found the interactive nature of the technology especially distressing, and we can use *Titus* to explain why. The rape and mutilation of Lavinia, horrific as it is, takes place off stage; it would elevate the violence of a production to show it; and, surely, an audience would soundly reject as morally reprehensible a version that invited them to don virtual reality gear and play the role of the assailants—as a game.

A majority of the Court nevertheless had little trouble finding the statute unconstitutional. Its reasoning was pretty straightforward: A well-settled principle of First Amendment doctrine holds that, as a general proposition, the government can't restrict access to speech based on its content. Over the years, the Supreme Court has grudgingly recognized some exceptions, for example with respect to sexually obscene material. But the Court has never held that speech falls outside of First Amendment protections because it contains violent passages or images.

Furthermore, minors have many of the same First Amendment rights as adults. The California statute could therefore pass constitutional muster only if it met the demanding "strict scrutiny" test, adopting a narrowly tailored method for advancing a compelling state interest. The Court held that the law failed that test, an unsurprising result given that most laws to which the Court has applied strict scrutiny have died under its weight.

I should note in passing that any government effort to restrict speech based on its violent content would face other serious challenges as well. Among them, it's not at all clear how a law could draw a workable and sensible line between the violence that we deem acceptable and socially valuable and that which we deem excessive and socially dangerous. And the risks of getting the line wrong are substantial because so much violence appears in so many works that we view as not only important but as cornerstones of civilization. Those works include the Bible, the *Iliad*, the *Odyssey*, the *Aeneid*, and, now that you mention it, the plays of Shakespeare.

Brown answers a legal question and, in my view, does so correctly. But no court can answer the moral question that I posed above, and that I think *Titus Andronicus* places squarely before us. Granted, we may have the right to read such material and see it performed. But why is doing so, especially for entertainment purposes, ethically justifiable? What value does such a work bring into our lives, assuming that it brings any at all?

A cynic might argue that we protect the wide dissemination of such works because they cultivate an attitude toward violence that our society finds sinisterly useful. A society that glorifies violence, and desensitizes people to it, has an easier time rallying its citizens to go to war and kill on its behalf. We will encounter this idea again when we consider *Coriolanus*, where various figures struggle with how to think about a man who they fear and view as dangerous—but who they also reluctantly come to recognize as necessary to their survival.

In my view, however, *Titus Andronicus* has its value elsewhere, in a very different and actually subversive dynamic. I think that the questions called by the play force us to recognize our own complicity in its violence. Shakespeare could not make us direct participants in the drama, like modern video games do; but he could do the next best thing. He could make us into voyeurs, leaving us to grapple (or not) with the significance of having come to such a play for its "pleasures."

A contemporary analogy may help here. If you had to give an award for "most disturbing film ever made," you might be able to make the case for a 1997 Austrian movie called *Funny Games*. In the film, two young men—who present as clean-cut and normal—manipulate their way into a family's home, torture them, and eventually murder all of them, right down to their pet dog. The violence is brutal and nauseating, even though some of it is conveyed only by suggestion.

What makes the film so haunting is that from time to time—including at the very end—one of the murderers looks directly into the camera and smiles slyly at the viewer. The creepiness of the effect lies in how it outs us as co-conspirators in the very violence that repels us. Any healthy person feels disgust at the young men's ghoulish use of bloodshed for entertainment; and, yet, there we are, doing the same thing.

As I suggested in the last section, *Titus Andronicus* leaves us with lots of unsettling questions about the law and revenge. But perhaps its most disturbing questions ask what kind of person finds entertainment in so horrible a play. In this sense, *Titus Andronicus* does not, in the words of Prince Hamlet, hold the mirror up to nature. It holds the mirror up to *our* nature.

And we may not like what we see.

If we could meet Shakespeare at the bar, we could ask him whether he had anything like this in mind. Given the pervasive and casual violence of his time, it may seem unlikely that he did. But who knows?

"In my mind's eye," I imagine posing the question to Will and then watching as he turns his gaze from mine. He carves something into the tavern wall. He sips his drink. He smiles an enigmatic smile.

And so it goes. Never telling. Always asking.

2

"These Dangerous Days"

Henry VI, Part 2

Backdrop

In his book *Young Shakespeare*, Russell Fraser describes a strategy used by fowlers in Elizabethan times. In order to keep from spooking their prey, bird hunters hid behind "an old nag or a piece of painted canvas" as they crept along through the forest. When they got close to their game, they'd peek up from behind their cover and take their shot. The practice gives us our phrase "stalking horse," which has come to mean any device someone uses to camouflage their true purpose.

Trial lawyers use stalking horses all the time. Granted, every good advocate has to face head on the challenges that their cases present. But gifted litigators are also masters of the art of misdirection.

I make the point every term during one of the first meetings of my law school Evidence course. At the start of class, I perform a simple magic trick: I mysteriously transform a soap bubble into a solid glass ball. The students burst into applause.

I tell them: "If I fooled you, it's because I made you look the wrong way." I explain that this is exactly what many lawyers try to do during trials—they try to make the jury look the wrong way. Our evidence rules exist to keep lawyers from getting away with it, or at least from getting away with too much of it.

Fraser observes that in many of his plays Shakespeare employed a stalking horse of his own: history. In Will's time, writing a play that expressly portrayed current or recent events was fraught with personal and professional peril. In 1581, Queen Elizabeth ordered that all plays proposed for performance had first to be submitted to the Master of Revels for inspection for political and religious sedition. Sedition was severely punished, so a misstep could result in the loss of a job, an audience, or a head. Because young Will favored keeping as many of these as possible, he needed a strategy.

He found it in the past. Early on, he discovered that he could write about many of the themes and ideas that interested him as long as he set his play in another age. So, for example, although we don't have plays from him entitled *Queen Elizabeth* or *King James* that discuss the delicate process by which rule moved from the former to the latter, many of his plays use historic events to explore issues of succession and the transfer of power—issues that Will knew were of keen interest to his audiences.

As Stephen Greenblatt observes in his book *Tyrant: Shakespeare on Politics*, Will "carefully kept at least a full century between himself and the events he depicted." A change of locale afforded even more distance and insulation. So, if Will wanted to write a play about contested governance, he could set it in ancient Rome, call it *Titus Andronicus*, and write pretty much whatever he wanted—precisely what he did in the opening chapter of that play.

With that said, theater audiences in sixteenth- and seventeenth-century London were not made up of idiots. They must have understood a great deal of what Will was doing. The trick didn't even fool Queen Elizabeth, who is said to have recognized herself in the protagonist of the play we'll discuss in the next chapter, *Richard II*. That she did so came dangerously close to shortening Will's career, if not shortening Will himself.

Nevertheless, as a general proposition the relatively safe cover of history gave Will plenty of opportunity to launch the arrows he wanted. Plus, the audiences loved the plays and came to see them in droves. A practical man always eager to make a good living, Will responded accordingly.

A commonly proposed timeline of Shakespeare's works indicates that four of his first seven plays were English histories. If you accept his authorship of *Edward III*, then that's yet another. As Greenblatt notes in *Tyrant*, "The [three] parts of *King Henry VI* are now among his least-known plays, but they first made him famous." That includes his inaugural history play, *Henry VI, Part 2*, the play we look at together in this chapter.

Scholars believe that Shakespeare wrote *Henry VI, Part 2* around the same time he wrote *Titus Andronicus*, perhaps even a couple years earlier. If you're wondering why the first play he wrote in the series is called Part 2, it's because he later wrote a prequel that we call Part 1. The *Star Wars* films may have perfected the prequel, but they didn't invent it.

Unlike *Titus Andronicus*, this play draws on a small number of easily identifiable sources. For historical background, Shakespeare turned to the 1587 edition of Holinshed's *Chronicles* and Hall's *The union of the two noble and illustre families of Lancastre and Yorke*, written in 1550. Shakespeare would go back to these sources again, especially the *Chronicles*, in writing some of his most famous plays, like *Macbeth* and *King Lear.*

Let's try to imagine young Will's life at the time. His family remained in Stratford while he labored away on plays in London. We don't know exactly where in London he lived when he first arrived, but by 1596 he had taken up residence in the small parish of St. Helen's Bishopsgate. We can say this with confidence because records indicate he failed to pay his taxes there—a lapse for which his biographers are grateful.

Will probably spent a lot of his time in tough, hardscrabble neighborhoods because that's where most of the theaters and other performance venues were located, by design. Entertainment was a popular industry, but it was also a disreputable one, especially through the eyes of the Puritans. As a result, it got pushed off into the Elizabethan equivalent of red-light districts.

Plague closed the theaters in 1593, compelling Shakespeare to turn his efforts to poetry. But by 1594, when Will probably wrote *Titus*, things were up and running again and he helped found a theater company called the Lord Chamberlain's Men. This group would later become the King's Men, with Richard Burbage serving as its lead player when he wasn't busy drinking with Will at the Tabard Inn.

We can envision Will sitting in a dirty and fairly dangerous post-plague part of London, his head swirling with ideas. He needed a great story to seize and hold the attention of his audiences. Why not draw from English history and, particularly, from the grand and glorious tales of the English kings?

Someone who didn't know much about the history of England might imagine its kings as a succession of figures like the Arthur of legend—dashing, chivalrous, and romantic. But, as John Julius Norwich observes in his book *Shakespeare's Kings*, nothing could be further from the truth. He writes: "With the doubtful exception of Richard the Lionheart, Henry V is the only King of England who is still generally perceived as a hero. Whether he deserved the title must be open to question."

Even within this motley company, Henry VI might seem like an odd subject for a young playwright's first historical venture. Henry ascended to the throne at an age just shy of nine months, so, to say the least, at the beginning of his rule somebody else was running the country. As he grew older and into the job, it became evident to everyone that he was completely unfit for the doing of it.

He was ostentatiously pious, attending formal worship services several times a day. At feasts he wore a hair shirt underneath his robes, presumably to eliminate any risk that he might have a good time. But, Norwich argues, his "chief fault was that he was impressionable and almost pathetically easily led" by the various unscrupulous figures that surrounded him. "More dangerous still," Norwich adds, "he soon showed himself to be alarmingly lacking in political judgment." Over time, he also grew mentally unstable, at some points breaking down altogether. It was a disastrous combination of qualities for a king.

If a playwright in his twenties wanted to write a bit of happy pablum to propagandize the glories of English history, Henry VI would make for an odd choice. But that wasn't Will's agenda; he wanted to tell a good story. And the very disarray of Henry's rule—the instability it created, the opportunities for mischief it brought forth, the treachery it facilitated—offered endless possibilities to a creative mind, especially one that operated relatively free of the constraints of precise historical truth.

On that last point, we need always to remember that Will relied heavily on historical sources like Holinshed's *Chronicles* in identifying a worthy tale, spotting major themes, flagging the important players, and setting the general arc of the narrative. But he routinely departed from those sources for dramatic and other reasons. For example, as Marjorie Garber points out, the Jack Cade character we meet in this play is actually a mashup of multiple characters found in Holinshed's work.

On the question of how closely the three parts of *Henry VI* conform to historical fact, Norwich summarily answers: "not very." But, then, this is unremarkable; Will was writing drama, not biography. And, as Norwich emphasizes, he was trying to show his audience the "vast sweep of history." Such an exercise demands artistic license. In the wielding of that license, Shakespeare never made anything less interesting than it was in real life.

Henry VI, Part 2 poses challenges to the modern reader. Shakespeare's subject is the War of the Roses, the civil wars fought for control of the English throne between the houses of Lancaster and York from 1455 to 1487. The intrigues and personalities involved in that contest would have been familiar enough to a London audience, just as we Americans have a sufficient grasp of our own history to enjoy *Hamilton*. But current audiences may find the plot of this play—especially in its details—confusing and hard to follow. It give us lots of Lords with lots of conflicting agendas.

Furthermore, the play reflects the inexperience of its author. It is seriously long; the BBC film version, which leaves out some scenes, runs to three-and-a-half hours. Some characters feel less than fully developed. The story lurches about from one plotline to another. It includes a few painfully tedious passages. York's explanation of why he has the legitimate claim to the crown is so detailed and boring that one creative modern production has him present it as a PowerPoint.

Finally, while *Henry VI, Part 2* works as a stand-alone play, it's much better encountered as part of the cycle that begins with *Henry VI, Part 1* and ends with *Richard III*. Years ago, I had the opportunity to take in two days of Royal Shakespeare Company productions that presented the four plays sequentially, a magnificently immersive experience. Taken by itself, *Henry VI, Part 2* feels like what it is: a part of the story.

These challenges notwithstanding, in my judgment no book about Shakespeare and the law can ignore this play. *Henry VI, Part 2* is rich with talk of the law and with lessons about how law works—or, more often, how it doesn't. Plus, it includes the single most famous line that Shakespeare ever wrote about the legal profession: "The first thing we do, let's kill all the lawyers." In light of the familiarity of that quotation, ignoring the play might seem like a transparent effort to dodge a plausible suggestion for social reform.

So, pull up a seat at Will's table. Make yourself at home. Let's take a closer look at the play.

And let's consider two questions that I think *Henry VI, Part 2* puts squarely before us. The first is whether the law actually does what we want it to do and achieves justice. And the second is whether all of our grandiose talk about the law may, in the end, be utterly meaningless.

Our young Will is busily becoming Shakespeare. And in this play he's having some marvelous sport with law and lawyers.

Let's see how he does it.

Law, Law, Law, Law, Law

It might at first seem as if *Henry VI, Part 2* has a lot to do with political maneuvering but not a lot to do with the law. That would be a mistake. On close study, it turns out that the play offers up a fugue in multiple parts on the law and those who engage with it. Indeed, legal issues arise in every one of the play's five acts and the law has a critical role in driving the action at various points in the plotline.

By time we arrive at the end of the play, Shakespeare has shown us a lot about the law—about how the law gets tossed around, about how it goes wrong, about how it doesn't do what we say it does, and about how it isn't what we think it is. Dressed up as history, the play delivers a romp in institutional deconstruction. But let's not get ahead of ourselves; let's go act by act—as in this case we must do—and see how these various lessons about the law unfold.

Let's start by looking at Act I, specifically the third scene. Here, Will explores the tendency of everyone—everyone—to claim that the law is on their side. Indeed, the characters here invoke the word "law" as if it had some sort of magical, talismanic power. As a result, the law gets summoned to do all sorts of curious (and even mutually exclusive) things.

At the beginning of the scene, the major players gather, squabbles commence, and things quickly go downhill. Queen Margaret, who has had enough of the meddling of the Duke of Gloucester, the Lord Protector of the realm, asks why a king who has achieved adulthood needs a Lord Protector, anyway. She has a point: Gloucester took on the role while Henry was a child and that time has long passed.

Others pile on. Her question prompts accusations that Gloucester has raided the public treasury to build elaborate homes and to buy fancy clothes for his wife, Eleanor. Further accusations bubble up that he has enriched himself by selling off towns in France.

Then Buckingham does something remarkable: He invokes the law against Gloucester, declaring: "Thy cruelty in execution / Upon offenders hath exceeded law / And left thee to the mercy of the law." It's a surprising charge for two reasons. First, by dint of his position as Lord Protector, Gloucester represents the institution of the law—so Buckingham essentially invokes the law against the law itself. Second, Buckingham accuses Gloucester of breaking the law by enforcing the law too severely—a puzzling notion that intrigued Shakespeare, as we'll discuss more in a moment.

Gloucester responds to Buckingham's invocation of the law by invoking it on his own behalf. After the insult he storms off, but then returns. He has walked around, calmed down, done his equivalent of counting to ten, and wants to focus everyone on matters of shared concern. He cannot, however, ignore the accusations made against him. So he says: "As for your spiteful false objections, / Prove them, and I lie open to the law." Or, as we say in current parlance: "Bring it."

The next figure to invoke the law is, ironically, the lawless Duke of York. The Duke of Suffolk arrives with two men in custody: York's armorer and the armorer's servant. The servant has made statements suggesting that the armorer has engaged in treasonous speech against Henry by arguing that York holds the rightful claim to the throne. York calls his accuser a "base dunghill villain," a wonderfully Shakespearean insult, and begs the king punish him with "all the rigor of the law."

Henry needs help sorting the law, so he turns to Gloucester for advice. Gloucester responds that the law requires the armorer and his servant to engage in single combat to decide who's right. The servant protests that he cannot fight—even so much as a blow—but Gloucester is unmoved. He replies that the servant "must fight or else be hanged." With that, the two men are dragged off to prison until the day of the contest.

It's quite a scene, what with everyone invoking the law and claiming it for their own. And those invocations devolve into complete absurdity at that moment when York responds to the insinuation of treason made against him by insisting that the law come to his aid. After all, York has confessed to us the exact offense of which he's accused and that he so vigorously denies.

"The devil can cite scripture for his purpose," Will later writes in *The Merchant of Venice*. The same holds true for law. And the bad guys can invoke chapter and section just as easily as they can invoke chapter and verse.

❁ ❁ ❁ ❁ ❁

As Act I unfolds, Will shifts focus to show us how the law looks when we put it into action, specifically with respect to the dispute between the armorer and the servant. Gloucester certainly has the authority to prescribe the required procedure, so in that sense the process he dictates qualifies as "law." But that process has nothing to do with evidence-based justice and everything to do with physical prowess.

The case before him perfectly demonstrates the problem. It pits the brutal armorer, who looks forward to the fight, against his timid servant, who dreads the very thought of it. The outcome looks certain and certainly unjust: The armorer will obliterate his servant; the guilty York will have his reputation restored; and an innocent man will die to vindicate him.

The duel ensues and the servant manages to win the contest, but only because his master is staggeringly drunk. The armorer confesses as he dies, so we are confident that justice has been done, but it has been done only by accident. It's hardly an endorsement of the prescribed method of adjudication.

We have arrived at the end of Act I and Will has already given us at least two reasons to view the law skeptically. Everybody claims the law is on their side—even the villains. And, to the extent that the law results in anything like justice, it is the result of sheer happenstance.

But Will's not done with the law.

It gets worse.

Law makes its next appearance in the third scene of Act II, where Will explores the law's celebrated impartiality. In that scene, the authorities bring before the king all of the parties involved in the witchcraft ritual: Eleanor, the witch, two priests, and a conjurer. The king has reassured Gloucester, who is concerned for the well-being of his wife, that "justice's equal scales" will lead to a fair outcome.

From our twenty-first-century perspective, we may find unthinkable the idea that any witch trial would ever yield a reasoned and just result. It's not clear, however, that Will would have shared our assumptions on this front. A Witchcraft Act had been adopted early in the reign of Queen Elizabeth and a revised one would be adopted early in the reign of King James—a man so preoccupied with witches and demonology that he wrote a book on the subject.

In Will's time, witchcraft trials were not suspect as exotic proceedings. We have no particular reason—beyond the precociousness of his intellect—to assume that Will would have doubted the existence of witches or the efficacy of the prosecutions against them. Lord Coke, among the most distinguished of Elizabethan and Jacobean jurists and not generally given to complete lunacy, accepted them as a matter of course.

In any event, in this witch trial the king swiftly finds everyone guilty, which apparently they were, and sentences four of them to death: the witch by burning and the priests and conjurer by hanging. The king declares that biblical law demands the sentence: "Receive the sentence of the law for sins / Such as by God's book are adjudged to death." He's got this right. Exodus 22:18 declares "Thou shalt not suffer a witch to live" and brooks no apparent exceptions to the strict command.

Nevertheless, this inflexible biblical injunction becomes considerably more flexible when it comes to sentencing Eleanor. In her case, the king orders three days of open penance and then commands her to "live in your country here in banishment" with a lord in the Isle of Man. Now, it's true, Eleanor does indeed experience that sentence as an awful punishment, particularly because of her pride in her social rank. But banishment seems infinitely preferable to the measures ordered against her co-conspirators: roasting at the stake or hanging by the neck until dead.

The king makes no bones about the grounds for this differential treatment: Eleanor, unlike the other perpetrators, was "more nobly born." Justice thus varies by station, and stern biblical law blinks and looks the other way if the criminal holds a title. So much for that celebrated impartiality; so much for "justice's equal scales."

To paraphrase George Orwell, some witches are more equal than others.

Law returns to center stage in the first scene of Act III, this time in the voice of the Cardinal of Winchester, who loathes Gloucester and wants him out of the way. The Cardinal invokes law in his accusations against Gloucester, repeating Buckingham's charge that as Lord Protector he executed punishments too harshly: "Did he not, contrary to the form of law, / Devise strange deaths for small offenses done?" As I noted earlier, the paradox that a figure in authority can violate the law by enforcing it with undue rigor deeply interested Shakespeare; as we'll see, he explores the idea later in both *The Merchant of Venice* and *Measure for Measure.*

Will then introduces another theme. The Cardinal, warming to the idea of dispensing with Gloucester, declares that the law must be followed—in appearance. He says: "That he should die is worthy policy; / But yet we want a color for his death. / 'Tis meet he be condemned by course of law." By a "color" the Cardinal means a pretext, a cover.

In the Cardinal's hands, law thus becomes its own kind of stalking horse, something to hide behind while co-opting the government's power to destroy a human life. And so it goes: When we later encounter Gloucester in the second scene of Act III he is dead in his bed, preemptively executed in anticipation of his guilt.

As an aside, it's worth noting that the prosecution and death of Gloucester also introduces some interesting evidence issues. York tells Gloucester while arresting him that "tis thought" he took bribes from France. In the face of this vaguely sourced accusation, Gloucester angrily responds: "Is it but thought so? What are they that think it?"

Gloucester's challenge to the "evidence" against him is prescient. Just a few years later, in 1603, the crown would charge Sir Walter Raleigh with treason against King James. The prosecution relied in large measure on statements made by witnesses who were not present in court. Raleigh famously responded to the prosecutor's evidence by demanding, much as Gloucester does here, that his accusers come forward—a demand that the court rejected. Sir Walter Raleigh's plight—facing testimony from witnesses he could not examine—gave us the hearsay doctrine, an honor it seems likely Raleigh would happily have forgone given that it cost him his head.

Evidence may have failed in court, but it works in the public square. Commoners learn of facts indicating that Gloucester has been strangled. Outraged, they call for justice, and they threaten the life of the king if he does not deliver it. The shaken king honors their demands and the chief perpetrator, Suffolk, bears the consequences.

For the moment, it might seem as if Will is giving an approving nod to law arising from a grassroots moral imperative. We shouldn't get too comfortable with that idea. It doesn't last.

Any confidence we have in commoners erecting a fair and sound legal structure quickly gets undone in the person of Jack Cade.

In the fourth act, Will shifts focus yet again, now turning his attention to the consequences of doing away with law. We meet Jack and his army of workingman revolutionaries, including Dick the butcher and Smith the weaver. Cade rallies his troops, pumping himself up as being "of an honorable house," valiant, and fearless, a hero of the common folk intent on taking down the oppressive existing order. Cade and his followers can be played to great comic effect, but make no mistake: These are dangerous men.

An inspired Dick the butcher calls out: "The first thing we do, let's kill all the lawyers!" It was a laugh line for Shakespeare's audience, which routinely included members of the local Inns of Court, and it remains a laugh line today. It may be the Shakespeare quotation most commonly found on coffee mugs, T-shirts, and law school graduation greeting cards.

Nevertheless, the cry has a deeply sinister significance. It recognizes that political order depends upon the law and upon professionals who have expertise in it. Kill all the lawyers and you kill all the law; kill all the law and you can do whatever you want. An audience that is laughing too loudly may not hear Cade's bold and unsettling response: "Nay, that is what I mean to do."

And Cade promptly shows he's not joking. Shortly after Dick's quip, he orders a clerk executed. His crime? Literacy. The man knew how to read and write.

In his book *Kill All the Lawyers?*, Daniel Kornstein discusses this passage at some length. He notes that, in a dissenting opinion in the 1985 case of *Walters v. Radiation Survivors*, Justice John Paul Stevens quoted the line and emphasized that the statement was "spoken by a rebel, not a friend of liberty." Stevens went on: "Shakespeare insightfully realized that disposing of lawyers is a step in the direction of a totalitarian form of government." Kornstein concurs: "Lawyers tend to be a stable, lawful government's first line of defense. To have a successful revolution, you must get rid of the lawyers."

I agree with this analysis—to a point. My reservation lies with any suggestion that the play posits a choice between stable law, on the one hand, and chaotic lawlessness, on the other. Law in the time of Henry VI, at least as Will depicts it, was anything but stable. And Jack Cade doesn't stand on a platform of "no law"; he's not a true anarchist. He instead presses an agenda of "new law," of law that originates with his will and follows his whims.

As sources of legal authority go, the predilections of Jack Cade may not seem like a strong or even valid one. But the play invites us to ask ourselves why that's the case. If Jack Cade can secure the power to issue enforceable orders, then why are his random commands any less "law" than the random commands of a king, a queen, or a parliament?

Cade announces that he comes in the "spirit of putting down kings and princes." But, in the next breath, he talks about all the things he'll do "when I am king, as king I shall be." It's a familiar populist gambit. Cade opposes all absolute power—unless he's the one who's got it; he opposes all law—unless he's the one who makes it. It's a short and easy step from populism to tyranny.

Cade then details the social changes he has in mind. He will do away with money. Everyone will eat and drink on his "score." He will make it a felony to drink "small" (i.e., low-alcohol) beer. He will dress everyone in the same clothes, like monks, so they can worship him as their Lord. It's all delightful nonsense.

Still, as with Dick the butcher's cry, a serious issue lies embedded within the silliness. The abolition of order creates a vacuum, and something has to fill it. Whether the new order marks an improvement always remains to be seen. The new boss may be the same as the old boss; the new boss may be worse.

Cade hardly looks like an improvement. In the fourth scene of Act IV, a messenger reports to Henry on the rebellion and it's all bad news. Cade, who has declared Henry a usurper, plans to march into London and to crown himself in Westminster on arrival. And Cade's enemies list has grown: He intends to dispose of all scholars, courtiers, and gentlemen, too. Let's not just kill all the lawyers; let's kill everyone who uses language in the service of the social order.

By the seventh scene, still more of Cade's threats have become realities. His army has arrived in London. He orders the Inns of Court destroyed. At Dick the butcher's urging, he commands the burning of all the records of the realm—records, the very stuff of law. Cade declares that, from this point forward, the only law will be whatever comes out of his mouth.

Not everyone looks forward to the prospect. One rebel predicts that—unless they pull Cade's teeth out—these will be "biting laws," indeed. We will hear the phrase again, in *Measure for Measure*, to describe overly punitive legislation. Another rebel laments that the laws will stink—like Cade's breath does from "eating toasted cheese."

In the view of those who know him best, Jack Cade's program for law reform doesn't hold much promise. We can't argue with them. And, so far, law isn't looking good here—whether it comes from kings or commoners.

The first scene of Act V brings us the play's last reference to law. It may reflect Will's profound skepticism about the law that the statement comes from the play's most lawless character, York, and in the midst of his most lawless act, open treason. Confronting the king with his claim to the throne, York declares:

> "King" did I call thee? No, thou art not king,
> Not fit to govern and rule multitudes,
> Which dar'st not—no, nor canst not—rule a traitor.
> That head of thine doth not become a crown;
> Thy hand is made to grasp a palmer's staff,
> And not to grace an awful princely scepter.
> That gold must round engirt these brows of mine,
> Whose smile and frown, like to Achilles' spear,
> Is able with the change to kill and cure.

Here is a hand to hold a scepter up
And with the same to act controlling laws.
Give place. By heaven, thou shalt rule no more
O'er him whom heaven created for thy ruler. (V:1:94–106)

In York's view, law is power. Period. Only the powerful deserve the authority "to act controlling laws." And the authority exercised by the powerful? Well, that *is* the law.

Act by act, *Henry VI, Part 2* takes us on a journey through law. It starts with everyone invoking the law as their own. And then it shows us one failure of law after another. It closes with York declaring a monopoly on law because, well, he's the guy with the sword. The play leads us to a profoundly uncomfortable place, and then leaves us there.

Henry VI, Part 2 shows us law, law, law, law, law doing its business and none of it making for a pretty or reassuring sight. But Will's not done. Because this play doesn't just ask us whether law is what we say it is or does what we say it does.

It asks us whether the idea of law even makes any sense.

The Empty Idea of Law

In 1982, the *Harvard Law Review* published an article by legal scholar Peter Westen with a provocative title: "The Empty Idea of Equality." In the piece, Westen notes that the principle of equality—the idea that like things should be treated alike—"has been a fixture of Western thought for thousands of years." We view equality as a shared and revered value and we routinely summon it in support of our arguments for policies, principles, and processes.

Westen contends, however, that all this chatter about equality turns out to be meaningless. After all, for the idea that "likes should be treated alike" to make any sense, it must incorporate external values that determine which things and treatments are alike in the ways that matter to us. But, once we've identified and incorporated those values, the notion of "equality" becomes superfluous. On this basis, Westen urges us to abandon our familiar "rhetoric of equality" because it leads to nothing but confusion and logical error.

A simple example helps demonstrate his point. In our society, we maintain that the principle of equality should govern someone's ability to get a particular job—for instance, as an airline pilot. Now, if we take that statement to mean that everyone who applies for the position should have the same shot at getting hired, we reduce it to nonsense. I, for example, should not be able to land the job, given that I do not know how to land a plane.

Under Westen's theory, we can give meaning to the statement of principle only by adding information about the "likenesses" that we think are important. So, we might refine our idea here by saying that, as among those people who hold identical or substantially similar qualifications to serve as an airline pilot, we should not choose one over the other because of their race, religion, gender, or ethnicity. Once we've said that, though, reintroducing talk of equality doesn't seem to add anything. To the contrary, doing so may simply reintroduce confusion over what exactly the statement of principle means.

In *Henry VI, Part 2*, Shakespeare toys with an analogous argument about the rhetoric of "law." As we've seen, throughout the play (and especially at the beginning) one major character after another invokes the law as if the mere doing of it constitutes a substantive argument. They treat the word as if it magically endows the speaker with legitimacy and authority. To borrow Peter Westen's framing, law is a "fixture" in the thought and speech of the world depicted in the play—as it is in our own world—and everyone uses it as a cudgel.

But the very fact that everyone invokes the principle and claims it for their own creates a crisis of meaning. As a matter of logic, no coherent idea of law can represent the principles of both Gloucester and York, of both the king and Cade, of both the cardinal and the commoners. Those parties hold opposing views of the law, and the law can only mean all of those inconsistent and mutually exclusive things by meaning nothing at all.

The play also challenges us to ask what the idea of law adds to our understanding of things, just as Westen asks about equality. Throughout the play, law gets equated with power, with one person's capacity to impose his will on others. If that's wrong, then why? And, if that's right, then isn't the whole concept of law superfluous? Isn't it, to borrow a phrase from the philosopher Bernard Williams, "one thought too many?"

It is as if the play sends us on a treasure hunt, looking for those qualities that separate the things that are law from the things that are not. And this is where Will really starts to have fun with us. As the action unfolds, the play suggests a variety of characteristics that might qualify a social structure as "law" and give meaning to the word. But then Will merrily runs every one of these qualifying characteristics right off the rails. Watch how he does it.

We might think that "law" is characterized by its evenhandedness and impartiality, by the blindness of its justice to the identities of the participants. As you'll remember, the king relies upon just such a concept when he assures Gloucester that "justice's equal scales" will govern the disposition of the witchcraft charges brought against the co-conspirators. And, yet, the "law" gives something like community service to Eleanor, the most privileged among the accused, while burning and hanging the rest.

We might think that "law" is characterized by its institutionalization of process, by a reliance on established and sensible rules for resolving disputes. When the armorer and his servant exchange accusations, Gloucester advises the king that a procedure exists to deal with the controversy. Fair enough. And, yet, the law he announces has nothing to do with evidence, has everything to do with power, and yields justice only accidentally and because one of the parties is fall-down drunk.

We might think that "law" is characterized by its alignment with popular values, by its correspondence to the moral sensibilities of those who it governs. Here we get faint glimmers of hope when the common people call for justice against Suffolk. But the law as we encounter it in the hands of Cade and Dick the butcher becomes an instrument of murder and mayhem.

We might think that "law" is characterized by its efficacy at preserving order, by its capacity to protect us from those who would threaten our safety and destabilize our society. But, in the hands of Winchester and York, law becomes a stalking horse for assassins and traitors. And any notion that law guards us from abuses of power receives its firmest rebuttal from York, who maintains that law *is* power and power *is* law.

In short, by the end of this play we have nothing left of any reasoned concept of law. Every vessel is empty, every road leads nowhere, every winding passage brings us to a dead end. Our idea of law as a critical social institution has burned away like the morning mist. All that remains are the particular *ad hoc* behaviors of individual human actors. And we know what that gets us.

We might wonder why Will arrived at such a dismal view of law. Perhaps his own experiences led him there. After all, law kept the Shakespeare family from following their Catholic faith. Law drove Will's father from a respected public office. Law pressed Will's family perilously close to financial ruin. Law put the decaying heads of criminals on the pikes that Will passed on his way into the city. Perhaps, but given how little we actually know about him, drawing direct connections between Shakespeare's life and his work always makes for a risky and speculative business.

It could be that Will was simply having fun with the lawyers in his audience, of whom there were probably many. Seeing the venerable institution of the law presented, in turns, as impotent, corrupt, unjust, unequal, cruel, manipulable, and potentially even meaningless seems likely to have drawn winces of recognition and hollers of laughter from members of the Inns of Court. Again, perhaps, but it seems dreadfully reductionist to think of this play as the functional equivalent of an extended sixteenth-century lawyer joke.

In the preface, I observed that in much of Shakespeare's work the point lies in the asking. In that spirit, *Henry VI, Part 2* seems to me to pose hard questions to us, over and over again: How does law—this thing we see as essential to a civilized society—really work in the world? How does law fail and betray us? How does it go wrong? Can we do better? Or will these problems necessarily trouble any legal system we create, because all such systems reflect our human imperfections? What does it even mean to talk about the law, when in the end all we really have are the people who create it, enforce it, and interpret it?

We can't dismiss these high-level questions as abstract, metaphysical, or irrelevant. To the contrary, they are essential to any thoughtful approach to the law. We need to ask them, always, to ensure we don't become trapped inside our naïve or formulaic assumptions about what law is and how it actually plays out on the ground in the lives it affects.

These are exactly the kinds of hard questions we ask in law school classrooms, almost every single day. Starting in the first hour of the first meeting of my first-year first-term Civil Procedure course. It's a great place to begin our conversations.

First thing we do, let's kill all the illusions.

3

"And Tell Sad Stories of the Deaths of Kings"

Richard II

Backdrop

Most lawyers don't receive formal training as psychologists, but we practice an extraordinarily psychological discipline. In the course of litigating cases, I've often found myself trying to set up shop inside other people's heads. Judges, jurors, opposing counsel, witnesses, clients—I want to know what they're thinking and how I can bring them around to my client's way of seeing things. Litigators read minds for a living, and a lot of the reading isn't light.

I remember once, during a break in a trial, talking with some of my colleagues about whether our opposing counsel would ask a particular question of one of our witnesses. It didn't make any sense for him to do so: The question opened the door to testimony that could badly hurt his case. They were all convinced that he would opt against it.

But I suspected he wouldn't be able to resist. He liked to bully people; the question had a bullying quality to it; and the witness looked like someone you could bully. So, I prepared the witness to capitalize on the opportunity if it arose. And so it did. The question came flying in out of left field, just as I had predicted, and the witness mercilessly beat the lawyer about the head and body with her answer. I was still a relatively young lawyer then, and at that moment it occurred to me that I might actually know what I was doing.

As we've seen, even Will's earliest work reflects a keen interest in why human beings do what they do, and each new play reveals a deepening psychological sensitivity and understanding. By time we get to *Richard II*, the play we explore together in this chapter, we find him grappling with dazzlingly complex questions of character and identity.

It's the very stuff of which so much of legal theory and practice is made.

Scholars generally agree that Shakespeare wrote *Richard II* around 1595, sometime after he wrote *Henry VI, Part 2*. In the historical chronology, however, the events of *Richard II* come first. Indeed, *Richard II* portrays the usurpation of power that haunts the *Henry VI* cycle and ultimately spurs the Wars of the Roses. *Richard II* thus sits at the opposite end of English history from *Henry VI*.

Richard II opposes *Henry VI, Part 2* in other ways as well. In *Henry VI*, we met a protagonist who proved himself an incompetent king because of his excessive piety, his malleability, and his mental frailty. The king we meet in *Richard II* suffers from an abundance of weaknesses, but not those. Materialistic, vain, reckless, and impetuous, he rides roughshod over people as habitually as Henry VI steers around them. In the end, those abuses cost him the crown.

Richard II and Henry VI also have very different holds on authority. As York tiresomely explains to anyone who will listen, Henry VI's claim to the throne was subject to dispute. In contrast, Richard II's claim was impeccable. He could trace his line directly to Edward III, whose legitimacy as king was unquestioned.

That fact matters a lot in this play, because it makes clear that what we're watching unfold is a full-on usurpation, an unsanctioned seizure of a power that was believed to come from God. If such an act can be justified at all, it's therefore not by the pedigree of the usurper's claim, but by the failures of the sitting king to serve his land and subjects. And that raises provocative questions: Can you toss a king out for such inadequacies? If so, then what happened to the God-given-power part of being king?

The raw arrogation of power depicted in *Richard II* made it a riskier undertaking for Will than the earlier history plays. Shakespeare lived in dangerous times, and the wolves who scratched at Queen Elizabeth's door needed no encouraging. If we'd met Will at the bar when he was writing the play we might have tried to talk him out of it: He could wake up to discover that his stalking horse had wandered off and left him exposed to an angry monarch.

It may have been good advice. In 1601, Lord Essex—a disaffected royal who had once been a favorite of Elizabeth—led an utterly incompetent rebellion against the queen. As part of it, his co-conspirators approached Shakespeare's company and asked them to revive *Richard II*. The conspirators seem to have believed that the play's portrayal of a successful usurpation would inspire London audiences to go forth and do likewise. It didn't work, of course—it's impossible to imagine why it would—and Essex was arrested, tried, and messily beheaded in the Tower of London.

Elizabeth apparently saw similarities between the fragility of Richard's rule and her own: "I am Richard II," she is said to have declared, "Know ye not that?" The actor Augustine Phillips, representing the company during the subsequent investigation, testified that they had no part in any conspiracy. Someone offered them forty shillings more than the usual fee to put on the play, so they did it. The explanation and plea of ignorance satisfied those in power, but it's fair to assume that Will experienced these events as an uncomfortably close shave.

In writing *Richard II*, Will appears to have drawn upon several sources, including Holinshed's *Chronicles*, Edward Hall's history of the houses of Lancaster and York, and a long poem about the civil war by Samuel Daniel. As always, he exercised considerable artistic license with the material, reworking it for dramatic purposes and making it distinctly his own. In his hands, events that took months to play out are compressed into single scenes and various figures become fuller and more (or less) sympathetic than we find them in Holinshed.

One could sensibly argue that during this period the more mature writer we think of as William Shakespeare begins to take form. Stephen Greenblatt, in his book *Will in the World*, observes that "*Richard II* marked a major advance in the playwright's ability to represent inwardness." When I teach the play I'm always struck by the complexity of Richard's character and our conflicted reactions to him as the action unfolds. I think Richard II is one of Shakespeare's great parts and I've seen many wonderful portrayals of it, including by Christopher Walken in the late 1970s when I was a college student. His performance was not at all lessened by sounding like the king came from Queens.

The play is complex in many other respects as well. *Richard II* shows us a naked seizure of authority; but we're not sure we can condemn it. It shows us the fall of a flawed and corrupt king; but we're not sure we can cheer it. As Emma Smith observes, the play depicts a "momentous transfer" of power and the beginning of a new dynasty, but "we really don't know whether it was a good thing or not." Will drops us into circumstances of profound moral ambiguity and leaves us to find our own way; he'll return to this model again and again in later works. It's prime material to look at through the lens of the law, where profound moral ambiguity is our stock-in-trade and our business as usual.

❁ ❁ ❁ ❁ ❁

As with *Titus Andronicus* and *Henry VI, Part 2*, this play may not at first seem like an obvious candidate for legal analysis. Among other things, *Richard II* is one of Shakespeare's most poetic plays. We can feel Will stretching his artistic muscles and marveling at their newfound capacities. The play's rich and elaborate language, combined with its remote historical setting, might seem to distance it from the prosaic and pragmatic sensibilities of the law.

When I teach my Shakespeare & the Law seminar, however, many students identify *Richard II* as one of their favorite plays and say they find it highly relevant to their studies. I can see why. It delves into questions of character—a concern of lawyers and of the law, especially the law of evidence. It gives trials a central role in the plotline at critical moments. And it explores the concept of sovereignty, a notion of continuing interest to the law and legal scholars.

We've got a lot to work with here. Let's get started.

A Matter of Character

Let's begin by stepping back from *Richard II* for a moment and by talking about the concept of character. Bear with me: This discussion will take us a bit afield for a while. But I promise to lead us back to *Richard II* and to Shakespeare, who we will—as usual—find waiting for us.

In everyday life, we make lots of decisions based on assessments of character. Some of those decisions are among our most important. We rely on judgments about character when deciding who to date, who to marry, who to befriend, who to hire, who to work for, who to support politically, who to respect, who to emulate, and who to trust and believe. Ignoring or misjudging character can have dire consequences. We all have examples from experience.

Most of us don't have a fully and formally developed theory of character. We do a fair amount of this work by hunch. But the ways we think and talk about character suggest that we tend to believe three things are true about it.

First, we believe that character is discernable. Granted, in some instances we may face challenges in figuring out exactly what someone's character is. We may have less information than we'd like or may receive conflicting signals. But believing that we need to make character judgments necessarily entails the assumption that in at least some cases it's possible for us to do it.

It also necessarily entails the assumption that we have the tools necessary to get it done. And, indeed, we tend to think that what someone says, what someone does, and how they say it and do it typically tell us a lot about who someone is. Many of us like to say that we're good judges of character, and maybe we are. Or maybe character generally isn't that hard to judge.

The second thing we believe about character is that it's stable. We think it's stable across time, and we express that idea through a variety of idioms and clichés. You know them: People don't change. Once a [fill in the blank], always a [fill in the blank]. A leopard doesn't change its spots—a biblical expression that finds its way into *Richard II*.

We also tend to think that character is stable across contexts. A parent whose child lies to them about doing their homework will worry that the child will lie about other things, too. A liar's a liar, period. Only the pants on fire thing is variable.

Third and finally, we believe that character has powerful predictive value. We think that people typically act in a manner consistent with their character and only rarely depart from it. If I know who you are, I can predict what you will do. If I know what you've done in the past, I have a pretty reliable sense of what you'll do in the future. In the law, we call this "propensity reasoning." When I predicted that the bullying lawyer would probably ask a bullying question because he had a propensity to bully, that's exactly what I was doing. And I was right.

In our everyday interactions, we don't just indulge propensity reasoning; we embrace it and mobilize it for our own use. The undergraduate who exhaustively documents all of their prior accomplishments in their application to law school does so for a reason. They hope to persuade the admissions director that their track record reflects a collection of relevant character traits—like intelligence, diligence, dedication, and initiative—that they will carry into their next endeavor. "What's past is prologue," Will writes in *The Tempest*, and that's the theory behind every curriculum vitae that gets written and emailed.

Indeed, someone who tried to keep others from applying propensity reasoning to them would quickly run into serious trouble. Imagine telling a prospective employer that they had no right to review your prior performance and background credentials because those were irrelevant. Or imagine saying on a first date that you refused to disclose anything about your past because it had no bearing on the present. As I wrote in an article on this subject in the ABA journal, *Litigation*: "These seem like reliable prescriptions for unemployment and dining alone."

Despite our pervasive reliance on this manner of thinking, the evidence rules that we apply in court reflect a deep skepticism about propensity reasoning and generally forbid the use of character evidence in civil and criminal trials. Granted, the law grudgingly recognizes a few exceptions. For example, a criminal defendant can offer evidence of their good character—an opportunity rarely pursued because it opens the door for the prosecutor to offer evidence of the defendant's bad character. But, for the most part, the law of evidence tries to keep character out of the courtroom.

If you describe this legal principle to a layperson they'll shake their head in disbelief. They'll balk at the idea that you can't offer evidence that X killed A, B, C, D, and E in order to show that he has a propensity to kill people and therefore probably also killed F. I sympathize with their puzzlement. At first blush, it seems bizarre that our evidence rules should so roundly reject a type of reasoning we depend on all the time when making countless important decisions.

But it turns out there are good reasons to exercise caution in making and relying on judgments of character—both inside and outside of the courtroom.

Let's start with the inside of the courtroom part. In the context of a trial, we worry that jurors will misuse evidence of *bad* character. For example, a jury that learns a criminal defendant has done unsavory things in the past may decide to convict in order to get him off the street. They may not care whether he actually committed the crime with which he's charged; they'll just feel better if he's behind bars.

We worry about admitting evidence of *good* character at trials, too. Such evidence may occupy more time than it's worth and may distract the jury from the central factual issues it needs to decide. This seems particularly likely where the other side will respond to evidence of good character by offering evidence of bad character, leading in turn to efforts to rehabilitate character. All these detours into character can make the jury lose sight of what the trial is actually about.

Even outside of the courtroom we have reasons for concern about judgments of character. First, it's not clear how we can reliably determine what someone's character is. Asking them seems fruitless. Asking others may give us a sense of the individual's reputation, but public reputation and inner character may substantially differ. Also, reputation depends on hearsay, which usually signals trouble.

We might think we can discern character by looking at specific instances of prior conduct. But that's fraught with peril, too. All of us, at one time or another, have felt unfairly treated because someone judged us on the basis of one or two acts rather than on the longer arc of our behavior.

A continuing and consistent pattern of behavior may offer more dependable evidence of character than a few isolated incidents. But how many acts do we need to make up such a pattern? Over what period of time? And how similar do the acts have to be, and in what ways, for them to count as relevant?

A second concern is that character, if it exists, turns out to be significantly less stable than we think it is. In his book *Experiments in Ethics*, philosopher Kwame Anthony Appiah discusses how contemporary social science challenges our assumption that character is fixed. He cites studies showing that even relatively minor environmental changes can significantly affect people's behavior. One of these studies suggests that how generous a person is may depend on something as apparently trivial and unrelated as whether there's a pleasant smell in the air.

Furthermore, Appiah observes, many psychologists today don't believe that character traits exhibit much "cross-situational stability." A person who is rude or cruel or unforgiving in one context may behave very differently in another. This is good news for the parent who learns that their child has lied; a child who lies to their teacher may not lie to their parents or otherwise be a liar in any general sense. But, of course, it's also bad news for the parent who proclaims their child a sweet kid based on a single, isolated act of compassion. That may be a fluke, too.

Those first two concerns give rise to a third: If it's not clear how we can arrive at a reliable judgment of what character is, and if character is unstable and context dependent, then character would seem to have much less predictive power than we assume it does. Some people will be better than their prior conduct would suggest, some will be worse, and some will act as expected. Every human decision about how to behave will contain within it a potential element of surprise.

❖ ❖ ❖ ❖ ❖

What's all this have to do with *Richard II*? Well, I believe, quite a lot.

The elusive nature of character fascinated Shakespeare, who explored the subject in numerous plays. If we met Will at the Tabard Inn for a few friendly ales, it seems likely that the conversation would sooner or later wander around to the topic. And he had much more than a theoretical interest in it; he understood that the complexities of character made for good theater and therefore bustling box offices.

As I suggested earlier, I think *Richard II* signals Will's blossoming interest in character's Delphic dimensions. Sure, the earlier plays, like *Titus Andronicus* and *Henry VI, Part 2*, include some deeply interesting figures, but they mostly act just as we'd expect them to act and our assessments of them probably don't change much as the plays unfold. In *Richard II*, however, Will takes us into entirely new territory.

We'll start where the play does and see what happens as it moves along.

❖ ❖ ❖ ❖ ❖

Will's audiences would have come to the play with preconceived notions about both King Richard II and Henry Bolingbroke, Duke of Hereford and later King Henry IV (who in this chapter I'll just call "Henry" for simplicity's sake). Let's begin with Richard.

From histories and popular lore, the audience would have known that Richard was a fussy dandy; he was famous for it. As John Julius Norwich notes in *Shakespeare's Kings*, "It is perhaps a measure of Richard's vanity that he is the first English king whose true likeness has come down to us—and not with one contemporary portrait, but with two." He ushered in an age of male fashion that featured ostentatious dress, turbans, and crazy quantities of jewelry. Biographers credit him with inventing the handkerchief and also the codpiece, the latter suggesting an irresistible quasi-Shakespearean joke about Richard wanting his clothing to stand out.

In most performances of the play, these facets of Richard's character are made apparent before he even speaks a word. As the lights come up, the audience finds him dressed elaborately, even by the standards of a king. His hair is neatly coiffed and he carries himself with a conspicuous superiority and arrogance. Most directors and dramaturges capitalize on this familiar iconography of Richard II.

Will's audience also would have known Richard to have been self-dealing and dishonest. He was famous for that, too. As Norwich discusses, while still a teenage king Richard II performed the rather extraordinary act of putting down a dangerous popular rebellion. He achieved the feat, however, by essentially capitulating to all of the mob's demands and making promises for reform. When things calmed down, he broke his word. Norwich observes: "If the King were to be properly respected and revered by his subjects, it was essential that he should be seen to be a man of good faith. In this Richard had failed, and it was a failure that would not be forgotten." Shakespeare's audiences wouldn't have forgotten it, either.

That's the Richard we meet at the beginning of the first act. The Henry we meet there seems like his polar opposite in almost every respect. If Richard is effete and dandyish, Henry is bold and combative. If Richard is weak and deceptive, Henry is solid and straightforward. If Richard is wavering and impetuous, Henry is steady and purposeful. Nothing would have surprised Will's audiences in the way the first scene of the first act presented either Richard or Henry; it was for them like playing Abraham Lincoln in a stovepipe hat is for us.

Throughout the first act, both of the principal players stay in those characters. Henry exudes honor in all things, even in banishment. Richard, in contrast, gives us exactly zero reasons to warm to him. When Henry and Mowbray, the Duke of Norfolk, come before the king to resolve a dispute, Richard adjudicates it ineptly. He orders them to make peace, then he allows them to fight, and then he changes his mind again and interrupts the contest and banishes them both. He vows impartiality in making his judgment but then gives Henry a substantially more lenient sentence, either out of favoritism or out of fear of Henry's popularity. He hides his complicity in the death of Gloucester, which has taken place before the play begins. He enviously grinds his teeth over Henry's common touch. As I say, not much to like here.

The first act's portrayal of Richard's character closes with an exclamation mark. The play presents John of Gaunt (Henry's father) sympathetically, but when Richard learns that Gaunt is dying he rejoices over his imminent demise. Richard seems as contemptible as he is contemptuous, and that takes some doing.

This pattern holds for most of the second act, with Richard enthusiastically persisting in open villainy. He upbraids the dying Gaunt for presuming to criticize him. He shrugs off the news that Gaunt has passed: "So much for that." Against the advice of the Duke of York, who sees it as a disastrous error, he seizes all of Gaunt's possessions and property, effectively disinheriting the exiled Henry. He burdens the people with grievous taxes, fines nobles "for ancient quarrels," and yet still manages to spend more money than he takes in. "Most degenerate king!" cries the Earl of Northumberland, to no dissenting voices, including our own.

But, toward the end of the second act, things start to get a bit trickier with respect to questions of character. Henry, the "loyal subject," has returned to England despite the fact that he is still under the king's banishment, and with an army no less. When York confronts him and accuses him of acting the traitor, he offers an excuse of lawyerly technicality: "As I was banished, I was banished Hereford, / But as I come, I come for Lancaster." That is: The king banished someone with a living father, but I'm someone with a dead father.

Henry goes on to raise a much stronger point that rests on basic notions of fairness. He argues that his new title—dearly acquired because of his father's passing—carries with it certain rights and entitlements, which the king has without justification taken from him. He's acting only to protect that which is his. Henry presents himself as the ultimate pro se plaintiff, who just happens to have an army along for the ride.

The difficulties we face in assessing Henry's character at this juncture come less from his conduct than from Richard's. If the king hadn't seized Gaunt's possessions, we'd have no question about Henry's intentions in returning with armed forces in tow. But Richard's calamitous decision to disinherit Henry makes it much harder to figure things out. Perhaps Henry does indeed want only what law and inheritance guarantee him. Or perhaps the king's colossal error has provided a convenient stalking horse for an ambitious upstart looking for an excuse to oust an unpopular ruler. At this point, who knows?

The first scene of the third act, however, signals that Henry may well have an agenda beyond the restoration of his property. Sitting as prosecutor, judge, and jury, he condemns the king's two favorites—Sir John Bushy and Sir Henry Green—to death. This gets dressed up as an effort to save Richard from two manipulative sycophants who have led the king into trouble. But, like his reentry into England under banishment, Henry knows full well that it's an exercise of power and authority that Richard would condemn.

Marjorie Garber has noted that many of Shakespeare's plays follow a kind of chiastic structure in which the plotline looks something like an X. As one character falls, another character rises. Shakespeare being Shakespeare, he often adds an additional dimension by having the descending character rise in some respect and having the ascending character fall in another.

If *Richard II* observes this structure, and I think it clearly does, then the third act provides the axis of the X. It now becomes plain that Richard's fortunes have taken a sudden, spiraling downturn. In scene 2 he asks: "Is my kingdom lost?" And this seems to say a great deal not just about the state of his sovereignty but about his unwillingness to take responsibility for his condition: The passive sense of his inquiry puts aside the possibility that he's the one who lost it.

Richard resists the conclusion at first. He tries to convince himself that as king he is "the deputy elected by the Lord," who God himself will protect and no man may depose. But the bad news of Henry's increasing power quickly forces him to abandon the fantasy. A lesser playwright would assign to Richard one category of emotional response to the events—anger, for example—and stick with it. But Will understood that humans who experience profound loss often have a host of conflicting emotions, so that's what we get.

When Sir Stephen Scroop (wonderful name) delivers the "tidings of calamity" to Richard, we get a series of reactions in quick succession. He feigns indifference, then embraces fatalism, then blames others for betraying him, and then descends into poetic despondency. He rails against the vanity of all he has been and has represented, and then—awash in self-pity (his favorite thing to be awash in)—he pleads his humanity. His speech may not move us all the way to a place of sympathy, although perhaps it does so for people with bigger hearts than mine. But even the crustiest among us has to acknowledge that the Richard we find here feels different from the Richard we encountered in the first act.

The next scene then gives us yet another take on the character of Henry. The king has retreated to Flint Castle, and Henry and his supporters have assembled there. Henry makes a great show of his continued loyalty to the king, but he also has demands. He wants his banishment repealed and his lands restored. Uh, or else.

To be clear, this is not just an invitation into a negotiation, which would be offensive enough given their respective positions. Rather, Henry makes an unambiguous threat of violence while pretending that doing so is the farthest thing from his mind. Although Richard initially responds defiantly, he quickly accedes to Henry's demands "without contradiction."

As the scene unfolds, Richard may seem to us oddly quick to conclude that he must surrender the crown. He goes on a bit of a rant about how he'll happily eat from a wooden bowl and die in an obscure grave. In the face of all this operatic surrender Henry continues to insist that he "comes for but [his] own," but Richard responds: "Your own is yours, and I am yours, and all."

What's going on here?

Applying conventional propensity reasoning to Richard's behavior in this scene would give us an easy answer. Richard is weak. That's his character. It's fixed, it's stable, it doesn't change, and it holds true across differing contexts and circumstances. His premature surrender is therefore completely predictable. It's exactly who Richard is: weak, weak, weak, and more weak. Surely, no one expected a different outcome.

Will may, indeed, have had just that message in mind, but I don't think so. It seems to me important to recognize that Richard (and Henry) would have understood that at this point the king has already lost power. Richard's authority depended on an unwavering recognition of his absolute sovereignty—and no truly loyal subject would unilaterally impose terms on or threaten a true sovereign. So, Richard does here what many of us do when we've lost something that matters dearly to us: We pretend we have given it up voluntarily; we disclaim any desire to keep it; we rationalize. In short, we try to deceive ourselves. The deception may work at first, but it does not always age well.

Indeed, it quickly becomes clear that Richard has had second thoughts about his capitulation. When Henry summons Richard before him, the king doesn't promptly and voluntarily hand over the crown. That's what Henry needs him to do, but Richard shows himself in no great hurry to do it.

He gives us another self-pitying speech, in which he compares himself to the betrayed Christ. Then he senses an opportunity to toy with Henry. He takes the crown in hand and invites Henry to "seize" it. An alarmed Henry replies: "I thought you had been willing to resign." And back and forth they go: "Are you contented to resign the crown?" "Ay, no; no, ay." Finally, after all this messing about, Richard surrenders: "God save King Henry, unkinged Richard says, / And send him many years of sunshine days. / What more remains?"

By the end of these exchanges Henry has grown weary of Richard and, perhaps, so have we. But then Northumberland reveals some fine print to the resignation: In order to ensure that the people think Richard "worthily deposed," he must confess to a list of "grievous crimes" committed by him and his followers. Richard does not deny wrongdoing, and we know that his misfortunes are his own damn fault, but the insistence upon a confession may strike us as piling on. It certainly felt that way to Richard, who again compared himself to Christ as he condemned the "Pontius Pilates" around him.

The next moment is one of the most famous in the play. A broken, tear-filled Richard puts aside Northumberland's list of offenses and calls for a mirror. No one does a thing until Henry sends for one—a subtle but powerful signal of how little authority Richard retains. Northumberland presses Richard to review the paper while the mirror is fetched, but Henry instructs him to "urge it no more." After studying his face and musing over his fall, Richard smashes the glass.

His identity has been shattered. He is not who or what he was. And, when he pitifully asks leave to go, Henry grants it—by putting him in custody.

By the conclusion of this scene, Will has artfully scrambled any easy judgments of character we had put in place way back in Act I. Yes, of course, we may still think of Richard as a lousy king with an exhaustive catalog of unattractive traits; but, somehow, he has transcended the fickle dandy who appeared in the first scenes. Maybe even against our will and better judgment, Richard has in our eyes become human, and his suffering is real and beautifully expressed. He has grown painfully, if maybe also only partially, aware of his own responsibility in a disaster that has befallen not only him but the station of the monarch and the principle of sovereignty.

At the same time, Henry has moved beyond the simple portrait painted of him at the beginning of the play. He holds Richard in disdain and will happily take a willingly offered crown. But it matters to him that the king surrender it voluntarily, and not just for purposes of public relations. He feels pity for Richard and takes no delight in humiliating him. But he also knows that he cannot let a freshly deposed king freely roam the land and he needs Richard out of the way. That Henry seems to have persuaded himself that Richard's murder would not promptly and unavoidably follow constitutes its own kind of self-deception.

Then, in the fifth and final act, Will really mixes things up. We now see Henry in power, adjudicating the treason of the Duke of Aumerle, York's son. His performance may leave us less than fully impressed. His decision to pardon Aumerle, dressed up as an act of Christian charity, comes only because the Duchess of York adequately bends his ear. And he provides no explanation for why Aumerle's fellow co-conspirators deserve less forgiveness and must die. The first act placed the former king in the role of judge and showed him to be changeable, biased, and unfair; the final act places the new king in the same role and puts the same qualities on display.

In the penultimate scene, Richard gives us a long and despairing soliloquy on his circumstances. When confronted by murderers, however, he does "not go gentle into that good night." He battles bravely and effectively, killing two of the would-be assassins before Sir Pierce of Exton strikes him down. Richard dies with the monarchy on his lips, decrying the spilling of "King's blood" on the "King's land."

When Henry receives news of Richard's death, he readily acknowledges his confused feelings: "Though I did wish him dead, / I hate the murderer, love him murdered." It's an honest enough remark, but his candor doesn't win him much credit. Surely, Henry understood that Richard couldn't stick around, eat out of wooden bowls, and die of old age in an abbey.

To usurp the king is to kill the king. It is perhaps a symbolic death at first, but a literal one must come sooner or later to put a ribbon on things and keep the new king safe. Henry heads off on a crusade to purge himself of the guilt. It is guilt that he has earned.

❂ ❂ ❂ ❂ ❂

What are we to make of all this? Well, there are lots of possibilities, aren't there?

We may arrive at the end of the last act with the sense that the characters of our two protagonists changed in the course of the play. Henry appears to have started as a loyal subject with no thought of seizing the crown. When the opportunity arose, however, he found a burgeoning ambition within himself that he couldn't suppress. He lived with the newfound lust uneasily, perhaps, but he also cheerfully marched toward wherever it led him.

Richard, in turn, started as a protean, deceptive, calculating, intolerable brat. But the brutal alchemies of loss and suffering transform him, just as they transform many of us. Richard never becomes a heroic figure, not even in his final battle for his life, but somewhere along the line he acquires the capacity to evoke sympathy.

Scholars have argued that Richard never quite qualifies as tragic. I'm not so sure. Harold Bloom describes him as a victim of his own self-indulgence. I've known people like that; they seem to me about as tragic as people get.

But wait a minute: Is any of that right? Can we say with confidence that either man changed at all? How do we know that events didn't simply reveal qualities that they already had but that weren't obvious in different circumstances? Do Henry the usurper and Richard the poet really come out of nowhere? Extreme situations can show us a lot about who people are. Most commonly, however, they just make people more of whatever they already were. In this play, does character change—or does it simply come to light?

And then there's this: In the end, how differently do we view the characters of our two protagonists? At the beginning, they seemed like polar opposites. Do we still have that impression at the conclusion? Or are they more alike than we had imagined? Consider, for example, how the unequal treatment reflected in Richard's judgments of Henry and Mowbray in Act I gets echoed in Henry's judgments of Aumerle and his fellow conspirators in Act V.

I've read about a modern production of *Richard II* where, right before the play gets underway, a member of the audience randomly chooses which of the two lead actors will perform each role. Is that finally how we should view Richard and Henry? Are kings, or at least these kings, for all practical purposes interchangeable?

I've asked lots of questions here with no plan to answer any of them. And that's because I don't think Will had any plan to answer any of them, either. As I say, for Will the asking is often the point.

Richard II resists any simple formulations of what character is, how it works, whether it changes, and where it leads us. It does so because the play sets out not to tell but to inquire. And, through that questioning, in its own subtle and subversive way, it counsels caution and humility when it comes to judging character.

Just like our evidence rules do.

Dilemmas of Sovereignty

In *Richard II*, Will explores not just character but also the related concept of identity. For both Richard and Henry, identity turns out to be intertwined with the idea of sovereignty. We watch Richard go from God's Own Lieutenant Whose Word Is Law to an impotent has-been who can't get anyone to fetch him a mirror. Sovereignty is absolute power and so, for those who hold it, absolute identity.

The idea of sovereignty may seem antiquated and irrelevant to us today, but it continues to occupy space in our legal theory and language. We talk about the sovereignty of countries and states and have built confounding bodies of legal doctrine and political practice around the concept. In his book *Sovereignty RIP*, my colleague Don Herzog argues—to my mind persuasively—that the notion has lost its utility. We have moved so far away from the classic concept of sovereignty, he contends, that it doesn't do any work that we can't do better through more manageable concepts like state, jurisdiction, and authority.

The classic concept, as Don describes it, holds that "to have an orderly society, you have to have a locus of political authority that's unlimited, undivided, and unaccountable." In Don's telling, this theory was born of necessity, a response to early modern Europe's wars of religion. He sees it as a sensible enough measure to deal with extraordinarily violent and dangerous circumstances. But the concept has worn poorly; in the hands of fascists and dictators it has become the handmaiden of endless injustices and atrocities.

The classic concept, articulated in various ways throughout the sixteenth and seventeenth centuries, tends to situate sovereignty in a monarch, although it could reside anywhere as long as authority remains unlimited, undivided, and unaccountable. Whatever its shortcomings, this view of sovereignty does have the virtue of answering all sorts of questions, especially about law. What is law? Whatever the king commands. Can the king break the law? No, that's nonsense; the king's voice is the law. Does an authority exist over the king? None; indeed, the king is God's ambassador on earth.

In *Richard II*, Shakespeare takes the idea of sovereignty in hand, turns it over and over, and inspects it from every angle. Granted, the classic concept gets its cheerleaders, Richard chief among them. When, in the third act, Northumberland approaches Richard at Flint Castle to present Henry's demands, the king reminds him that nothing short of the divine will can wrestle him from his station:

> If we be not [your king], show us the hand of God
> That hath dismissed us from our stewardship.
> For well we know no hand of blood and bone
> Can gripe the sacred handle of our scepter. (III:3:79–82)

It's a pretty little speech, but it feels like bringing a knife to a gunfight—or, perhaps more accurately, the memory of a knife. The very making of demands reduces Richard's sovereignty to nothing, Henry's disclaimers notwithstanding. And, within fifty lines of the speech, Richard has capitulated to all of those demands. Sovereign shmovereign.

That capitulation leaves us with a bit of a puzzle. Granted, the concept of complete authority may as a matter of logical necessity have to include the power to surrender it. But it does seem hard to reconcile (A) an appointment to kingship by the Very Hand of the Living God with (B) willful abdication. "I am in this role by command of the Most Powerful Force in the Universe. And, now, I must be going."

The other figures in the play who stand by the classic concept of sovereignty don't fare much better than Richard. Gaunt invokes it in the second scene of Act I when the Duchess of Gloucester pleads for him to avenge Richard's role in her late husband's death. He summarily dismisses the idea:

> God's is the quarrel; for God's substitute,
> His deputy anointed in His sight,
> Hath caused his death, the which if wrongfully
> Let heaven revenge, for I may never lift
> An angry arm against His minister. (I:2:39–43)

The king murdered someone? Sorry, Gaunt says, leave him to heaven; that's above my pay grade. But, then, watch what becomes of Gaunt, so loyal to the classic concept of sovereignty: The sovereign celebrates his death and steals his son's property. How's that sovereignty thing working for you now?

Or consider the Bishop of Carlisle's rant, in the first scene of Act IV, upon Henry's announcement that he'll ascend the throne. "What subject can give sentence on his king?" he cries, "And who sits here who is not Richard's subject?" Carlisle pronounces Henry a traitor and unleashes a prophecy of full-on apocalyptic dimensions. "The blood of English shall manure the ground," peace will flee the country, "disorder, horror, fear, and mutiny" will rule the day, and the land will be named for "dead men's skulls."

Sounds pretty bad. And what does good Carlisle get for his full-throated defense of the classic concept of sovereignty? Arrested.

Henry, a practical politician, has little time on his way up for theories of any kind, let alone theories that might hold him back. Making demands of the king—"God's lieutenant" in the words of Coke—may make for bad form, but Henry wants his land. When it comes around to his turn, though, Henry will have some of that sovereignty stuff if it comes with the job. So, he does not just declare that he'll ascend the throne—he says he'll do it "in God's name."

The God that Henry invokes seems like a changeable sort, but surely no more changeable than York. When York first learns that Henry has returned—although still under banishment—he upbraids him and reaffirms his loyalty to his sovereign, Richard. Henry's arguments don't move him much—he subscribes to the classic concept of sovereignty—but he recognizes that support has shifted away from Richard and so says he'll remain "neuter." That neutrality doesn't last long: his reservations notwithstanding, York invites Henry and crew into his castle for bed and breakfast; in short order, they have become allies.

For obvious reasons, Will couldn't write a play that directly challenged the classic concept of sovereignty. But, using historical events as his stalking horse, he could write a play about what becomes of that concept in practice, amidst the skirmishes of realpolitik, in the hands of men capable of molding it to their own ends. *Richard II* puts the full range of possibilities on display.

When we look at *Richard II* through the lens of the law, we see Will wrestling with a concept that makes little sense in our own time and was of limited utility even in his own. After all, it may be true that the classic concept of sovereignty gets a society some much-needed stability, order, and peace in especially perilous times. But if the locus of authority—the monarch—proves incompetent and destructive to the social good, if the cure proves worse than the disease, then we need a Plan B.

The problem, of course, is that every Plan B must, by necessity, violate the purportedly inviolable sovereignty we put up in the first place. Talk of sovereignty that can be lost when the sovereign misbehaves is incoherent under the classic concept; it makes the absolute contingent. If we continue to pledge our allegiance to the classic concept, at least in principle, then Plan B can never fully shake off the charge that it is nothing more than treason most foul—even if sometimes we need a little friendly treason to get by.

Where does that leave us? Where history always leaves us.

Sitting on the ground.

Telling sad stories of the deaths of kings.

4

"A Cold Decree"

The Merchant of Venice

Backdrop

I suppose you could write a book or teach a course about Shakespeare and the law and not touch on any of the first three plays we've examined together—although I think it would be a mistake. But you absolutely couldn't do so without discussing *The Merchant of Venice*. The central scene in the play takes place during a legal proceeding. The fate of several of the play's key characters turns on a legal argument. And the advocate who makes that argument, Portia, has long been celebrated as a model of courtroom brilliance and resourcefulness—although, as we'll discuss, reasonable people can disagree about what to make of her.

Nevertheless, any sensible person who writes on or teaches *Merchant* approaches the project with a respectable helping of dread. Tradition classifies the play as a comedy, which doesn't make sense to modern audiences. More on that later. And, for good reasons, scholars have categorized *Merchant* as one of Shakespeare's "problem plays." More on that later, too. But the biggest obstacle to our unalloyed enjoyment of the play lies in the powerful antisemitic poison that courses through its veins. More on that later as well? Oh, yes. Quite a bit.

But first things first.

Will wrote *Merchant* in the late 1590s. It was registered for publication in 1598 and its references to a particular Spanish ship suggest authorship in

1596 or 1597. For Will, these were years of both dazzling light and crushing darkness.

At the professional level, Will had arrived. He followed up *Richard II* with two masterpieces, *Romeo and Juliet* and *A Midsummer Night's Dream.* He had demonstrated his command over the theatrical genres of history, tragedy, and comedy, a stunning achievement. Michael Wood writes: "By the summer of 1596, Shakespeare was already the greatest poet in the English language, and he would be still regarded as such today even if he had written nothing more after *Romeo and Juliet*."

But, in the summer of 1596, Will suffered two staggering losses in quick succession. In July, his patron Lord Hunsdon passed away, leaving the survival of Will's company in doubt. And then, in August, his eleven-year-old son Hamnet died. We don't know the cause for certain, but plague is the prime suspect.

Divining someone's intentions over the distance of more than four centuries is a dicey proposition, but it appears that Will responded to the tragic loss of his son by tightening connections with family. In October of 1596 he applied for a coat of arms, an honor for which his father had yearned. And in 1597 he bought a sprawling house in Stratford, a bit run down but endowed with ten chimneys and one of the area's most impressive homes, which he set about updating for his wife and surviving children.

The Stratford investment notwithstanding, Will's work required that he reside primarily in London. From tax records, scholars have concluded that it was around this time he moved to the sketchy Southwark area of town—where the Tabard Inn was located. It seems likely that Will shared in the rough and bawdy life of Southwark, given how far out of his way he'd have had to go to avoid it. So, when Will convincingly conveys to us the scents and sensibilities of London dive bars, we can fairly assume that he drew from personal experience and not from hearsay.

Will looked to a variety of sources in writing *Merchant*, but two influences are particularly pronounced. First, a story told in Fiorentino's collection of tales, *Il Pecorone*, printed in 1558, supplied the primary narrative and general outline for many of the characters. Second, Will was undoubtedly familiar with a play written by his rival Christopher Marlowe, *The Jew of Malta*, which had met with considerable success. The Jew at the center of Marlowe's play, the extravagantly sinister Barabas, who boasts about poisoning wells and going around town killing sick homeless people, has little in common with Will's vastly more complex Shylock. But both playwrights traded on antisemitic tropes in crafting their characters.

As always, a great distance lies between Will's influences and his own take on the story. Indeed, *Merchant* may leave us with the sense that Will breathed so much additional life into some of the play's characters that he couldn't quite figure out what to do with them. As we will see, that's not the only trouble he gets himself into here.

A modern audience member can sit through a lot of *The Merchant of Venice* without laughing, or for that matter smiling, so its traditional classification as a comedy may seem puzzling. It helps to think about comedy as a structural concept and to view the play backwards: *Merchant* ends with a couple united—indeed, in a typically Shakespearean flourish, two couples united—despite all the formidable obstacles the plot throws in their way. That structure make *Merchant* a comedy, indeed a conventionally framed one.

But *Merchant* is also a "problem play." In an 1896 book called *Shakespeare and His Predecessors*, literary scholar Frederick Samuel Boas coined that phrase to describe *All's Well that Ends Well*, *Troilus and Cressida*, and *Measure for Measure*, the last of which we'll consider in a later chapter. Scholars have disagreed about which plays qualify as problem plays, and about what exactly makes a problem play problematic. *The Merchant of Venice* shows up regularly on lists of problem plays, even though Boas did not include it in his.

For our purposes, we can think of a problem play as one that fits uncomfortably in the category of comedy. Sure, in a general sense the play honors the formula: It has yearning lovers, seemingly insurmountable challenges, mix-ups and misunderstandings along the way, and a uniting of the couple at the end. But the play also raises complex moral dilemmas and a thick darkness broods over its action. Conventional comedies amuse us, but they don't haunt us; problem plays do. By this standard, *The Merchant of Venice* qualifies as whoppingly problematic.

As I noted above, for contemporary audiences the most daunting problem the play presents is how to think about its strident antisemitism. I have my own views, which we'll get to later, but at present I'd like to offer something akin to a preliminary jury instruction. No matter what you know, or think you know, about *The Merchant of Venice*, please keep an open mind until all the evidence is in. Then, inside of the sealed room where authors and readers freely and confidentially talk things through, we'll deliberate to a verdict.

I can't promise it will be a unanimous one.

Get comfortable. Take a sip of mead. We've got a lot to discuss, and Will's got a lot of explaining to do.

An Argument and Some Ethical Puzzles

The first scene of the fourth act gives us Will's most famous depiction of a trial. Antonio has been arrested for failing to pay his debt to Shylock—a debt secured by a pound of Antonio's flesh. He has been brought before the Duke and a collection of Venetian nobles. The Duke tells his cohort that he has tried to dissuade Shylock from insisting on the gruesome payment but to no effect. Not one to mince words, the Duke describes Shylock as "a stony adversary, an inhuman wretch, uncapable of pity, void and empty from any dram of mercy."

When Shylock enters, the Duke takes another run at him, suggesting that perhaps Shylock has decided to hold out until the last possible moment in order to antagonize Antonio. "We all expect a gentle answer," the Duke declares hopefully, but he doesn't get one. Shylock reiterates that "by our holy Sabbath" he has sworn to have his bond satisfied with a pound of flesh. And he issues a warning: Failure to strictly enforce the bond will undermine Venetian law and the Duke's authority.

In the course of these exchanges, the question naturally arises as to why Shylock wants a pound of flesh, anyway. What good does it do him? At first Shylock refuses to explain. The debt belongs to him and he can collect it as he chooses. But then he relents and offers a reason: He hates Antonio. Antonio's beloved friend, Bassanio, on whose behalf he borrowed the money, argues with Shylock and doubles the offered payment to six thousand ducats, but Shylock holds firm. He stubbornly insists: "I would have my bond."

The Duke explains that he has asked Bellario, a distinguished legal scholar, to advise him in adjudicating the dispute. Nerissa appears and introduces herself as clerk to a "young and learned doctor" of the laws, who Bellario has sent in his stead. Enter Portia, dressed as said young and learned counselor, Balthazar.

A simplified version of what happens next goes something like this: Portia poignantly explains the nature of mercy to Shylock, but he refuses to hear it. Having failed to persuade him, she advances a brilliant legal argument that exploits a loophole in the bond. And, lo, justice gets done.

If we look at this scene through the lens of the law, however, we discover many more layers of subtlety and complexity. Let's dig in.

Portia does indeed offer up a lovely speech about mercy, beginning with these famous verses: "The quality of mercy is not strained. / It droppeth as the gentle rain from heaven / Upon the place beneath. It is twice blest: / It blesseth him that gives and him that takes." On and on she goes, extolling the virtues of grace and forgiveness.

Of course, on its face it looks for all the world like Portia is directing this poignant argument toward Shylock. Shylock certainly takes it that way, because he promptly responds to her. "I crave the law, / The penalty and forfeit of my bond," he declares. If Portia hoped to persuade Shylock with this pretty speech, it plainly didn't work.

But is Portia really talking to Shylock? Does she really think she's going to change his mind? We have reasons to think not, on both counts.

In my view, it's fair to assume that Portia knows Shylock has already refused Bassanio's efforts to pay the debt and has rebuffed the Duke's arm-twisting. Indeed, if the Duke or Bassanio had been able to settle the matter, then there'd be no need for a trial and no need for her to appear. I think it's also fair to assume that Portia doesn't really believe that poetry will succeed where ducats and a Duke have failed. Such a belief would require boundless—and uncharacteristic—naivete on her part. It therefore seems implausible that she's trying to move the immovable Shylock or, for that matter, that she's even addressing her remarks to him.

Here's what I think is going on.

Every litigator will tell you that, in court, the person to whom you're speaking isn't necessarily the person you're trying to persuade. When at trial a lawyer cross-examines a hostile witness, he's not really talking to the witness; he knows the witness isn't going to agree with him. He's talking to the jury, giving them reasons to doubt the witness's credibility. When, at an appellate argument, a lawyer answers a question from a hostile judge, she's not really talking to that judge; she knows she can't get his vote. She's talking to the friendlier judges on the panel, trying to draw them firmly to her side.

I suspect that Portia has a different audience in mind when she offers Shylock her grand poetic tribute to mercy. She isn't talking to Shylock; she's talking to the Duke. She wants the Duke, who will serve as the ultimate decision maker, to see Shylock's cold indifference to her beautiful words. She wants the Duke to witness the black depths of Shylock's malice. After her speech, she drives the point home by giving Shylock several more opportunities to show mercy, which he summarily rejects.

Portia believes that if she puts Shylock's cruelty and callousness on full display it will make the Duke more receptive to the legal argument she plans to make. She needs all the help she can get on that front, because her argument is almost comically technical—even more technical than Henry's claim in *Richard II* that he has complied with the king's order because he was banished under one title but returns under another. Thinking of Portia's strategy this way significantly changes how we assess her performance.

If we see Portia's efforts here as trying to persuade Shylock of anything, then she fails; but if we see it as a strategy to soften up the Duke, then she succeeds—magnificently.

Of course, Shylock's vindictiveness bears no relevance to the legal question at issue. If he's entitled to the pound of flesh, then he should get it. But every litigator understands that decision makers are influenced by irrelevant considerations. That's why I do a magic trick in front of my Evidence students: to help them understand the strategic advantages of misdirection.

Lawyers call this tactic "poisoning the well," a striking coincidence given that Marlowe's evil Jew, Barabas, went around the city of Malta literally doing just that. A lawyer who "poisons the well" tries to get facts in front of the jury that make their opponent look bad. For their purposes, it doesn't matter that those facts are utterly immaterial to the dispute.

Many years ago, toward the beginning of my career, I was in a meeting with a crusty old litigator who could barely restrain his delight over a very bad fact that we had discovered about the other side. He couldn't wait to watch the faces of the judge and jurors when they heard about this evidence. I had reservations; I couldn't figure out why the evidence was relevant to the case—unsurprising, perhaps, given that it plainly wasn't. After a bit of back and forth between us, he finally sighed, gave me a bemused look, and said: "Young man, this evidence is admissible pursuant to the Uniform Well-Poisoning Act."

The evidence came in. It had the predicted effect.

Having softened up the Duke, Portia deftly makes her next move. Bassanio begs the Duke for relief from Shylock's demand for a pound of flesh, but Portia intercedes: "It must not be." Failing to enforce a lawful bond, she argues, would create a dangerous precedent, destabilizing the state. Her point aligns perfectly with the very argument Shylock made to the Duke so, needless to say, Shylock loves it.

A brief detour: It's worth noting that Shakespeare's plays reflect a deep interest in this argument—the argument that the state must enforce even destructive and unfair laws lest anarchy ensue—and that he does not appear to have been impressed by it. We'll encounter the idea again in other plays and it will receive similarly critical treatment. *Merchant* itself perfectly displays the internal contradiction that often exists within the argument. If moral regard for the law is what we're after, it seems unlikely we're going to get it under a system that forces a man to give up a pound of flesh to settle a debt.

Okay, back to the main thread: As this scene unfolds, Portia reiterates again and again that the bond must be enforced according to its literal terms. At this point, the intended audience for her remarks reverses: It seems like she's talking to the Duke, but she's actually talking to Shylock. She's goading him on, luring him into fully and publicly embracing the most literal reading possible of the terms of the bond. He takes the bait, praising her wisdom and discernment.

But when Shylock seems poised to start cutting, Portia intervenes. She notes that the bond awards Shylock one pound of flesh—but no blood. If Shylock draws any blood in the process of collecting the flesh, he will have violated the terms of the agreement. A bewildered Shylock wants to know where this detail appears in the bond, but of course that's not the point. The point is about what the bond doesn't say, not about what it says, and what it doesn't say is that Shylock has the right to collect any of Antonio's blood along with the flesh.

Legal scholars have noted that, as arguments go, Portia's is weak, bordering on silly. Every contract comes with implied terms. When I agree to sell you a house, that includes the roof and the walls. When I agree to sell you a car, that includes the wheels and the engine. When I agree to repay you in a pound of flesh, that includes the skin and the blood. As Kenji Yoshino notes in his book *A Thousand Times More Fair*, critics have described Portia's argument as a "wretched quibble," a "miserable pettifogging trick," and a "shoddy technicality."

Perhaps, but I don't think those critics give Portia enough credit. In my view, her argument works, but it works only because she ensures that Shylock can't credibly object to it. She coaxes him into stipulating—repeatedly, openly, insistently—that nothing other than a strictly literal construction of the agreement will do. She gets him to play one-move chess and then mates him with his own absolutism: You get your pound of flesh and that's that? Fine. Then you get your pound of flesh—and that's that. He who lives by the literal construction shall die by the literal construction. (In a later play, Macbeth will find out how the literal construction of a prophecy can get you into trouble, too.)

Every trial lawyer who reads this scene recognizes Portia's strategy. The litigator draws the opposing party into agreeing with something that seems benign or perhaps even advantageous—and then they reveal the trap. An old adage holds that the best lawyers prove their case through their opponent, and that's just what Portia does here; she uses Shylock's uncompromising literalism to serve her own ends. Call it a "pettifogging trick" if you like, but it works in the play and it often works quite wonderfully in practice.

I find much to admire in Portia's strategy, at least to the extent we've explored it so far. But she may have had even better legal arguments, especially under contract law as it exists now. Contemporary lawyers and judges have delighted in inventorying them.

For example, Daniel Kornstein argues that no court today would enforce the penalty provision of the bond because it violates public policy. The idea that public policy forbids certain types of agreements is the stuff of basic first-year law school Contracts courses, so when I talk about *Merchant* with lawyers and law students this is often the first point they raise. And, indeed, at the risk of stating the obvious, current law doesn't countenance debts secured by living human flesh. A few years ago, a creative student of mine wrote a paper suggesting that a related federal law prohibiting the sale of human organs might prohibit the enforcement of the bond as well.

Kornstein further contends that, under current legal doctrine, the contract wouldn't be valid because Shylock used fraud to induce Antonio to sign it. He has a point. In their initial conversation about the loan, Shylock tells Antonio that the bond is being done "in merry sport," suggesting that the penalty provision amounted to nothing more than a joke. And Antonio had good reasons to take it as such, given that a pound of flesh presumably wouldn't have any utility or value for Shylock.

In a fascinating essay on *Merchant*, Judge Richard Posner raises yet another argument. He contends that, even if the agreement was valid and the bond had come due, Shylock was entitled only to demand payment. Bassanio stood ready to fulfill that obligation, several times over. Shylock therefore had the right to collect the ducats owed him, but no right to insist on the pound of flesh.

These various efforts to out-Portia Portia are great fun, at least for the nerdiest among us, but I think they obscure her achievement. Almost any lawyer can win a case when they have a great argument, and most of these latter-day arguments are indeed pretty good. But it takes a truly skilled advocate to prevail when all they have is a lousy one.

And that's what Will gives Portia here: a lousy argument of ridiculous technicality that would hold little or no persuasive force in any other context. But Portia makes it work. And she makes it work by getting Shylock to embrace it and by giving the Duke abundant, if legally irrelevant, reasons to find in her favor.

In these respects, Portia's performance is a dazzlingly good one.

Will could have ended Shylock's misadventures there. We can imagine a version of the play where Shylock gets back his 3,000 ducats (a penalty in itself because Bassanio has used the money interest-free) and stalks off the stage in frustration to the mocking laughter of everyone around him. Indeed, the scene almost ends that way: A frustrated and defeated Shylock throws his hands up and begins to exit.

If we understood Shylock as an absurd character—and Shakespeare gives us plenty of those in his plays—such an outcome might make sense. This is, after all, a comedy. But the play has painted Shylock as a villain, and villains must get their comeuppance, especially if we need a truly happy ending, so obviously Will can't allow him to depart the stage scot-free.

"Tarry, Jew," Portia calls out. She notes that Shylock, an "alien," has attempted to take the life of a Venetian citizen, a crime that carries with it specific and severe penalties. The party whose life the alien threatened gets half of the defendant's goods; the other half goes to the state; and the Duke can condemn the alien to execution. The Duke swiftly orders half of Shylock's goods to the state and half to Antonio, but spares Shylock's life.

The roles flip and Shylock now pleads for mercy from Antonio, and he gets some, although not much. Antonio will take half of his goods, but hold them in trust for his daughter, Jessica, and her betrothed, Lorenzo. The state will impose a fine on Shylock, but not take all of his remaining property. Shylock will bequeath any property he has at death to his daughter and her husband. Oh, and one last thing: Shylock must "presently become a Christian."

It seems unlikely that Will's audiences would have found anything especially troubling in Shylock's punishment. The Duke spares Shylock's life and Antonio asks for a lesser financial penalty than the law allows. It's hard to begrudge Antonio his cut, so to speak, given that Shylock came perilously close to killing him. (In the words of the personal injury lawyer television ads, Antonio "may be entitled to compensation.") And the primary financial beneficiary of the forfeiture isn't Antonio, but Shylock's daughter and his son-in-law.

Nor does it seem likely that Will's audiences would have been offended by the compulsory conversion. King Edward I had banned Jews from England in 1290—some three centuries earlier—so antisemitism was effectively a longstanding matter of national public policy. No one in Will's audiences may ever have met a Jew, let alone acquired any understanding of them beyond the prevailing pernicious stereotypes. And, if Will's audiences were not put off by Shylock's punishment, then they would not have been put off by Portia's facilitation of it.

All of this sits quite differently with current audiences, who may experience the penalty as breathtakingly severe. It obliterates Shylock's identity as a financially successful Jew. He loses more than half of his wealth and all control over what becomes of his estate. He can no longer practice his faith. And the religious dimension of the punishment puts him in a double bind: He could claim to convert to Christianity while remaining a Jew at heart, but doing so would require him to violate the commandment against false testimony.

These events may also lead modern audiences to puzzle over Portia's character and integrity. Once a voluble advocate for mercy, Portia doesn't press Antonio to lighten further the sentence imposed on Shylock. To the contrary, she assists in the ruthless enforcement of Antonio's will. She asks Shylock if he is content, perhaps because his conversion to Christianity would be meaningless unless voluntary, and, when he says yes, she directs the clerk to draw up the necessary forms. So, given the unapologetic antisemitism of the punishment she helps implement, what do we think of Portia today?

Looking at Portia's conduct through the lens of the law, especially the lens of legal ethics, brings several issues into focus. As an initial matter, Portia has an obvious conflict of interest. The Duke sent for help in adjudicating the case and "Balthazar" answered that call to government service, so Portia is ostensibly working as a dispassionate instrument of justice. But, of course, she has skin in the game (literally): She wants Antonio to prevail, and she works hard to make that happen by—among other things—manipulating the Duke.

We might instead think of her as legal counsel to Antonio, which more accurately captures her role, but ethical problems persist. One such problem is that Portia isn't a lawyer at all; she's just pretending to be one. It seems a rich irony that Portia, long idolized as a brilliant legal strategist, was apparently engaged in the unauthorized practice of law.

But let's put aside the nettlesome fact that Portia wasn't a lawyer and let's assume that Portia was acting as Antonio's legal counsel. Under those circumstances, is there anything ethically wrong in Portia working to achieve whatever Antonio wants—even if what Antonio wants strikes us as morally obnoxious? Isn't that what lawyers are supposed to do?

Modern legal ethics rules hold that a lawyer's representation of a client does not constitute a personal endorsement of their conduct or position. Today, when an offended layperson asks a lawyer "How can you represent someone like that?," the sort of question we might pose to Portia, the attorney typically responds that their job is to help their client, not to judge them. Judging their client is somebody else's job.

In explaining the point, legal ethics experts have occasionally compared lawyers to taxicab drivers: The client tells the lawyer where they want to go and the lawyer's role is to get them there. (I once heard law professor and ethicist Geoffrey Hazard joke that lawyers are more like New York cab drivers—they take the client by the longest and most expensive route.) The analogy emphasizes the neutrality of the lawyer, whose "conveyance" of the client doesn't signal their approval of the client's chosen destination.

When I teach my Legal Ethics course, I test the boundaries of this analogy by asking my students whether this means that a cab driver has to do everything their passenger asks of them. Of course, they say no. They recognize that a driver shouldn't speed recklessly, go over sidewalks, bump pedestrians out of the way, or ignore ambulance sirens just because the passenger demands it. Sure, I tell them, the passenger gets a lot of control over where the cab goes and how it goes there. But I add: Never forget—you're in the cab, too.

Modern audiences may wonder whether Portia has forgotten that she's in the cab, too. We cheer her on as she cleverly extricates Antonio from his perilous situation. But when the switch flips, and she becomes less angel of justice and more instrument of revenge, we may feel considerably less enthused. When she outmaneuvers Shylock, we see evidence of her brilliant mind. When, on Antonio's behalf, she goes on to destroy Shylock as a human being, we may find ourselves looking for evidence of her soul.

Antonio has his virtues; he sticks his neck out to help a friend he loves. But he is ferociously antisemitic and, in the end, he demands nothing less than the destruction of Shylock's identity. Why does Portia go along with it? Why does she help him get to that destination? How can a person of conscience represent someone like that?

It's an old dilemma. As old as the profession itself.

And as current as the next unsavory client who walks into our office.

"A Jewish Heart"

The Merchant of Venice unquestionably includes powerful and unsettling elements of antisemitism. It features antisemitic speech, antisemitic imagery, antisemitic tropes, and antisemitic humor. The play has even given rise to its own antisemitic epithet: Calling someone a "Shylock" labels them as a Jew who loans money at usurious rates or engages in other sharp practices.

But can we fairly call *Merchant* an antisemitic *play*—meaning a play with an antisemitic *message*? And, if so, can we fairly conclude that, whatever his other admirable qualities, William Shakespeare was himself an antisemite? These questions dog readers of the play, especially in a post-Holocaust world that has seen the unspeakable tragedies that follow from unchecked hate and scapegoating.

Different literary scholars, directors, and actors have expressed divergent views on these questions. Some have argued that, although certain characters in the play clearly hold antisemitic attitudes, the play itself is not antisemitic. Among other things, they contend that Will gives Shylock too much humanity, and makes the Christians around him too cruel and flawed, for us to conclude that the play endorses antisemitic impulses.

Others reach very different conclusions. Harold Bloom, for example, doesn't mince words in expressing the opposing point of view. He writes: "One would have to be blind, deaf, and dumb not to recognize that Shakespeare's grand, equivocal comedy *The Merchant of Venice* is nevertheless a profoundly anti-Semitic work." Bloom argues that the play only makes sense if Shylock comes across as a comic villain, and portraying him as such necessarily depends on antisemitic tropes and stereotypes.

Those who reject an antisemitic reading of *Merchant* sometimes point toward Will's personal experience. They note that Will grew up in a family of religious outsiders, Catholics forced to abandon their faith under strict

Protestant rule. They argue that someone familiar with the burdens of religious persecution wouldn't write an antisemitic play.

We might be able to confirm this theory if we could meet Shakespeare at the bar and talk things over with him, but we can't. And all the things that we don't know make the theory problematic. We don't know what Will thought about the ban on Catholicism. If he opposed it, we don't know whether that opposition translated into respect for the religious freedom of Jews. We don't know how the prevailing antisemitism of his age affected Will. As noted earlier, antisemitism had been a matter of public policy in England for three centuries, and Will may have fallen prey to the prejudices of his time. Even the best among us do.

Assessing the antisemitism in *Merchant* through the lens of the law requires us to resist the tempting speculations of biography and to focus on the most reliable evidence we have: the text itself. But it turns out that the text complicates things, too. And it does so not just by what it says, but by what it doesn't say.

Emma Smith has aptly observed that Shakespeare's plays have a "gappiness" to them. That is, the plays leave unspoken lots of details about staging and presentation. How we fill those gaps can make a significant difference in what we think the play tells us. This holds particularly true for *Merchant*.

Consider an example. Toward the beginning of *Merchant*, Shylock says that—among many other abuses—Antonio has spat upon him. It's a repulsive image, and one that invites us to sympathize with Shylock's anger. But a production that *shows* Antonio spitting on Shylock, as does the 2004 film version of the play starring Jeremy Irons and Al Pacino, may give us an even greater understanding of Shylock's rage and Antonio's responsibility for it.

So, how we fill the gaps can help determine the meaning of the play and how we think about its antisemitism. But the gaps are also just that—gaps. And our project is to assess the text that we have, not to imagine all the things that the gappiness of that text might allow us to do with it.

So let's focus on the text of *Merchant* and see where it leads.

One important piece of evidence is the stunning quantity of antisemitic language that *Merchant* contains. Of course, the presence of such language doesn't in itself make a play antisemitic. A play that wanted to show us an antisemitic society, without endorsing that antisemitism, could include such language—indeed, it would probably have to do so. So, for that matter, would a play that wanted to critique and subvert antisemitism. The novels of many contemporary Jewish authors include viciously antisemitic language, but toward the goal of disassembling antisemitism, not toward the goal of shoring it up.

But the text of *Merchant* makes it hard, if not impossible, to conclude that the play reflects a neutral or critical view of antisemitism. Such an argument might hold up if Will gave antisemitic lines only to characters in the play who he casts as villains or fools, but he doesn't. For example, Gratiano—who otherwise seems likable enough—calls Shylock a "harsh Jew," a "currish Jew," and a "damned inexecrable dog." Furthermore, the epithets directed against Shylock go well beyond Will's typical over-the-top insults; they expressly link to religious identity and portray their target as less than human.

Scholars have argued that even the use of the single word "Jew" takes on a charged significance in *Merchant.* As D. M. Cohen notes in his 1980 essay *The Jew and Shylock*, the word "Jew" is used in the play fifty-eight times. Variations on the word, like "Jewish," fourteen more times. In the entire play, someone addresses Shylock by his name only seventeen times; on every other occasion, they call him "the Jew." Cohen writes: "The reason for this discrimination is, of course, to set Shylock apart from the other characters. This it successfully does. Calling the play's villain by a name which generalizes him while at the same time ostensibly defining his essence is, in a sense, to depersonalize him."

But the text goes further. At a few points, it moves us from passive observers of the play's antisemitism to active participants in it. In part, it does so by inviting us to laugh along with humor that plays on ugly stereotypes. Consider, for example, the scene where two of Antonio's friends, Salanio and Salarino, mockingly describe Shylock running up and down the streets calling in distress for his ducats and his daughter—as if both held equal value to him. Contemporary audiences may recoil at using antisemitic caricatures as a source of amusement and laughter, but we have no reason to believe Will would have expected his own audiences to react the same way.

The play's portrayal of Shylock, which relies on pernicious stereotypes about Jews, further rebuts the argument that the play takes a neutral stance on antisemitism or seeks to undermine it. Shylock lends money at usurious rates. He hates Antonio in part because Antonio has undercut Shylock's loan-sharking business. He loathes Christians. He dreams of bags of money. He places law and commerce and the strict enforcement of rules over compassion and forgiveness and grace.

So far the case against the play looks pretty strong, and the analysis would end there if the text did nothing to humanize Shylock. But, as we've seen and will discuss further in future chapters, Will never shows much interest in uncomplicated villains. Shakespeare may have created no character more monstrous than Aaron in *Titus Andronicus*, and he endows even this heartless brute with tender feelings for his infant son. And so it goes with Shylock.

The play gives texture to the portrait of Shylock. He has lost his wife, who he clearly loved. He cares deeply for Jessica, despite her abundant shortcomings; and, if he smothers and alienates her, he's not the first or last father to make that mistake. It's not clear, though, how much these considerations help. After all, the play doesn't have to portray Shylock as the embodiment of evil in order to qualify as antisemitic.

It has often been noted that Will gives Shylock one of the best speeches in the play—and a speech in which he inventories the qualities of his humanity, no less: "I am a Jew. Hath not a Jew eyes? Hath not a Jew hands, organs, dimensions, senses, affections, passions? . . . If you prick us do we not bleed? If you tickle us, do we not laugh? If you poison us, do we not die?" It's powerful stuff.

On closer inspection, though, the speech has sharp edges: Shylock begins and ends it with talk of revenge. He precedes the speech by explaining why he insists on the pound of flesh: "It will feed my revenge." And then, after the poignant lines quoted above, he adds: "And if you wrong us, shall we not revenge? . . . The villainy you teach me, I will execute. And it shall go hard, but I will better the instruction." As I noted in our conversation about *Titus Andronicus*, the line between law and revenge is a blurry one, and Shylock shows himself happy to dance across it.

Okay, but what are we to make of that? We might think that these references to revenge drain Shylock's otherwise moving speech of the very humanity it invokes. I'm not so sure. Granted, if we subscribe to the "official" position, as Bill Miller calls it, then Shylock should lose us when he starts talking about revenge. But, as we've discussed, the official position doesn't align with the satisfaction we experience in seeing vengeance done when the situation justifies it. We love a good revenge story, and the plot of *Merchant* seems to have set one up for us.

Antonio's abuses leave him with a debt to Shylock far in excess of the 3,000 ducats, and we can sympathize with Shylock's powerful compulsion to collect on it. Furthermore, Antonio's abuses have made up only a small part of what Shylock has had to endure under the pervasive antisemitism within Venetian society, as *Merchant* extravagantly displays it. Will doesn't give us Marlowe's psychopathic Barabas; he gives us Shylock, a human being who has abundant reasons to crave revenge, to cast a cold eye on pleas for mercy, and to thumb his nose at the society that pleads for a grace it has never shown to him.

In the end, though, our sympathy with Shylock can only extend so far. As discussed in the chapter on *Titus Andronicus*, we cheer the avenger on—but only as long as the revenge feels proportional to the debt. Granted, Antonio's mistreatment of Shylock has earned him a big old steaming pile of misery. But death by meat cleaver is something else altogether.

In Shylock, Will's rich imagination and preternatural gift for empathy created an unmanageable character—one entitled to revenge, but not the revenge he wants; one with whom we can empathize, but not entirely; one who is fully human, but also fully monster, just as those potentials exist within us all. No wonder Will had to get rid of him in the fourth act.

Where does this leave us? What do we learn by considering the antisemitism of *Merchant* though the lens of the law? Here are my verdicts, respectfully submitted, acknowledging that yours may differ.

First, I think a preponderance of the evidence supports the conclusion that the play is antisemitic. In my view, the quantity of antisemitic epithets, stereotypes, and tropes, the distribution of antisemitic remarks and actions across so many characters, the use of antisemitic caricatures as "laugh lines," and the stereotype-driven villainy of Shylock add up to make a compelling case. Indeed, the case against *Merchant* seems to me so clear that I wonder whether we'd even debate the issue if a less beloved playwright had written it.

Second, I believe that the question of whether *Merchant* is antisemitic is separate and distinct from the question of whether Shakespeare was himself an antisemite. Even Bloom, who thinks the case against the play proved beyond any question, declares: "That Shakespeare himself was personally anti-Semitic we reasonably can doubt." I agree, and I think that the law provides useful insights on the point.

Every day of the year, parties vigorously litigate discrimination cases across the country. Overwhelmingly, those cases focus on questions about what the defendant did: how the defendant treated the plaintiff, what the defendant said to the plaintiff, whether the defendant deprived the plaintiff of equal opportunity based on a protected characteristic like race, gender, or religion, and so on. The law asks the jury to make lots of different kinds of judgments.

But in those cases the law doesn't ask the jury to make a judgment about the character of the defendant. The special verdict form that the jury fills out, which poses a series of questions about the decisions they made that led to their verdict, doesn't ask: "Do you find the defendant to be a bigot?" or "Do you find the defendant to be an antisemite?" We might say that the law puts aside the more complex (and potentially irrelevant) question of character in favor of the more straightforward (and plainly relevant) question of what the defendant did. If we think about *Merchant* in these terms, then—once we've concluded that Will wrote an antisemitic play—our inquiry ends.

I think that's an appropriate place for it to stop. We don't, and can't, know what went on in Will's heart or head. Indeed, we might not know those things for certain even if we had the opportunity to talk with him at length in the tavern over multiple rounds of drinks. In any event, we certainly don't, and can't, know those things over the distance of more than four hundred years.

This candid recognition of our limitations neither convicts nor absolves him. It just acknowledges that we don't pursue certain claims because we can't carry the burden of proof that goes along with them. I think the claim that Will held antisemitic views is one of those claims.

If that leaves you unsatisfied, well, I take some comfort in my good company. I think unsatisfied is where Will leaves everyone at the end of *Merchant*, too. Perhaps he does it by design.

We can at least make the character judgment that leaving us with lots of unanswered questions is a completely Shakespearean thing to do.

5

"How That Might Change His Nature"

Julius Caesar

Backdrop

Scholars believe that Shakespeare wrote *The Tragedy of Julius Caesar* around 1599, a year or two after *The Merchant of Venice*. Will returned to ancient Rome throughout his career, setting four plays there. We've already looked at one of those plays, *Titus Andronicus*, and toward the end of this book we'll consider another, *Coriolanus*. Each benefits in its own way from an examination through the lens of the law.

It's unsurprising that Will felt at home in classical antiquity. His early education likely consisted of endless drills on the Latin language and Roman history, and many members of his audiences may have suffered through similar ordeals. Shakespeare biographers tell us that the question at the heart of this play, whether Brutus and his co-conspirators were justified in murdering Caesar, was common fodder for instruction in rhetoric during the Elizabethan era.

Teachers trained their students to argue both sides of that question, much as we now prepare law students to argue both sides of a case. The exercise is commonplace in legal education: "Good job arguing the plaintiff's position. Now, please persuasively argue the exact opposite." The doing of it cultivates a skill essential in practice. Your chances of winning a case if you can't articulate the other side's best arguments are slim to none.

It turns out to have been excellent training for a playwright as well. It provided solid preparation for the moral complexity that Will puts on display for us in his plays, especially this one. And, for reasons I'll discuss more later, it's helpful to remember that Will's audiences would have come to a play about Caesar's assassination expecting just that sort of ethical ambiguity.

In writing *Julius Caesar*, Will drew heavily on Plutarch's *Lives of the Noble Grecians and Romans*, specifically as translated by Sir Thomas North. His play closely aligns with the major events and characters that Plutarch describes. But of course Will, who didn't hesitate to take liberties even when writing a historical play, certainly didn't feel constrained by the facts when writing a tragedy. *Julius Caesar* accordingly includes numerous departures from reality in the service of drama.

It seems clear, however, that Will didn't turn to this subject matter simply because he felt comfortable there and because Plutarch gave him a rich store of promising source material. The story of Caesar's assassination must have appealed to him for other reasons as well. It raises issues of political power, the peaceful (or not) transfer of that power, and public anxiety over the instability of rule—all issues of intense and immediate concern to Will's audiences.

At the time Will wrote *Julius Caesar*, Elizabeth was elderly and growing infirm. She had no child or other obvious successor. Plots and conspiracies, real and rumored, churned away. People worried, and they had reasons. At the same time, talking openly about these issues entailed considerable risk and invited the kind of trouble that could put your head on a pike. In the story of Julius Caesar, Will found a stalking horse behind which he could safely explore problems that were very much on everyone's mind.

Will employed a variety of dramatic devices to connect the ancient world with his own, including the use of anachronism. A famous example comes when Brutus asks Cassius how many times the clock has tolled—a question that doesn't make sense in the play's historical context because chiming clocks hadn't yet been invented. Critics like Marjorie Garber doubt that this was just a mistake on Will's part. They argue that it reflects an effort to blur the lines between past and present, just as costume and set designers do by dressing the players in contemporary outfits or by populating the stage with modern furniture and décor.

Will found the story of Julius Caesar meaningful to his time, and in the centuries that have followed we have found *Julius Caesar* meaningful to ours. The questions of how tyranny arises and what we can and should do to resist it have remained regrettably pertinent. Each generation has discovered in the play useful insights, lessons, and cautionary tales.

Examples abound. In a famous 1937 production of the play, Orson Welles portrayed Caesar as a Mussolini-like Fascist. When, in the 1970s, a copy of the complete works of Shakespeare secretly circulated among the political prisoners on South Africa's Robben Island (including a prisoner named Nelson Mandela), some of them underscored lines from *Julius Caesar* for inspiration. The 2025 Broadway hit about Edward R. Murrow's fight against McCarthyism, *Good Night & Good Luck*, quotes repeatedly from the play.

Of course, drawing connections between *Julius Caesar* and current events has not always worked out well. An actor named John Wilkes Booth—obsessed with the play and identifying closely with the character of Brutus—is said to have shouted "sic semper tyrannis" ("so it is always with tyrants") when he shot Abraham Lincoln. Angry theatergoers walked out of a 2017 production that conspicuously modeled Julius Caesar on Donald Trump. Shakespeare is not alone in his use of stalking horses.

Julius Caesar is also a play filled with puzzles, starting with the title. For a play called *Julius Caesar, Julius Caesar* isn't much about Julius Caesar, who gets none of the best speeches in the play and who dies in Act III. And yet the play does indeed revolve around Caesar. His actions create the dilemmas that the play sets out to explore. And the principal players—Brutus, Mark Antony, and Cassius—are in large measure defined by their competing perceptions of who Julius Caesar is and what he may become.

In a sense, every life consists in at least two stories. One is a story of historical fact. The other is a story about influence, about the effects that a life has everyone around it. We might see *Julius Caesar* as primarily the second sort of project. Caesar haunts the play throughout, and not just by making a late cameo appearance as an unwelcome ghost.

But, even if we follow the most obvious interpretive tack and treat *Julius Caesar* as an anti-authoritarian anthem, we find ourselves awash in difficulties, many of which come special delivery from the text itself. Will never met a scenario that he didn't want to make more nuanced, and *Julius Caesar* gives us a master class in the exercise. We therefore find here not so much an unqualified condemnation of tyranny as a collection of provocative questions about it. I'll pursue just two of them in this chapter, but they'll give us more than enough to ponder.

The first question we'll consider is whether we are morally permitted, or perhaps even obligated, to break the law in order to save the institutions that make law possible. To put it more simply: Must we sometimes ignore the law to keep the law? That question necessarily entails others, such as who we should trust to make so delicate and complicated a judgment. We'll take a close look at how Brutus in particular thinks these things through—or fails to do so.

The second question we'll consider is this: What type of arguments have the best chance at persuading people? It's a question that both Brutus and Mark Antony must answer at a critical moment in the play. And it's a question that practicing lawyers ponder every day of their professional lives. We'll look at how these two skilled orators approach the task, we'll assess their performances, and we'll try to see what we can learn from it all.

The tavern door is open. There are tankards on the table and there's a fire in the fireplace. Let's throw a leg over a bench and start the discussion.

A Suicide Pact

We'll begin, as all good tavern chatter does, with a story.

In the 1940s, Arthur Terminiello, a onetime Catholic priest who had been suspended by his Bishop, came to Chicago from Birmingham, Alabama, to give a speech. Inside the building, he spoke to a capacity crowd that was largely sympathetic to his views. Outside the building, an opposing crowd gathered to protest his messages, which they (correctly) condemned as racist and Fascist. Terminiello's speech agitated everyone, although for different reasons.

Circumstances grew increasingly tense and confrontational. Inside, attendees called for violence against the groups that Terminiello's speech villainized. Outside, protestors threw bricks and rocks and the Chicago police struggled to maintain order. Terminiello was charged with breach of the peace, convicted, and fined. He appealed his case all the way to the Supreme Court of the United States, which reversed his conviction.

The Supreme Court acknowledged the inflammatory nature of Terminiello's speech (it would have been tough to do otherwise) but also concluded that the city ordinance in question ran afoul of the First Amendment. Certainly, the Court said, the city had the power to adopt a law that prohibited disorderly conduct. In this case, however, the trial judge instructed the jury that a "breach of the peace" under the ordinance included any manner of speech that "stirs the public to anger, invites dispute, brings about a condition of unrest, or creates a disturbance." This interpretation, the Supreme Court declared, rendered the ordinance unconstitutionally vague and overbroad.

In my view, the Court clearly got this right. The definition of "breach of the peace" used by the trial judge was much too expansive. After all, speech that "invitees dispute" or "brings about a condition of unrest" would include a fair number of the words exchanged during peaceful protests, at sporting events, and around holiday dinner tables. To survive constitutional scrutiny, the ordinance needed to cut more surgically.

Nevertheless, several justices dissented, including Justice Robert Jackson. Before coming to the Court, Justice Jackson had held a variety of political posts, and he later took a leave of absence to serve as the chief U.S. prosecutor at the Nazi war crimes trials at Nuremburg. He was a pragmatist with a firm grasp on how the world actually works, but also had a gift for memorable, almost poetic, turns of phrase.

Justice Jackson expressed deep concern about Terminiello's speech, the effect it had on those in attendance, and the threat to public order it posed. He concluded his opinion with these words: "This Court has gone far toward accepting the doctrine that civil liberty means the removal of all restraints from these crowds . . . There is danger that, if the Court does not temper its doctrinaire logic with a little practical wisdom, it will convert the constitutional Bill of Rights into a suicide pact."

The risk that the law might become a "suicide pact" could arise in a variety of circumstances. Justice Jackson claimed to have identified one of them: where the law gives dissidents the freedom to vandalize the very legal order that ensures that freedom in the first instance. Liberty, Justice Jackson argued, does not include the liberty to tear it all down.

Justice Jackson may have overstated the dangers presented by Terminiello's speech, but the dilemma he identifies is a real one. The Court has often struggled with it, especially in connection with speech promoting Communist, anarchist, and Fascist ideologies. We have here a puzzle with an aftertaste of paradox: Why should the First Amendment protect speech that promotes the destruction of (among other things) the First Amendment? But, if it doesn't, then does it actually afford true freedom of expression?

Julius Caesar explores a different circumstance in which the law could become a suicide pact: where the law protects the life of a tyrant whose seizure of power will destroy the very institutions that give us law. We get strong hints of paradox here as well. We can save the law from the tyrant, the argument goes, only by killing the tyrant and breaking the law. I'll call this "the argument from tyranny."

In the United States, we don't just understand the argument from tyranny. As a nation born out of revolution, we think it has a central place in our history, political philosophy, and national identity. The argument gets a famous summation in a letter of Thomas Jefferson: "The tree of liberty must be refreshed from time to time with the blood of patriots and tyrants. It is it's natural manure."

Still, the argument from tyranny leaves us in an uncomfortable place, perhaps even a profoundly confused one, because it requires us simultaneously to do two things that feel inconsistent: (1) elevate the rule of law to an absolute value and (2) qualify the rule of law as contingent on the current circumstances and players. And then there's the problem of knowing when the conditions justify abandoning the rule of law—and who gets to decide that such a moment has arrived. Will seizes on these dilemmas, wraps them up and puts a bow on them, and delivers them unto Brutus and his brethren—but with no operating instructions.

As I noted in the introduction to this book, Will could have written a play that clearly cast Caesar, Cassius, and Brutus as good guys or bad guys, that purported to solve these dilemmas and resolve these paradoxes, and that tidily answered our questions. But Will wasn't interested in such easy clarity. His play wants us to slosh around in the swampy moral ambiguity of things. And it wants us to do so not just because that makes for a more engaging theatrical experience (although it does), but because that's what these sorts of circumstances demand of us in the real world.

Let's think about how Will makes things so complicated.

The trouble starts with the person of Julius Caesar himself. The issue of Caesar's character is central because the argument from tyranny depends on the conclusion that Rome has a tyrant on its hands—no tyrant, no excuse for breaking the law. As to this issue, however, the play delights in sending us conflicting signals.

Those signals start early. In the second scene of Act I, the cynical Roman senator Casca reports that at a public gathering Mark Antony offered Caesar the crown three times—and three times Caesar refused it. One would think a leader eager to seize power would, well, seize power (a point Mark Antony makes later). Those who admire George Washington—and I count myself among them—often raise his repeated refusals to become king as proof of his high moral character and his dedication to the democratic experiment. Does Caesar deserve similar credit?

Perhaps, or perhaps only hopeless naivete could lead someone to think so. We do have reasons for skepticism: Caesar was a man accustomed to conquering whatever he saw, and seizing power gets a lot easier if you can convince the people that you're not trying to do it. As reported, Caesar's serial refusals of the crown also have a highly performative quality to them. In any event, we don't know for certain how things might have played out at this public ceremony because Caesar's dramatic displays of forbearance are interrupted when he falls into an epileptic seizure.

As the play unfolds, it gives us evidence from which we can conclude that Caesar wanted the crown, his strategic refusals of it notwithstanding. Perhaps the most compelling proof comes in the second scene of Act II. Caesar's anxious wife, Calphurnia, has persuaded him to stay home on the Ides of March, but Caesar abruptly changes his mind when the manipulative Decius Brutus tells him that the senators stand ready to crown him that very day—and may change their minds if he doesn't show up. Think of it as Decius Brutus putting Caesar to a test that he fails: His decision to go to the Capitol confirms the hunger for power that the conspirators (Decius Brutus among them) fear.

Still, before we pronounce Caesar a tyrant we have to acknowledge an additional complication. Kingship and tyranny don't necessarily go hand in hand, or at least they wouldn't have done so in the minds of Shakespeare's audiences, who were after all ruled by a monarch. In his plays, Will gives us kings who qualify as tyrants but also kings who don't. So, even if Caesar had set his sights on becoming king, the question of how he would have ruled remains open and immensely important.

As I noted earlier, Shakespeare's audiences would have come to the play—as we do—understanding that the situation was morally complicated. That complexity distances us from a number of the principal players, including Cassius (who has already made up his mind) and Mark Antony (who is steadfastly in Caesar's corner). Brutus becomes the voice of our uncertainty, the sound of us thinking out loud about what to do under such fraught circumstances.

In the first scene of Act II, Brutus outlines his reasoning in a soliloquy that test-drives the argument from tyranny. Will invites us to ride along and see what we think. I'll quote the passage at length because the details matter:

> He would be crowned:
> How that might change his nature, there's the question.
> It is bright day that brings forth the adder,
> And that craves wary walking. Crown him that,

And then I grant we put a sting in him
That at his will he may do danger with.
Th' abuse of greatness is when it disjoins
Remorse from power. And, to speak truth of Caesar,
I have not known when his affections swayed
More than his reason. But 'tis a common proof
That lowliness is young ambition's ladder,
Whereto the climber-upward turns his face;
But, when he once attains the upmost round,
He then unto the ladder turns his back,
Looks in the clouds, scorning the base degrees
By which he did ascend. So Caesar may.
Then, lest he may, prevent . . .
Therefore think him a serpent's egg,
Which, hatched, would, as his kind, grow mischievous,
And kill him in the shell. (II:1:12–36)

As reasons for abandoning law and murdering a political leader go, these may strike us as pretty anemic.

Brutus acknowledges that Caesar is not a tyrant now. Nor, Brutus admits, does Caesar's "nature" particularly suggest he'll become one. The idea that Caesar will behave like a tyrant rests on speculation: The words "may" and "might" appear throughout the soliloquy, and Brutus describes how being crowned "might change [Caesar's] nature" as "the question"—not as a forgone conclusion.

Furthermore, as his soliloquy makes clear, Brutus doesn't base his reasoning on an assessment of Caesar's own character, about which he remains ambivalent. Instead, he bases it on his view of ambitious people generally. This seems like an especially suspect form of character evidence—the kind of evidence discussed in the earlier chapter about *Richard II*. Consider: It's risky enough to assess someone's character based on what they've done. It's exponentially more dangerous to assess someone's character based on the behavior of others—especially if you're trying to justify murdering that someone in cold blood.

In this soliloquy, Brutus doesn't consider the preliminary question of why he has the right to decide Caesar's fate. He seems to take it as a given.

Perhaps he attributes it to his place as a descendent of the founder of the Roman Republic. Perhaps he thinks his rock-solid integrity and his absence of self-interest qualifies him. He knows his own motives, or at least he thinks he does, and he finds them pure.

He may have a point. Everyone (except, I suppose Caesar) appears to agree that Brutus is "the noblest Roman of them all." But Will shows us that even distinguished, noble, and well-intentioned human beings remain human beings, and therefore imperfect and prone to error. The argument from tyranny tells us what must be done but not who has the standing and the qualities to do it, and we meet in Brutus someone who appears totally fitted for the job. And yet we have reservations even about his doing of it.

As I mentioned earlier, we enter the play aligned with Brutus, sharing in his uncertainty, and distancing ourselves from the resolute and calculating Cassius, the principal conspirator in Caesar's assassination. To borrow a wonderful phrase from one of Justice Antonin Scalia's opinions, Cassius is a wolf that comes to us as a wolf. It's hard to imagine anyone warming to his lean and hungry look. And, yet, over and over again the play proves Cassius right and Brutus wrong.

Brutus lets Mark Antony live after Caesar's assassination, invites him to address the people, and leaves him alone with the crowd when he does so—all dreadful mistakes that Cassius recognizes as such. Cassius warns Brutus over and over, but Brutus blunders forward just the same. In this play rich in paradoxes, we might reach the uncomfortable, if also unassailable, conclusion that if Brutus is right about the ends, then Cassius is right about the means. But then we have to ask ourselves: Do we really want the terrible decision that the argument from tyranny requires to be made by someone like Cassius? Does that make us sleep any more soundly than the image of Caesar in a crown?

As a matter of political theory, we can defend the idea that we may have to break the law in order to save it. This includes the notion that we may need to murder a tyrant to preserve the very rule of law that makes murder a crime. But what is pretty in theory is often grotesque in application, and *Julius Caesar* shows us all of the things that can go tragically wrong as Brutus and Cassius try to put the concept into operation. Little wonder it all unfolds so poorly. After all, laws exist precisely because none of us does a very good job of figuring these things out on the fly and completely free of guardrails.

At the end of the play we may be no clearer about what's right and wrong than we were at the beginning. I think that's precisely where Will wants to leave us. But we can't ignore the finally shared fate of the two men. In the end, Brutus and Cassius both kill themselves.

They thought they were working together to save the Republic.

It turns out to have been a suicide pact, after all.

Persuading the People

In the opening scene of our play, the commoners have taken the day off work to celebrate Julius Caesar's triumphant return to Rome after his victory over Pompey. Their festivities offend two tribunals, who tell the people to clear the streets and get back to their labors. When a few members of the crowd balk at the order, the tribunals soberly remind them of how they once revered Pompey, whose death at the hands of Caesar they now treat as an occasion for a holiday.

The play thus begins by introducing two themes that reappear throughout *Julius Caesar* and, indeed, throughout much of Will's work. The first is that the common people are fickle and feckless. And the second is that they can be—and often are—moved by things other than logic and reason.

We encountered those themes earlier in this book when we talked about the misadventures of Jack Cade and his motley crew of rebels in *Henry VI, Part 2*. And we encounter them again at a number of points in *Julius Caesar*, for example when a collection of frenzied citizens attack and kill the poet Cinna, who they have mistaken for the conspirator of the same name. When Cinna protests that they have the wrong man, they shrug and decide to tear him apart anyway—"for his bad verses."

The persistent presence of these themes in his plays has led some critics to cast Will as an elitist with an edgy distrust of the lower classes, especially when they gather in crowds and somebody whips them up. Those critics point to a number of scenes in *Julius Caesar* as evidence of Will's condescending view of common folk. Those include the opening scene and the scene involving Cinna, both of which appear to support the accusation.

Of particular interest to us here, these critics also cite as evidence of Will's attitude toward common folk the well-known second scene of Act III, where the gathered plebians are initially persuaded by Brutus's oration justifying the murder of Caesar but then shift their allegiance after hearing from Mark Antony. In this scene (the argument goes), Will casts a cold eye on the rabble and portrays them as silly, shallow, and suggestible. It's not a wholly unreasonable interpretation of the scene.

Nevertheless, I want to push back against these arguments for two reasons. First, I think they oversimplify what's going on in the play generally. Second, I think they oversimplify what's going on in the funeral oration scene specifically. I'm particularly concerned about the latter oversimplification, because in my view the second scene of Act III has a lot to teach us about the art of persuasion, and I think we lose those lessons if we believe things unfold the way they do simply because common folk are dopes who can't tell a good argument from a bad one. But let me start with the first point.

I don't think it's fair to read *Julius Caesar*, taken as a whole, as an indictment of the common folk because they sometimes make bad, or even tragically bad, decisions. After all, in this play plebians aren't the only people who are persuaded by considerations other than logic and reason. Decius Brutus persuades Caesar to go to the Capitol—despite the risks and against all good advice—by appealing to his lust for power. Cassius persuades Brutus (and Brutus persuades himself) to join the conspiracy by invoking a romanticized vision of the Republic that, as scholars have noted, hadn't existed for some time, if it ever existed. In *Julius Caesar*, falling prey to faulty reasoning doesn't identify someone as a commoner as much as it identifies them as a human being.

I also don't think it's fair to see the commoners as weak-minded simply because they find the second speaker more persuasive than the first and change their minds after hearing from him. In the law, we often assume that the final argument someone hears takes on an outsized importance; that's why we generally give the last word to the party with the burden of persuasion. The opportunity to leave a jury or a judge with the final thoughts it gets on a subject gives the speaker a powerful advantage.

And, of course, there's nothing intrinsically wrong with altering your views after hearing additional argument. To the contrary, if the second argument has greater persuasive force, then favoring that argument is what rational decision-making requires of us. In and of itself, the crowd's shift from Brutus to Mark Antony gives us no grounds for criticism. To the contrary, we can assess the quality of the crowd's decision-making only by assessing the quality of the process around it and the quality of the respective arguments.

With that in mind, let's look at the process the plebians follow here. The scene starts with them expressing their dismay over Caesar's assassination and insisting on an explanation that they find satisfactory. Their demands suggest that the people view the burden of proof as resting on the conspirators, which I find deeply interesting because this aligns with how we think about things. Under our laws, the prosecutor has the burden of proving the elements of murder, but a defendant who claims that the murder was justified (for example, because they acted in self-defense) has the burden of offering proof to support that claim. It's up to Brutus to convince the people he acted properly, and a failure to do so will seal his guilt.

The plebians make another interesting decision about process as well—one that often goes unnoticed. Brutus is not the only conspirator who speaks: Cassius gives a speech, too, although the play doesn't tell us what he says. But some of the plebians peel off to hear Cassius separately, so they can later compare notes with those who've heard from Brutus. The process looks a lot like sequestration, where we try to ensure the reliability of testimony by having witnesses testify outside of the hearing of each other. In short, the much-maligned plebians take at least two important steps here to help ensure they reach the right decision.

With those observations about process before us, let's turn to the merits of the arguments. As an effort at persuasion, Brutus's speech has a primitive clunkiness to it. It comes to us in the most pedestrian of prose:

> Romans, countrymen, and lovers, hear me for my cause, and be silent that you may hear. Believe me for mine honor, and have respect to mine honor that you may believe. Censure me in your wisdom, and awake your senses that you may better judge. If there be any in this assembly, any dear friend of Caesar's, to him I say that Brutus' love to Caesar was no less than his. If then that friend demand why Brutus rose against Caesar, this is my answer: not that I loved Caesar less, but that I loved Rome more. Had you rather Caesar were living, and die all slaves, than that Caesar were dead, to live all freemen? As Caesar loved me, I weep for him. As he was fortunate, I rejoice at it. As he was valiant, I honor him. But, as he was ambitious, I slew him . . . (III:2:14–28)

Plainly—or perhaps I should say even more plainly—stated, the speech comes down to this: "Everybody shut up and listen. Look, I loved Caesar, but he was ambitious. So, I killed him to keep Romans—such as [insert your name here]—free." The burden is on Brutus to make his case, and by all appearances he fails both in substance and style.

We might therefore say that the remarkable thing about Brutus's argument is not that Mark Antony's speech ultimately eclipses it, but that it manages to attract any followers in the first place. And, yet, we can understand why it does so and why it almost works. Brutus appeals to the patriotism of his audience and such appeals often get traction—regardless of their intellectual merit or lack of it.

Appeals to patriotism push lots of different buttons. They elevate a communal value above individual interests, which sounds noble. They rely on shared symbols, traditions, or folklore, even when those things have more basis in mythology than historical fact. They feed our tribal impulses: Brutus's speech divides those who love Rome from those who do not—"Who is here so vile," he asks, "that will not love his country?" And then he places himself at the head of the class because he loves Rome the most—as he must, he declares, having murdered the Caesar that he loved so dearly in order to save it.

Appeals to patriotism have continued to work with audiences throughout history and to the current day. Just one (relatively) recent example came after the terrorist attacks of September 11, when Congress passed a massive and opaque piece of legislation called the PATRIOT Act. Because those tragic attacks called for a swift government response, and because the proposed legislation was biblical in its heft, many members of Congress voted for the law without reading it—as some of them later admitted when serious problems with the statute emerged. We can understand why they did so. What politician in his or her right mind would vote against something called the PATRIOT Act?

Brutus's appeal to patriotism runs into two problems that often arise when we try to persuade people of something based on an argument from principle. First, the precise principle that Brutus invokes here is less than completely clear. When Brutus talks about "loving Rome," what exactly does he mean? Loving a status quo that Caesar threatened? Loving the Republic as a form of government? Loving the freedom that Roman citizens enjoyed? When you rally people behind an idea there may be some advantages in keeping that idea a bit vague, but sooner or later such mushiness may prove a vulnerability.

Second, Brutus fails to make the principle he invokes—whatever it is—truly personal to those he hopes to persuade. Yes, he points out that Caesar posed a threat to their freedom. And, yes, he gets the plebians to call out that they love their country, too. But none of this establishes an intimate connection between the common folk and the principle on which Brutus builds his argument.

I want to contrast Brutus's speech here with the famous St. Crispin's Day speech that Will gives us in *Henry V.* Recall the context and content of that speech: It is the eve of the Battle of Agincourt, which will fall on St. Crispin's Day. The French troops significantly outnumber the English and Henry V's men are worried. When the Earl of Westmoreland gives voice to those concerns, Henry responds.

Now, note what Henry doesn't do and what he does do. He doesn't tell his men to fight for love of England. He doesn't point out that an English victory will benefit them in some abstract political sense. Instead, he makes the battle personal to them. He talks about how, for the rest of their lives, they will have bragging rights for their role in a victory over lopsided odds. He talks about how their scars will testify to their heroism—which, he adds with a smirk, they will no doubt describe "with advantages."

I'm going to quote the speech at length because it makes the contrast with Brutus's oration all the clearer. Besides, the speech deserves quoting at length whenever one gets the chance. So here's what Henry—or, all the more personally, "Harry" as he calls himself in these lines—says:

> If we are mark'd to die, we are enough
> To do our country loss; and if to live,
> The fewer men, the greater share of honour.
> God's will! I pray thee, wish not one man more . . .
> No, faith, my coz, wish not a man from England.
> God's peace! I would not lose so great an honour
> As one man more methinks would share from me
> For the best hope I have. O, do not wish one more!
> Rather proclaim it, Westmoreland, through my host,
> That he which hath no stomach to this fight,
> Let him depart; his passport shall be made,
> And crowns for convoy put into his purse;
> We would not die in that man's company
> That fears his fellowship to die with us.
> This day is call'd the feast of Crispian,
> He that outlives this day, and comes safe home,
> Will stand a tip-toe when this day is nam'd,
> And rouse him at the name of Crispian.
> He that shall live this day, and see old age,
> Will yearly on the vigil feast his neighbours,
> And say "To-morrow is Saint Crispian."
> Then will he strip his sleeve and show his scars,

And say "These wounds I had on Crispin's day."
Old men forget; yet all shall be forgot,
But he'll remember, with advantages,
What feats he did that day. Then shall our names,
Familiar in his mouth as household words—
Harry the King, Bedford and Exeter,
Warwick and Talbot, Salisbury and Gloucester—
Be in their flowing cups freshly rememb'red.
This story shall the good man teach his son;
And Crispin Crispian shall ne'er go by,
From this day to the ending of the world,
But we in it shall be rememberèd—
We few, we happy few, we band of brothers;
For he to-day that sheds his blood with me
Shall be my brother; be he ne'er so vile,
This day shall gentle his condition;
And gentlemen in England now a-bed
Shall think themselves accurs'd they were not here,
And hold their manhoods cheap whiles any speaks
That fought with us upon Saint Crispin's day. (IV:3:23–69)

Brutus's speech may temporarily persuade people not to rip him asunder for murdering Caesar, but it's far too prosaic, abstract, and impersonal to give his listeners anything like inspiration. Henry, on the other hand, makes you want to grab the nearest sword and start swinging. He even makes you wish for a few visible wounds along the way.

In some legal cases, a party may have a very strong argument from principle, but their lawyer may hesitate to make it the centerpiece of their claim or defense. An example comes from my own experience. For roughly forty years I've defended media entities—newspapers, television stations, and online platforms—against defamation claims. I've been an active member of the relatively small national bar that handles these sorts of cases and have had endless conversations with my colleagues about matters of strategy.

In jury trials, most media lawyers focus on proving the truth of the reporting at issue, on demonstrating the care taken by their client to get the story right, and on attacking the plaintiff's character and reputation. They avoid any long speeches about the importance of the First Amendment because they think they'll likely fall flat with the jurors. You might say they don't want to risk sounding like Brutus: prosaic, abstract, and impersonal. They fear that the Mark Antony on the other side may eat their lunch.

But for every rule about things you shouldn't do in court there are lawyers who know how and when to break it. So, one of the wiliest and most formidable media defense lawyers I know prevailed in a difficult high-profile defamation case by reminding the jury over and over again that under our Constitution everyone has the right to their own opinion. He found ways to make the principle poetic, concrete, and personal to their own experience. In all candor, I'm not convinced the argument should have carried as much weight as it did—the reporting in question in that particular case was more factual than editorial. But the lawyer liked the appeal to principle, and apparently so did the jury because they came back in his favor after a relatively short deliberation.

✲ ✲ ✲ ✲ ✲

When we turn from Brutus's speech to Mark Antony's, we encounter a very different collection of persuasive strategies. Mark Antony understands that the crowd has rallied behind Brutus and that any direct attack on him will run into stiff opposition. He therefore begins by appearing to align himself with Brutus, disclaiming any intention to honor Caesar and casting Brutus as a "noble" and "honorable man."

He repeats Brutus's charge that Caesar was ambitious. But, as his speech unfolds, he starts to undermine the accusation. Note all the subtle shifts he makes here, gradually introducing questions about Caesar's ambition and examples of Caesar's love for the people. And note that—unlike Brutus's speech—this one comes to us in verse:

> Friends, Romans, countrymen, lend me your ears;
> I come to bury Caesar, not to praise him.
> The evil that men do lives after them;
> The good is oft interrèd with their bones;
> So let it be with Caesar. The noble Brutus
> Hath told you Caesar was ambitious:

If it were so, it was a grievous fault,
And grievously hath Caesar answer'd it.
Here, under leave of Brutus and the rest—
For Brutus is an honourable man;
So are they all, all honourable men—
Come I to speak in Caesar's funeral.
He was my friend, faithful and just to me:
But Brutus says he was ambitious;
And Brutus is an honourable man.
He hath brought many captives home to Rome
Whose ransoms did the general coffers fill:
Did this in Caesar seem ambitious?
When that the poor have cried, Caesar hath wept:
Ambition should be made of sterner stuff:
Yet Brutus says he was ambitious;
And Brutus is an honourable man.
You all did see that on the Lupercal
I thrice presented him a kingly crown,
Which he did thrice refuse: was this ambition?
Yet Brutus says he was ambitious;
And, sure, he is an honourable man.
I speak not to disprove what Brutus spoke,
But here I am to speak what I do know.
You all did love him once, not without cause:
What cause withholds you then, to mourn for him?
O judgment! Thou art fled to brutish beasts,
And men have lost their reason. Bear with me;
My heart is in the coffin there with Caesar,
And I must pause till it come back to me. (III:2:82–117)

And then we find this stage direction: "He weeps." That's important.

I once had an expert witness, who we had called to testify about the tragic death of a teenage boy, break down in sincere and heartfelt tears in front of a jury. I watched the jury watch him cry and then watched tears form in their own eyes as well. At that instant we knew we had won the case.

Mark Antony has more to say and he says it. He reads to them from Caesar's will. He displays to them Caesar's bloodied corpse. But, make no mistake about it, he has already prevailed.

And when toward the end of his remarks Mark Antony tells them, "I am no orator, as Brutus is," and when he disclaims any capacity "to stir men's blood," we have to laugh. As the saying goes, if an attorney tells you they're just a "simple country lawyer" you should beware. And you may want to check to make sure you still have your wallet.

Depending on how much cynicism we manage to muster, we might describe Mark Antony's speech as "moving" the people or as "manipulating" them. But even the more suspicious of these verbs doesn't require us to think Mark Antony is insincere or to deem his argument intellectually inferior to Brutus's. To the contrary, Mark Antony sees something here that Brutus does not: Love of principle is a powerful thing; but the suffering our principles bring down upon ourselves and others make the irrebuttable argument for thinking twice. In contrast, a story of individual suffering can tell us things that all the statements of principle in the world cannot.

Years ago, I served as a member of a legal team that defended a university's affirmative action program. The case was conducted as a bench trial and involved lots of talk of abstract principles like equality and opportunity and diversity. But, by my reckoning, the most powerful moment in the trial came in a personal story.

A young woman who was called as a witness testified to the disadvantages she had encountered as a student from an impoverished Detroit high school seeking admission to an elite university. She had wanted to learn to play a musical instrument in high school, both because of her passion for it and because she thought it might strengthen her application to college. Her family had no money to buy or rent an instrument, but her high school informed her that she could choose one from the inventory of instruments that they maintained.

She waited excitedly for the day when she could get her musical education underway. When it finally arrived, she reported to the room the school specified. Passing through the door, she discovered herself in a space that was less a room than a closet. And the closet did not contain a single complete musical instrument. Not one. Instead, the shelves and floor were covered with boxes of parts. To no avail, she spent hours looking through them for something she could learn how to play.

When she finished the story, you could have heard a pin drop in that courtroom. The story broke her heart afresh. And it broke everyone else's right along with it.

Critics of our legal system, and particularly of large verdicts, often lament the degree to which decision makers—especially juries—are persuaded by appeals to emotion. I understand the concern. But we might read *Julius Caesar* to suggest that there are worse things, and that perhaps one of them is a society in which people have lost their susceptibility to such appeals.

Maybe that is why the play starts where it does: with a people who have forgotten their love.

With a people who have given love up in favor of a holiday in the streets.

6

"Who's There?"

Hamlet

Backdrop

In May of 2009, the University of Chicago Law School convened a roundtable discussion on the theme of Shakespeare and the law. The participants included Justice Stephen Breyer, who selected the three plays that served as the focal point for the event. Those plays were *As You Like It, Measure for Measure*, and *Hamlet*. When asked why he had chosen these particular works, Justice Breyer offered fairly detailed rationales as to the first two, but then as to the last said: "Why *Hamlet*? Well, why *Hamlet*, that's an absurd question."

I'm not sure why Justice Breyer thought the question was absurd, but I know why I do. In *Hamlet*, Will gives us fodder to think about almost everything worth thinking about within the realm of human experience: grief, love, friendship, family, rage, revenge, justice, deception, manipulation, introspection, initiative, hesitation, art, betrayal, doubt, faith, memory, madness, the supernatural and abstract, the concrete and practical, life, death. This makes pretty much every occasion a good one to bring *Hamlet* into the conversation. And, as we will see, the play provides us with a rich storehouse of material to examine through the lens of the law.

Most scholars think Shakespeare wrote *Hamlet* around 1600 or 1601, just a year or two after he and his partners built the Globe in Southwark and toward the end of the reign of Elizabeth. It appears that the play's immediate source was an earlier work, probably by the great revenge dramatist Thomas Kyd, that told essentially the same story and that has not survived the passage of time. But *Hamlet* has other roots as well, reflecting the influences of Scandinavian sagas, Montaigne's essays, and a literature of melancholy that was popular in Will's time.

While many critics over the centuries have viewed *Hamlet* as among Shakespeare's greatest works, opinions have varied, particularly with respect to the character of Hamlet himself. T. S. Eliot declared the play "an artistic failure," in large part because of a disconnection he sensed between the events depicted in the play and Hamlet's emotional response to them. Harold Bloom, in contrast, said that "The phenomenon of Hamlet, the prince without the play, is unsurpassed in the West's imaginative literature."

Whatever else holds true, both the tragedy and its central character have infused themselves into our popular culture. Those who can quote no other Shakespeare play can rattle off a half-dozen lines from this one, many of them spoken by the Prince, even if they don't know the source. "To be, or not to be," "Alas, poor Yorick," "What a piece of work is man," "The play's the thing," "to the manner born," "Frailty, thy name is woman," "cruel to be kind," "Hoist with his own petard," and many others have become part of our collective vocabulary. We have more film versions of *Hamlet* than any other Shakespeare play and it has been parodied in countless cartoons and television shows. At least one imaginative entrepreneur offers for sale a Hamlet action figure—a delightful oxymoron, given the Prince's reputation for inaction.

In this chapter, we'll follow these leads and concentrate largely—though not exclusively—on the character of Hamlet. It pains me to leave behind so many promising threads. A play of this complexity and length (more than 4,000 lines, Shakespeare's longest) could take us in lots of interesting directions. But, to my mind, *Hamlet* raises two sets of questions that particularly benefit from consideration through the lens of the law, and both sets relate primarily to the melancholy Dane.

The first set of questions concerns Hamlet's responsibility for the various deaths that pile up as the play progresses. I use the term "responsibility" here advisedly, recognizing that it can refer to a variety of things, including direct physical cause, moral accountability, and legal guilt. We'll need to explore all of those different dimensions of the idea.

It significantly understates matters to say that the law is interested in issues of responsibility. Questions of when, why, and whether we hold someone accountable for the direct and indirect consequences of their actions lie at the heart of any legal system. As we'll see, in this play Will takes us on a grand tour of all the different ways we might think about the concept of responsibility.

Of course, how we view Hamlet's responsibility—at least in the moral and legal sense—may depend on how we assess his sanity and his capacity for rational judgment. Hamlet says he puts on his madness like a mask, but that doesn't settle the matter. After all, what else would we expect a madman to say? His disclaimers aside, what does the evidence tell us?

Any fair and merciful system of criminal justice will allow a defense of mental illness or incompetence. It would be cruel and pointless to punish someone for a mental state they don't have the capacity to possess. But such a defense introduces the risk of fakery. By necessity, the law is therefore also interested in how we can tell when a mental state is real and when it is feigned.

A famous scene from the book and film *Anatomy of a Murder*, often used in law school ethics courses, gets at this problem—and the lawyer's potential role in aggravating it. In the scene, a seasoned defense attorney is trying to lead his client, who is charged with murder, to say he was temporarily insane when he shot the man who sexually assaulted his wife. The lawyer doesn't want to tell him what to say, because that might amount to suborning perjury, so he delicately talks around the subject.

The client, finally picking up on the hints, says: "Well, I must have been mad." Seeing that the lawyer has given him an interested look, he adds: "Am I getting warmer?" As the attorney heads out the door, he says: "Well, I'll tell you that after I talk to your wife. In the meantime, try to remember just how crazy you were." *Hamlet* asks us to figure out "just how crazy" the Prince is.

The second set of questions concerns Hamlet's notorious indecisiveness. The film version of the play that stars Sir Laurence Olivier begins with a voiceover of the actor sonorously declaring: "This is the story of a man who could not make up his mind." That theme may feel disconnected from the concerns of the law, but it definitely is not disconnected from the concerns of lawyers.

Hamlet is a highly intelligent, well-educated person who suddenly finds himself facing a decision of great moral complexity. Practicing lawyers often fit this description, even if the decision before them doesn't involve murdering their stepfather. Prosecutors and criminal defense lawyers make choices that are quite literally matters of life or death. Government lawyers advise their clients on everything from public health policy to the constitutionality of torture. Even an average workmanlike litigator has to decide whether to call a witness who they think will lie on the stand, or to offer a piece of evidence they suspect has been falsified, or to impeach an innocent but adverse witness by disclosing an embarrassing fact that will probably harm their public reputation and disrupt their lives.

Of course, lawyers hold no monopoly on making tough decisions in ethically difficult circumstances. Having to do so goes with the territories of being everything from an emergency room physician to the owner of a business to the parent of a child. In this chapter, I consider the indecisiveness problem in *Hamlet* through the lens of the law, but I think the play has something to teach almost everyone about the dilemma of deciding when deciding gets hard.

As you'll see, in the course of discussing that issue I'm going to challenge the notion that Hamlet waffles as much as his critics say he does. I'm even going to push back at the idea that what we're looking at here is simple indecisiveness. I think something very different, and vastly more interesting and instructive, is going on.

Will has given us a lot to unpack. Let's get started. And let's begin, in fine Shakespearean form, with a few murders.

Murder Most Foul

No fewer than nine major characters in *Hamlet* meet violent ends. Hamlet has a role in the vast majority of these killings, but the roles vary considerably, and the variations invite us to ponder what it means to be accountable for the death of another human being. Indeed, those variations are so numerous and so creative as to suggest that Will viewed this play as an opportunity to explore the range of possibilities in one long and discursive meditation on the theme.

❋ ❋ ❋ ❋ ❋

Hamlet starts with a murder, but not one that we see. The ghost of Hamlet's father, a part that Shakespeare himself sometimes played, appears to Hamlet and reveals that he was killed by Claudius, who married his widow and now sits on the throne. That accusation has the natural effect of directing our attention toward Claudius. We therefore may not think to ask whether Hamlet may have felt some responsibility for his father's death. But did he?

Hamlet obviously had no direct or physical role in his father's demise. But guilt doesn't always follow the rules of logic, and a feeling of moral responsibility can set in even where it makes little or no sense given the facts. This holds especially true for someone with Hamlet's hardwiring—a tendency toward self-criticism that occasionally seeps into self-loathing.

We can pretty easily conclude that Hamlet must have felt guilty if we go full frontal Freudian and assume that he lusted after his mother and wanted his father dead. Those Oedipal impulses would probably have elevated any simmering sensation of guilt to a full boil. But I don't think we have to subscribe to any elaborate psychoanalytic theories to understand why Hamlet might have experienced painful twinges of responsibility around his father's death.

When Hamlet gets the news, he's off at Wittenberg reading, studying, thinking great thoughts, and presumably doing all of the frivolous things that university students do. His dad, in the meantime, was busy ruling the kingdom and dying an untimely death. I suspect that every child who gets summoned home from school after the passing of a parent experiences at least some pangs of guilt. I can't imagine why Hamlet—prone to mental self-flagellation under the best of circumstances—would be an exception.

To the extent Hamlet had any feelings of responsibility for these events, they must have escalated dramatically when he learned that his father had been murdered. We can imagine him asking himself: What if I'd been at Elsinore? Would Claudius have dared to murder the king under my nose? Would I have noticed something—some piece of evidence, perhaps—that would have prevented the crime or led to its quick revelation?

I suggested above that, in *Hamlet*, Will sought to inventory and explore all the different kinds of responsibility that human beings experience. If that's so, then he'd certainly need to include the *feeling* of responsibility, even where the circumstances don't justify the emotion. And I think that's exactly where the play begins.

Practicing lawyers encounter the phenomenon of the client who wants to engage in some ill-advised action because of guilt they feel—but probably shouldn't. And we encounter its opposite as well, the client who denies responsibility for what they've done and who feels no guilt about it—but probably should. *Hamlet* starts where we often have to start with those we represent: by sorting the complexities of responsibility not as a causal, moral, or legal principle but as a mental state that is disconnected from reality, even if it has a reality all its own.

We don't get to our next murder until much later in the play, in the fourth scene of the third act, when Hamlet kills Polonius, advisor to Claudius and father to Ophelia and Laertes. This murder lands at the other end of the spectrum of responsibility: If Hamlet had no physical responsibility for the death of his father, he obviously has complete physical responsibility for the death of Polonius. The matters of his legal and moral responsibility, however, are considerably murkier.

Recall what happens in the scene. Hamlet visits the Queen, Gertrude, and makes her profoundly uncomfortable with his questions and provocations. When his mother feels threatened and calls out for help, Polonius shouts from behind the curtain where he's been hiding. Hamlet thrusts his sword through the fabric and kills Polonius, thinking he's slain the target of his revenge, Claudius.

Before we turn to the issues of legal and moral responsibility, permit me a word about timing. The traditional critique of Hamlet is that he's endlessly and frustratingly indecisive, that—in the words of Olivier—he cannot make up his mind. Well, perhaps, but clearly he's made it up by this point in Act III because he thinks he's killing Claudius and he proceeds to do it without hesitation.

In this connection, we might recall that the conspirators don't get around to killing Julius Caesar until the third act—and no one has ever accused Cassius or Brutus of chronic indecisiveness. As I'll discuss in the next section, I recognize that Hamlet has a problem, but I think it goes much deeper than a tendency toward inertia. More on that to come.

On the question of Hamlet's legal responsibility for killing Polonius, the play tells us almost nothing. Indeed, unlike *Henry VI*, *Part 2*, where no one can seem to talk about anything but the law, we find precious little consideration of it here. After learning of his murder of Polonius, Claudius announces that he will send Hamlet to England, but he purports to do so less to punish Hamlet than to keep him safe. That's a convenient solution for Claudius, who finds himself increasingly nervous about Hamlet's behavior.

It might seem as though the question of Hamlet's legal responsibility is complicated by the fact that he didn't intend to kill Polonius. Shakespeare may well have found that issue intriguing, but today's legal principles solve the problem through the doctrine of transferred intent. That doctrine allows a prosecutor to satisfy the mental state requirement of a crime by shifting the defendant's intent from the intended victim to an accidental victim.

Interestingly, the legal doctrine of transferred intent helps explain why the question of Hamlet's moral responsibility might be more complex than it first appears. To understand why, we need to turn our attention to Claudius for a moment. And we need to ask ourselves whether, in Shakespeare's world, Hamlet was morally justified in attempting to kill the king.

Hamlet is (in part) a revenge play, so let's start by thinking back on the principles of vengeance we discussed in connection with *Titus Andronicus*. As we noted there, revenge may have a plausible claim to moral justification where three things hold true: the offender has committed a grievous wrong; the law will not remedy it; and the avenger's response is proportional. Hamlet can check all three boxes: Claudius has murdered the king; it appears no law in Denmark will get justice done; and Hamlet wants only Claudius's life in return.

If Hamlet would have been justified in killing Claudius, then why would we hold him morally responsible for killing Polonius by mistake? If we transfer intent that is blameworthy, why shouldn't we transfer intent that isn't? To use an analogy, how would we think about someone who, while engaging in a legitimate act of self-defense, killed the wrong person?

A skeptic might argue that Hamlet should have exercised greater care before using the deadly force that killed Polonius. But why would Hamlet think that anyone other than Claudius would be hiding in the curtains of his mother's chamber? And wouldn't he reasonably have expected Claudius to be armed and dangerous? There's also a delicious irony to any argument that Hamlet should have been more cautious and less impulsive, given the traditional charge that he's much too hesitant and deliberative.

Here's an intriguing thought experiment to explore the issue a little more deeply. Assume that Hamlet finds Polonius maddeningly irritating. (This doesn't require much imagination, given that after slaying him Hamlet describes Polonius as a "wretched, rash, intruding fool".) Seeing movement in the curtain, and suspecting it is the meddlesome Polonius, Hamlet shoves his rapier through the fabric—a morally unjust killing. But say it turns out that Hamlet was wrong; the spy was none other than Claudius himself. Does Hamlet's "moral luck" transform the cold-blooded murder into a defensible act of revenge?

I'm not making here the strong claim that Hamlet gets a pass for killing Polonius because he'd have been justified in murdering Claudius. But I do want to suggest that the question of Hamlet's moral responsibility has more dimensions to it than we might at first expect. As *Titus* and other plays show us, Will was a sophisticated and experienced student of the dynamics of revenge. I think he understood full well that the matter of Hamlet's moral responsibility for Polonius's death is less clear than initially appears. And I think that he wanted us to puzzle over it—and perhaps to find the puzzle unsolvable.

If Hamlet suffered from insanity or some other form of extreme mental incompetency at the time he stabbed Polonius, then we'd have another reason to rethink his responsibility for the killing. Up to this point, however, the textual evidence portrays him as of sound mind. He describes his madness as calculated, and we have no reason to believe otherwise. He knows what he's doing.

This is not to say that Hamlet is mentally healthy and clear-thinking. He plainly isn't. And his troubles manifest in multiple forms.

He suffers from wild mood swings. In some ways, the most interesting thing about Hamlet's most famous soliloquy ("To be, or not to be") is what comes right before it. In his grand soliloquy, we get a potent dose of the melancholy Dane: He ponders the burdens of life, frets over the paralysis bred by thought and conscience, and mulls the possibility of self-destruction. It comes to us as the readable thought bubble of a profoundly anguished human being.

But, if we've been paying attention, we have to ask ourselves: Wait! Where did this come from? What happened? When we last saw Hamlet, he was excited—uplifted, even—about the idea of using a play, "The Mouse Trap," to ferret out his uncle's guilt. How did he fall so hard, so far, and so fast?

A number of contemporary critics and psychologists have suggested that Hamlet's behavior aligns fairly closely with manic depressive, or bipolar, disorder. The American Psychiatric Association's *Diagnostic and Statistical Manual of Mental Disorders*, commonly known as the DSM-5, includes an extended discussion of this disorder, or more properly this family of disorders, that tends to support the conclusion. Hamlet seems like a textbook example of someone who experiences the convulsing leaps from listlessness and depression to overactivity and excitedness (and back again) that the psychological literature describes. But psychiatrists have provided other long-distance diagnoses as well.

Hamlet also struggles to come up with and execute plans that actually make any sense, often engaging in the kind of foggy thinking we associate with shock and trauma. Consider his plan to feign madness. Granted, doing so may make Claudius uneasy, but to what end? One would think that a scheme to murder Claudius would have a better chance at success if the king felt comfortable around his would-be assassin. Odd behavior would seem like a surefire way to put Claudius on high alert, which it in fact does.

Or consider his decision to tell his friends Rosencrantz and Guildenstern: "I am but mad north-northwest; when the wind is southerly, I know a hawk from a handsaw." Having cleverly outed Rosencrantz and

Guildenstern as Claudius's spies, why does he tell them that his madness is performative? Surely, he must have understood that they would take that information directly to the king, raising suspicions and prompting Claudius to take preemptive action.

Or what about his strategy to use "The Mouse Trap" to reveal Claudius's guilt? He says he needs more evidence because the ghost who appeared to him may be a devil. But his newfound skepticism about the spirit doesn't seem to rest on any fresh developments. And, if he needs compelling new proof to confirm the guilt of Claudius, then watching how the king responds to a play hardly seems to fill the bill. As things turn out, Hamlet misbehaves so badly during the play that it's hard to tell whether Claudius stalks out because he feels guilty or because the Prince's antics grate on him. I'll confess that they grate on me.

Hamlet's behavior does sometimes seems odd to a point bordering on sociopathology. For example, his accidental murder of Polonius doesn't appear to trigger anything that looks even remotely like healthy remorse. He blames the victim ("Take thy fortune / Thou find'st to be too busy is some danger"). And he treats the corpse like an object—"I'll lug the guts into the neighbor room."

Indeed, he treats the body like an object of mirth. After Gertrude reports the murder, Claudius summons Hamlet and demands to know where Polonius is. Hamlet responds with a series of sarcastic replies: at dinner, being eaten by worms; in heaven, where your messenger can find him—or you can go look for him in the other place yourself; at the top of the stairs in the lobby, and, don't worry, he'll wait for you. Hamlet seems disturbingly detached from the tragic consequences of his actions. In fact, he seems to get a kick out of the whole thing.

Finally, our inventory of Hamlet's mental challenges has to include his deeply unhealthy relationships with women. I've already alluded to his uncomfortably confrontational episode with Gertrude, but his abusive interactions with his beloved Ophelia may make us squirm even more. Hamlet tortures Ophelia; he is, by turns, dismissive, mocking, and cruel. His scenes with her can be played with a range of intensity, but I think the almost physically violent rendering offered by Kenneth Branagh and Kate Winslet in the 1996 firm version gets it right.

It appears that he antagonizes Ophelia at least in part so she will tell Polonius that's he's mad. Hamlet knows the old man will promptly run to Claudius to share the gossip. The plan works, but it does so at the cost of using Ophelia as a pawn in his game of chess. His manipulation of Ophelia violates the Kantian prohibition against treating a human being as the means to an end. More fundamentally, it has nothing to do with how you behave toward someone you love.

And this leads us to the third death in the play.

As with the murder of his father, Hamlet has no direct physical responsibility for Ophelia's death. But, here, he must own at least some accountability for the tragedy. The play strongly suggests that his berating made her fragile, and his murder of her father—even if unintentional—finally broke her.

A debate has long raged over whether Ophelia accidentally drowns or commits suicide. The death occurs offstage and we have only the report that Gertrude provides to Laertes, very likely based on hearsay, perhaps even multiple levels of it. If Gertrude's description of the events is correct, then it makes little difference whether she threw herself into the water or made no effort to save herself after falling in. In either case, she died because of a compromised state that Hamlet had an active role in causing.

Under contemporary law, a very aggressive prosecutor might charge Hamlet with Ophelia's death under an involuntary manslaughter theory. The elements of involuntary manslaughter differ among jurisdictions, but a typical version makes it a felony to engage in wanton or reckless conduct that involves a high likelihood that substantial harm will result to another person. Although the charge probably arises most often in cases involving reckless driving, prosecutors bring it in a wide range of circumstances.

Consider, for example, the much-discussed Massachusetts case of *Commonwealth v. Carter.* In that case, Michelle Carter—a 17-year-old girl—was charged with the involuntary manslaughter of Conrad Roy—her 18-year-old boyfriend—by encouraging him to commit suicide. Because they lived in different towns at the time, their conversation (which was extensive) took place entirely through text messages.

Carter argued that the involuntary manslaughter charge couldn't lie against her because she wasn't even physically present with Conrad when he killed himself. Under the unique facts of the case—including that Carter and Roy were in a relationship, that she knew about his emotional fragility and prior suicide attempt, and that her communications were manipulative and coercive—the Massachusetts Supreme Court upheld the charge. A vigorous debate over the case has ensued, raising among other things the question of whether an involuntary manslaughter charge based exclusively on speech passes muster under the First Amendment.

We can easily distinguish Hamlet's conduct from Carter's. Hamlet doesn't urge Ophelia to commit suicide and wouldn't seem to have any reason to believe she was at risk for doing so. Further, as noted, the question of whether she killed herself remains an open one. It requires a stretch of existing doctrine to hold someone criminally responsible for someone else's suicide. Holding someone criminally responsible for making another person so mentally confused that they didn't try to save themselves from drowning would seem to require an even greater one.

But the law doesn't, and doesn't purport to, condemn everything we think morally wrong. We might conclude that holding Hamlet legally responsible for Ophelia's death would set a dangerous precedent. But, from a moral perspective, we may at the same time have little difficulty siding with Laertes in believing Hamlet to have been materially at fault. And, when Hamlet angrily proclaims his great love for the dead Ophelia, we may feel like he protests too much.

Or that we can add love to the list of things that Hamlet struggles to understand.

❂ ❂ ❂ ❂ ❂

The second scene of the fifth act brings us all the remaining deaths and, as with *Titus*, they cascade down pretty quickly. First, we learn that Hamlet disposed of Rosencrantz and Guildenstern by switching the document they brought to the king of England. Claudius gave them a letter demanding Hamlet's head, but Hamlet substituted a mocked-up letter that instead demanded theirs.

Did Hamlet cause their deaths? Well, that's complicated. It's true that Hamlet prepared the document that prompted the killing of Rosencrantz and Guildenstern. But Claudius is the one who put the plot in motion. And whether the document had any effect depended entirely on what Rosencrantz and Guildenstern did with it—in this sense, the matter was out of Hamlet's hands.

Was Hamlet justified in substituting the mocked-up letter that doomed them for the original one that doomed him? Well, that's complicated, too. It may depend on whether they knew what was in the original letter. If they believed that they were delivering a letter that contained instructions to kill Hamlet, then it would seem they got their just desserts. But, if they didn't know, then capital punishment seems like an unconscionably harsh penalty. To run the moral calculus we need to know what they knew, and Will doesn't tell us.

Will leaves us in a magnificently ambiguous place here. Hamlet is, and is not, the cause of the death of Rosencrantz and Guildenstern. He is, and is not, responsible. He may, or may not, be blameworthy in their beheading. It's a puzzle worthy of the physicist Erwin Schrödinger and his famous cat, simultaneously dead and alive.

I tell my law students that when I draft final examination questions I often go back and cut out one or more facts that are critical to the analysis. I want them to spot the missing pieces of information and to tell me why that information matters—just as they would have to do if a client left those details out of their narrative. It's as if Will does the same thing with us here: He gives us a conundrum about responsibility, and then challenges us to notice the absent fact or facts that we need to solve it.

❂ ❂ ❂ ❂ ❂

While the play leaves us uncertain about the role of Rosencrantz and Guildenstern in the plot against Hamlet, no questions surround the scheme hatched between Claudius and Laertes. It seems simple enough, and they've even got a Plan B. Laertes and Hamlet will enter into a fencing match; Laertes will poison his rapier so that a single scratch will kill Hamlet; should that stratagem fail, Claudius will give Hamlet a poisoned cup of wine.

But their infallible plan proves fallible, and Plan A and Plan B collapse into a hodgepodge of primary and intervening causes. Hamlet meets with some success in the match, prompting Gertrude to toast him with the poisoned cup, accidentally killing herself. Consistent with Plan A, Laertes wounds Hamlet with the poisoned rapier, ultimately killing him. But before Hamlet dies a scuffle takes place, swords get exchanged, and he cuts Laertes.

Who causes the death of Laertes? Hamlet, by wounding him? Laertes, by poisoning the sword? "I am justly killed with my own treachery," Laertes confesses. Or, wait, is Claudius to blame? When Laertes points toward Claudius as the prime mover behind all this mayhem, Hamlet promptly slays his stepfather.

Taken by itself, Hamlet's killing of Claudius might seem like the relatively straightforward revenge transaction we have long awaited. At last, the play has come full circle and Hamlet has fulfilled the charge that the ghost gave him in the first act. The debt has been discharged, the task has been completed, and justice has been done.

Except.

Except that this revenge comes to us at a grotesquely elevated cost. Yes, Claudius dies, but so do Polonius, Ophelia, Rosencrantz, Guildenstern,

Gertrude, and Laertes. Hamlet, the avenging angel who in Act I lamented that the obligation to see justice done had landed on his shoulders, has some role in all of their deaths. And then the avenger himself perishes, hoisted by his own petard, we might say.

Questions of responsibility are the everyday fare of the law. In some cases, like *Carter*, the law stretches the concept beyond its ordinary boundaries—perhaps improperly and to the breaking point. In *Hamlet*, Will invites us to see the idea of responsibility in all its wild richness, reflecting the infinite varieties of ways in which human beings are connected with each other and, as a result, become responsible for what happens to each other.

Literary scholars often describe *Hamlet* as a revenge tragedy, and of course it is one, but I'm not persuaded that revenge is its primary theme. If *Hamlet* were about revenge then it would be half as long and half as interesting. And *Titus Andronicus* suggests that twice as many bodies would show up twice as soon.

No, I think that at its core *Hamlet* is about something else altogether. I think it is about the unexpected interconnectedness of human beings and our destinies. I think it is about all the various ways in which that interconnectedness makes us responsible for each other.

In matters of law, we limit the concept of responsibility. But in matters of morality, we do so at our peril. Our endless points of contact and mutual influence require universality. "Each man's death diminishes me," John Donne wrote, "for I am involved in mankind."

The punchline of the New Testament parable of the Good Samaritan is that everyone is our neighbor. This holds true, the parable tells us, even on the dangerous and violent Jericho Road. *Hamlet* adds: Yes, and that road passes through the whole wide world as we find it.

It even runs through the rotten state of Denmark.

When the Wind Is Southerly

To my mind, *Hamlet* is very much about something else as well. I think it is about identity. Or, more specifically, I think it is about the absence of identity.

Prince Hamlet never met an internal conflict he didn't like. The first act gives us a subtle signal on this front. After the ghost tells Hamlet that he must avenge his most "foul and most unnatural" murder, Hamlet responds by saying two things. First, he pledges to sweep in with swift wings and see justice done (I:5:35–37). And, second, he complains that the obligation to revenge his father's death has fallen to him (I:5:210–211).

The images of the speedy avenger and the reluctant assassin, of the dauntless minister of justice and the hesitant intervenor, don't reconcile very easily. Hamlet displays these sorts of tensions in character throughout the play. Contrasts live side by side within him, and by all appearances they do so uncomfortably.

When I teach the play, I ask my students if they'd like to meet Hamlet at the bar (with apologies to Will, who we'll catch there another time). The vast majority of them say yes. When I ask why, they talk about finding him interesting. When I ask why again (law professors do a lot of this), they provide a list of qualities that they believe would make him good company.

This prompts me to ask for a list of *all* his qualities, of *all* the aspects of him that we see in the play, good or bad. The final result looks something like this: Witty/serious. Excitable/melancholy. Serious/frivolous. Intellectual/impetuous. Vicious/sentimental. Religious/skeptical. You get the idea. For every quality Hamlet displays in the play, it seems that we can find instances of him exhibiting the opposing quality.

Take the characteristics most often associated with Hamlet. We imagine him as the indecisive intellectual who overthinks things and can't bring himself to act. Granted, Hamlet does indeed sometimes display these attributes. On more than one occasion he even berates himself for them. But perhaps we shouldn't be so fast to accept his self-criticism at face value.

As I noted in the last section, Hamlet had decided to kill Claudius—and had tried to do it—by the third act of the play. Granted, he later demurs when he has the chance to kill Claudius on finding him at prayer, but he has a reason: slaying him under those circumstances might propel his soul to heaven. And, given the depth and breadth of Claudius's corruption, Hamlet knows he'll have another opportunity in short order to dispose of him with zero risk: "When he is drunk asleep, or in his rage, / Or in the incestuous pleasure of his bed / At game, a-swearing, or about some act / That has no relish of salvation in't."

For someone who supposedly can't make up his mind, Hamlet does a lot of it. He quickly—perhaps too quickly—settles on the strategy of feigned madness. He concocts an elaborate plan to use a play to tease out the king's guilt. He dispatches Rosencrantz and Guildenstern without hesitation. Maybe he is an action figure, after all.

In my view, *Hamlet* isn't a story about a man who can't make up his mind. *Hamlet* is the story of a man who doesn't know who he is. And who can blame him? His nature includes too many conflicting impulses and inclinations.

This leaves Hamlet with a dreadful problem, because not *knowing* who you are makes it impossible to *remember* who you are during times of moral crisis. And remembering who you are is essential to making choices and decisions that align with your conscience. The play shows us Hamlet adrift, and we may feel tempted to attribute it to indecisiveness. But the real cause is an absence of the moral grounding that comes with knowing who you are.

In my Legal Ethics course, I ask students a question about mountain climbers. I don't mean people like me, who scramble up the beautiful but modest mountains of the Adirondacks and New Hampshire. I mean the resolute folks who go on expeditions to ascend the world's major peaks. I ask my students if they know when these serious climbers decide the point at which they have to turn around, give up on the summit, and head back down the mountain.

It turns out that serious climbers make this decision when they're still in base camp, before they set off up the mountain. They know that in base camp they can still think clearly, logically, and with proper safety protocols in mind. They know that if they wait until they're well up the mountain they're much more likely to make a mistake. The rarified air will confuse them. The false summits will seduce them. They'll forget what they once knew.

I invite my students to think of law school and the first few years of practice as their moral base camp. I explain to them that, as their success grows, so will the temptations toward ethical compromise. At greater altitudes they may struggle to know the right thing to do and to do it. Their best shot lies in figuring out, while they're still in base camp, the conditions that will prompt them to stop, turn around, and go the other way. But if we do not start up the mountain already knowing who we are, well, then we are lost.

Hamlet says that he is "but mad north-north-west." That may be true. And when the wind is southerly, he may indeed know "a hawk from a handsaw."

But I think the play leaves us with this problem:

He still won't have the foggiest idea who he is.

7

"To Vouch This Is No Proof"

Othello

Backdrop

In the film *The People vs. Larry Flynt,* attorney Alan Isaacman grows weary of the legally reckless escapades of his client, Larry Flynt. Exasperated with Flynt's latest stunt, Isaacman threatens to terminate their relationship. Flynt waves off the idea. "I'm the dream client," he declares. "I'm rich, I'm the most fun, and I'm always in trouble."

Many of us have had clients like Larry Flynt, if less notorious and more subdued. They can be inscrutable. Mysterious forces attract them to existential turbulence. Inexplicable impulses compel them to run merrily off the rails, over and over again, usually with the same unfortunate outcomes. They earn the legal services equivalent of frequent flier status, and they do it the hard way.

Such clients can indeed be fun, in the same way that watching a demolition derby affords a kind of perverse amusement. They can also be financially lucrative; nothing drives revenue like a client's bad decision-making. But, in the end, a lawyer may come to view clients like this as intolerably frustrating. Over the years, I've let a few go because I wearied of profiting from their staunch refusal to learn from their blunders and grow up.

If I could meet Shakespeare at the bar, I'd tell him that this is why for a long time I didn't care much for his play, *Othello*. I recognize that many scholars celebrate it as one of his greatest works. But I found it hard to warm to the play's protagonist because of his uncompromising—and finally tragic—fondness for unforced errors.

Granted, Iago manipulates Othello, so certainly part of the fault rests with him. But in my early encounters with the play I was always struck by how unnecessary the whole mess was and how little Othello needed to do to avoid it. Watching the play, like watching some of my most self-destructive clients, was like watching a china cabinet topple over onto a marble floor. In slow motion.

With all that said, I'd also tell Will that I eventually came to love and admire the play. Looking at *Othello* more closely through the lens of the law helped me discern in it qualities that I'd previously missed, including the two themes we will focus on in this chapter. But more on them momentarily; first, we need a bit of background.

❂ ❂ ❂ ❂ ❂

Will probably wrote *Othello* in 1604, drawing heavily on a novella by Giraldi Cinthio, an author to whom he'd later return. He either knew the work through hearsay or, more likely, read it in a French translation. Will's play closely follows Cinthio's plot, but there are significant differences, including the addition of the figure of Roderigo, and as always he makes the story uniquely his own.

Othello introduces us to Shakespeare as a Jacobean playwright. That the tragedy begins with a trial based on an accusation of witchcraft is particularly interesting given the new king's fascination with all things supernatural. As we'll see, this witch trial has its problems, but it does go vastly better than most of them went historically.

That opening trial introduces us to both of the law-related themes we'll explore here. The first is the theme of race and, specifically, the ways in which subtle (and unsubtle) uses of racist language shape society and individual experience. The law has struggled, particularly in recent years, with the question of how to address hateful speech of this nature. We'll struggle a bit more with it here.

The second theme relates to the question of what counts as proof of a fact. In the opening trial, the play explores the question in the context of the charge of witchcraft that Brabantio (the father of Othello's betrothed, Desdemona) formally lodges against Othello. But the context quickly shifts to the charge of adultery that Othello informally lodges against his own wife. These charges also raise intriguing questions about such legal concepts as presumptions, burdens of proof, and due process.

As with *Hamlet*, we can't pursue all of the law-related threads that run through this complex work. For example, *Othello*—like *Hamlet*—raises fascinating problems of responsibility, including Iago's responsibility for the death of Desdemona. But the themes of race and evidence will give us more than enough to ponder in the space we have.

Loosen your collar. Throw an extra log on the fire at the Tabard. We have work to do.

A Barbary Stalking Horse

As we discussed in an earlier chapter, the antisemitism in *The Merchant of Venice* is vicious, conspicuous, and pervasive. It drives the action of the play. The abuse that Shylock receives at the hands of Antonio (and others) moves him to demand a pound of flesh as his bond and impels him to insist on the gruesome remedy despite all pleas for mercy. The antisemitism in *Merchant* goes way beyond the use of offensive speech; it is the prime mover behind key events.

To my mind, Will approaches the issue of Othello's race with a significantly lighter touch. That's not to say that race doesn't have an important place in the play; it clearly does. For example, Brabantio accuses Othello of witchcraft in the opening act only because he can't imagine any other reason Desdemona would consent to marry him—given his race. And numerous scholars have pointed out that the play makes use of pernicious racial stereotypes around virility, violence, and jealousy. But what particularly interests me about the play is its use of racist slurs and insults.

The play heavily front-loads this language. The references to "thick lips," "an old black ram," "a Barbary horse," "lascivious Moor," and a "sooty bosom" all appear in the first two scenes, as does Brabantio's suggestion that nothing other than witchcraft could explain his daughter's attraction to Othello. This structure makes for a striking contrast with *Merchant*, where the antisemitic slurs and insults are a steady drumbeat that runs throughout the play, right up to the point where Shylock is dismissed with orders to become a Christian.

Also, most of this language comes from two figures, Iago and Roderigo—again, a striking contrast with *Merchant*, where almost every non-Jew resorts to antisemitic epithets. And Iago and Roderigo use the language strategically, to feed Brabantio's concerns about his daughter. The slurs thus largely occur outside of the hearing of Othello, yet another striking contrast with *Merchant*, where Shylock has to endure so much of the vile stuff.

As a matter of social hierarchy, all of this makes perfect sense. As a Jew and an alien in Venice, Shylock had no social standing. The various players could openly abuse him and flex their privilege over him. Little wonder they became keenly frustrated, and Shylock enjoyed it so thoroughly, when Antonio's default on the bond put the abused Jew in a position of power.

As a high-ranking and respected military leader, Othello occupied a very different social station. Iago could hardly insult to his face the man he wished would promote him. Even the Duke descends to flattery, presumably because he so badly and urgently needs Othello's services. In public, the thick-lipped black ram thus becomes "Valiant Othello"; outward respect becomes a stalking horse for racist contempt.

The enforcement of anti-discrimination laws has taught us that racism works this way. As people of color receive the opportunity to succeed—and do so—racist ideas, stereotypes, and language don't go away. They just go underground—although usually not very far. *Othello* signals to us, and early on, that its title character carries with him a social stain for which he holds no responsibility, over which he has no control, and that he can't erase.

Language plays a critical role here. Brabantio makes a show of power when he tells Othello that his daughter wouldn't marry anyone like him absent a magic spell. Othello can disagree, but he can't rebuke Brabantio for the insult. Iago and Roderigo use racial slurs outside of Othello's presence, but this constitutes a show of power as well. Those slurs feed old prejudices and keep ancient hatreds alive for use at an opportune time. Words have power, and everyone in this play knows how to mobilize it.

Today, we have a keen understanding of the personal and societal damage done by such hateful speech. That understanding has prompted numerous efforts to criminalize or otherwise punish this sort of language. In European countries, laws prohibiting various kinds of hate speech are not uncommon. In the United States, however, First Amendment doctrine has proven a formidable obstacle to such regulation. This is so for several reasons.

Free speech doctrine in the United States rests on the general principle that all ideas should have the opportunity to enter the "marketplace" and to compete for our allegiance. First Amendment jurisprudence has long recognized a number of exceptions to this principle, like defamation and obscenity. But, even in those cases, the law defines the exception narrowly and protects a great deal of speech that most people might think has little value. And First Amendment doctrine has never recognized any "hate speech" exception.

Indeed, the United States Supreme Court made clear that it had no interest in creating such an exception in its 2011 decision in *Snyder v. Phelps.*

In that case, protestors from the Westboro Baptist Church picketed on ground near the funeral of Marine Lance Corporal Matthew Snyder, who died in the line of duty. The members of Westboro believe that God hates the United States for its tolerance of homosexuality and punishes it through military casualties. Near Matthew's funeral church members carried signs with slogans like "God Hates the USA," "You're Going to Hell," and "Thank God for dead soldiers."

Matthew's father brought claims for intentional infliction of emotional distress and other torts against Westboro. A jury awarded him millions of dollars in damages, but the Supreme Court reversed. The Court acknowledged Mr. Snyder's "already incalculable grief" and conceded that Westboro's "contribution to public discourse" was probably "negligible." But the Court nevertheless held that the First Amendment protected Westboro's speech.

Snyder v. Phelps tells us a lot about the Supreme Court's view of things. If the facts there didn't provide an occasion for recognizing a "hate speech" exception to the First Amendment, then it's hard to imagine the facts that would. It seems unlikely we could encounter a more sympathetic plaintiff, a less sympathetic defendant, and speech of coarser content and lower value.

A substantial part of the problem lies in trying to explain what does, and doesn't, qualify as hate speech. We can't define it by reference to mere offensiveness, because the First Amendment protects lots of speech that reasonable people find insulting, repulsive, and upsetting. The definition also can't include any vague or ambiguous terms, because due process requires that people have reasonable notice of what a law allows and prohibits. And our definition can't sweep too broadly or it will fail under the First Amendment overbreadth doctrine.

A few years ago, I discussed these challenges in a talk I gave on hate speech at a conference on First Amendment law. I took questions right before we broke for lunch. A gentleman who was sitting in the first row with an unhappy expression on his face and his arms crossed (indeed, it felt as if his entire body were crossed) shot up his hand. "It isn't hard to define hate speech," he declared. "We just lack the political will to regulate this sort of thing."

I handed him a pen and paper. I invited him to do the non-hard thing he described and to write a definition over lunch. But, I explained, the definition couldn't rest on offensiveness alone, couldn't be vague, and had to punish everything that we wanted to punish but nothing that we didn't. I told him I looked forward to reading his draft. He didn't return after the break.

That we can't define hate speech with constitutionally sufficient precision and breadth doesn't mean that such speech doesn't exist or that it doesn't cause real harm in the world. It plainly does both those things. Indeed, such speech all too often takes place openly, frequently as an exercise of majority power over a minority, much as we find it in *Merchant of Venice.*

But *Othello* shows us something different. At the beginning of this play, we observe hate speech at work explicitly, although sometimes behind the back of its target. And then, after the first act, that language almost entirely disappears from the text of the play.

Like so much racism, it goes underground. But if we think it goes away, then we have missed the entire point of front-loading its presence. It's like the ghost in *Hamlet*: It gets things started, and it does not need to stay at center stage to haunt its target.

Our friend Will knew exactly how these things work.

To See Before You Doubt

As I noted earlier, *Othello* begins with a trial and a question of proof. Iago and his friend Roderigo have gotten Brabantio thoroughly agitated over the idea that Othello has stolen his daughter. Brabantio hauls Othello before the Duke on the charge that his daughter would not have taken up with the Moor "sans witchcraft." Brabantio has no evidence to support this charge, only his anger, his suspicion, and his accusation. The Duke rebuffs him: "To vouch this is no proof."

Othello has an explanation in his defense. He suspects that the adventurous stories he has told Desdemona may have swayed her. But, of course, this is just more speculation, so Othello suggests they summon Desdemona to explain things in her own terms. She appears and says that she loves Othello. This settles matters, and everyone moves on to other business.

In a sense, however, this evidence amounts to no evidence at all. If Othello had indeed put a spell on Desdemona, then we would expect her to say exactly what she says. The testimony of a truly bewitched witness would tell us nothing. The first act thus launches us into an extended exploration of what counts for proof of a fact and how we can go wrong in our thinking about evidence.

After Othello's brief witchcraft trial, another very different trial ensues—one that occupies the balance of the play. In it, Othello effectively charges Desdemona with adultery. As the drama unfolds, he considers the various items of proof that he thinks relevant to the charge, and Will implicitly invites us to ponder whether he weighs them properly. We'll look at each of them in turn.

But, before we get there, we should pause to note the qualities that made the witchcraft trial procedurally fair to Othello. He received the essential benefits of due process: He got notice of the charge against him and an opportunity to be heard. He spoke on his own behalf and had the chance to summon witnesses in his favor. The Duke declared that the accusation by itself amounted to "no proof," suggesting that Othello's innocence was presumed and the burden rested on Brabantio to prove his guilt.

Othello affords no such process to Desdemona. He starts off well enough, rejecting Iago's insinuations and demanding "ocular proof" of her infidelity. But, as the play unfolds, it becomes apparent that the presumption shifts against her, and in the end it becomes irrebuttable. Through much of the play, Desdemona doesn't even know she's suspected of anything, let alone that she lives under the dark cloud of an increasingly unalterable judgment. I'll have more to say about this later.

To help us think about the evidence offered against Desdemona, I'm going to borrow an idea from the law of civil procedure. To my mind, looking at the evidence through this lens clarifies the inadequacies of the evidence that Othello compiles. I think it also offers powerful lessons not only about this play and about the law, but about human relationships and about what we owe to those we say we love.

Let's start here. In order for a plaintiff to get a civil lawsuit going, they need to file a complaint that includes sufficient allegations to state a claim. If the complaint fails to do so, then the case is dead on arrival and the defendant can move to dismiss it.

For many years, federal courts applied a forgiving standard that made it very easy for a plaintiff to state a claim in their complaint. Then, in 2007, the Supreme Court decided *Bell Atlantic Corp. v. Twombly* and significantly changed the controlling standard, at least in federal courts. To understand how and why, we need a quick review of the facts and holding of that case.

Twombly arose in a world in which AT&T had monopoly power as a telephone service provider. As a result of the enforcement of antitrust laws in the 1980s, the company was broken up into a number of separate regional companies, colloquially referred to as the "baby Bells." The idea was that the baby Bells would compete with each other and expand into each other's territories and that consumers would enjoy lower prices as a result. But this didn't happen.

Twombly brought a lawsuit essentially alleging that the baby Bells had conspired against competition in violation of the federal antitrust law, the Sherman Act. The facts included in the complaint satisfied the old standard for pleading a case. But the Supreme Court held that the old standard left too much room for non-meritorious cases to proceed and adopted a tougher new standard, which it concluded Twombly's complaint didn't satisfy.

The Court pointed out that, in his effort to state an antitrust claim, Twombly relied on the fact that the baby Bells had engaged in "parallel conduct"—that is, that each of the companies tended to do what the others did. For example, if one stayed in their territory, so did the others. Twombly claimed that those facts showed a conspiracy between the baby Bells not to compete.

The problem with this argument, the Court pointed out, is that parallel conduct is equally consistent with both *noncompetition* and *competition.* Take the example of raising prices. If a company raises prices, and its competitor follows suit, then this may signal that they have entered into a conspiracy not to compete. But it's just as likely that it means something benign. It might, for example, indicate that the competitor also thinks that the market will support an increase in prices and that it wants to maximize profits, too.

Evidence of parallel conduct, taken by itself, therefore tells us nothing about whether these decisions resulted from the kind of anticompetitive conspiracies we forbid or the kind of competitive strategies we encourage. And evidence of parallel conduct was all that Twombly had. The plaintiff therefore didn't, and couldn't, state a valid claim for antitrust.

Scholars have criticized various aspects and implications of *Twombly*, but we can put aside those intricacies for present purposes. What matters to our discussion is *Twombly*'s insight that you can't prove a case by offering only evidence that is equally consistent with guilt and innocence. Indeed, under the reasoning of *Twombly* you don't even get the opportunity to *try* to prove such a case. If your complaint includes only those kinds of allegations, then it fails to state a claim and your case has come to a swift and inglorious conclusion. Don't let the door hit you on the way out of the courtroom.

Now, with *Twombly* in mind, let's look at the evidence that gets offered against Desdemona. And let's ask whether that evidence, if included in a complaint, would even state a claim against her. As we'll see, for the most part the answer is a clear and unequivocal "no."

The first item of evidence actually materializes at the conclusion of Othello's own trial. After Othello has prevailed, Brabantio cautions him: "She has deceived her father, and may thee." Brabantio's comment plants the seed of Desdemona's potential for betrayal, and in the third scene of the third act Iago strategically revives the idea, saying: "She did deceive her father, marrying you."

Brabantio's remark constitutes the kind of character evidence we discussed earlier in this book. In essence, he argues that Desdemona's deception of her father indicates a general propensity toward such conduct, making it more likely she'll betray Othello down the road. As noted earlier in the chapter on *Richard II*, for a variety of reasons our law takes a hostile view of such arguments, and contemporary psychology suggests that this hostility is warranted.

If we look at Brabantio's argument through the lens of *Twombly*, though, we see yet another flaw in his reasoning. Yes, Desdemona's deception of her father might be consistent with the idea that she'll later deceive Othello. But it's at least equally consistent with the idea that she won't. After all, Desdemona deceived her father because of her deep love for Othello, which would seem to make it less likely that she'll betray him. As proof of a potential for marital infidelity goes, Brabantio's seems woefully inadequate.

The remainder of the evidence against Desdemona comes almost entirely from Iago. It appears that Othello has no idea that Iago hates him, so Othello has no reason to doubt Iago's credibility. This may be naïve on Othello's part. After all, it appears that Othello may have cuckolded Iago and he might reasonably wonder whether Iago knew about it. But if the notion flashed through Othello's mind the text doesn't appear to give us any sign of it.

The next piece of evidence comes in the third scene of Act III, and consists in Othello's observation of Cassio walking away from Desdemona. Othello might have thought nothing of it, had Iago not said: "Ha, I like not that . . . I cannot think it / That he would steal away so guiltylike / Seeing your coming."

Of course, Cassio and Desdemona's presence in each other's company means nothing, absent Iago's insinuations. And any adverse inference we might draw from it would seem dispelled by Desdemona's prompt disclosure that she'd been talking with Cassio and her pleas that Othello call him back so he could express his regrets over his earlier misconduct. If Desdemona and Cassio were trying to sneak around behind Othello's back, they were doing a magnificently poor job of it.

Well into the third scene of the third act, Othello seems thoroughly and appropriately dismissive of Iago's innuendos. He says: "No, Iago, / I'll see before I doubt; when I doubt." And he adds: "I do not think but Desdemona's honest." He instructs Iago to tell him if and when he has more evidence.

But then Iago hears a little fissure in Othello's resolve: "Why did I marry?" Othello continue to resist Iago's charge of infidelity, and later in the act Othello will demand "ocular proof" of it. But in this instant something changes, and the change is not lost upon the calculating Iago.

Numerous scholars have objected to the more demanding pleading standard endorsed in *Twombly* on the grounds that, in certain types of cases, it makes the plaintiff's job impossible. Conspiracies, like the anticompetitive conspiracy alleged in *Twombly* itself, provide an example. As a general proposition, conspirators don't go around publicizing their conspiracy; they do their work in secret. Critics of *Twombly* argue that it hamstrings the plaintiffs in such cases to require them to know and plead facts they can't possibly know and plead.

Iago raises just this argument when Othello declares that he'll "have some proof." Iago asks: "How satisfied, my Lord? Would you, the [spectator], grossly gape on / Behold her topped?" Iago has a point: Clandestine romances don't lend themselves to direct proof. The argument moderates Othello's expectations, setting the stage for Iago to persuade him with circumstantial evidence.

Iago immediately produces some: Awake at night with a toothache, he recently had occasion to hear Cassio talking in his sleep. He describes his memory of the event in extraordinary detail:

> In sleep I heard him say, "Sweet Desdemona,
> Let us be wary, let us hide our loves."
> And then, sir, would he gripe and wring my hand,
> Cry "Oh sweet creature!" then kiss me hard,
> As if he plucked up kisses by the roots
> That grew upon my lips; then laid his leg
> O'er my thigh, and sighed, and kissed, and then
> Cried, "Cursed fate that gave thee to the Moor!" (III:3:475–482)

The credulous Othello, taking the testimony at face value, exclaims: "O monstrous! Monstrous!"

To our modern sensibilities, Iago's story sounds ridiculous. Think about it. While asleep, Cassio speaks in complete sentences. Deep in his dreams, he mistakes Iago for Desdemona. He then all but mounts Iago—toothache and all—while Iago lies there impassively and watches it all unfold. As a former partner of mine who practiced criminal defense law used to say to his sketchy clients: "Your story may be true. But it sure doesn't sound true."

If we accept Iago's description of these events as accurate, however, it proves nothing. As one court observed, "Admitting hearsay evidence of statements made while a person is sleeping, so-called 'sleep talk,' would run counter to one of the central principles governing the admissibility of evidence, namely, that the proffered material is reliable . . . Common sense dictates that while asleep, one cannot distinguish between reality and fiction, a touchstone of admissibility." *Commonwealth v. Almeida*, 433 Mass. 717 (2001). Even Iago says: "this was but his dream." Exactly so, and it was therefore as plausibly a fantasy as it was the nocturnal reliving of an actual sexual encounter.

At this point, Iago plays his strongest card: He tells Othello that he has seen Cassio wipe his beard with a handkerchief spotted with a pattern of strawberries. The evidence hits Othello hard, because it describes a handkerchief that his mother gave to him and that he gave to Desdemona. Indeed, it hits him so hard that at first he appears to take it as dispositive proof. He proclaims his love gone. He talks of "vengeance" from "hollow hell." "O, blood, blood, blood" he cries.

But Othello's next step suggests that perhaps some doubt remains and that he still needs confirmation of the accusation. He goes to Desdemona and asks to see the handkerchief, although he doesn't say why. Embarrassed that she has lost Othello's treasured gift, she makes a terrible mistake and lies: She says she still has the handkerchief, but not with her. The lie seals Othello's conviction of her infidelity.

If we stand back and look at the evidence objectively, we find abundant reasons to question how much weight Othello should have given this "ocular proof." It seems inherently unlikely that Desdemona would give her adulterous lover a gift so easily identified as hers and so conspicuously connected with her husband. And, if she did, it seems even more unlikely that her lover would go around town wiping his beard with it. Othello had good reason to doubt that Iago saw what he said he saw.

And, even if Othello credited Iago's testimony, Cassio's possession of the handkerchief might be innocently explained. Everyone knew that

Desdemona and Cassio had a warm friendship. A handkerchief hardly makes for compelling evidence that their connection had evolved into adultery.

In processing this evidence, Othello has one good idea and two bad ones. His good idea is to go in search of additional evidence to rebut or confirm the insinuations of Iago. He wisely wants more and better proof. But, as I say, his good idea quickly gets outnumbered.

His first bad idea is that he can get to the bottom of things by finding out whether Desdemona still has the handkerchief. Of course, that's not quite right. It's true that if Desdemona has the handkerchief in her possession, then this fact contradicts Iago's story. But it's *not* true that if she *doesn't* have the handkerchief, then this validates the charge against her. After all, Desdemona could have lost the handkerchief and never given it to Cassio in the first place; indeed, that's exactly what in fact happened.

Othello's second bad idea is that the various pieces of "evidence" he's assembled add up to a case against Desdemona. He sees a cumulative significance in them, for example saying that Cassio's alleged sleep-talk "may help to thicken other proofs." Iago feeds this idea, saying of the handkerchief: "It speaks against her with the other proofs."

Othello has a point, indeed one that every Evidence professor would endorse. As a general proposition, we don't expect any individual item of evidence to do all the work in proving a case. Evidence operates additively, like pieces filling in a jigsaw puzzle.

This especially holds true in those cases that we have to prove circumstantially rather than directly, like most charges of adultery. In his foundational treatise on evidence law, Professor McCormick famously observed: "A brick is not a wall." Othello sees himself as building a wall, one brick at a time, and he's spot on in thinking that evidence usually works this way.

That conceptual model assumes, however, that each piece of evidence—while not the whole in itself—contributes something to it. We can mathematically represent the notion through a simple equation like $1 + 1 + 1 + 1 = 4$. And lawyers do indeed generally assemble their cases this way, with each piece of evidence contributing a small part of a bigger picture.

But this model doesn't hold up if each piece of evidence is equally consistent with guilt or innocence. Under those circumstances, the mathematical representation changes dramatically; it becomes $0 + 0 + 0 + 0 = 0$. That's the key insight of *Twombly*—that you can't build a claim based on equivocal facts that fail to make a case plausible. And an implausible claim is precisely the type put together by Othello and Iago here.

When your process consists in one good idea, but two bad ones, then you need a different process. The way for Othello to get the evidence he actually needs lies in an entirely different approach than the one he takes. It lies in his being honest with Desdemona, telling her what Iago has suggested to him, and asking her to tell him the truth.

Such an approach would have had numerous virtues. It would have afforded her notice and an opportunity to be heard. It would have presumed her innocence. It would have allowed Desdemona to confront her accuser. It would have forced Iago to make his case. It would have given her the chance to offer evidence on her behalf. In short, it would have given her the essence of due process—simple fairness. Othello enjoyed such protections during his witchcraft trial; but he couldn't bring himself to share the same protections with Desdemona, who he claimed to love.

Law is one thing and life is another. Applying legal principles to everyday human experience doesn't always make much sense or yield favorable results. In some instances, injecting the standards of the courtroom into other contexts can be silly or even dangerous.

But, in *Othello*, Shakespeare shows us two trials. The first is a formal trial in which due process is observed. All goes well and justice gets quickly done.

The second is the sort of informal trial that often takes place in human relationships. Due process is not observed. And it all ends in tragedy.

We might think of it this way: Some significant part of life involves figuring out what we owe to those we love.

Othello suggests that we owe them at least as much respect and protection as we afford the average defendant.

8

"Strict Statutes and Most Biting Laws"

Measure for Measure

Backdrop

In February of 2022, I participated in an academic workshop at St. Andrews University in Scotland. The purpose of the workshop was to continue a project initiated by my late University of Michigan Law School colleague, Brian Simpson, who was described in his *Guardian* obituary as "one of the greatest academic lawyers of his generation" in the fields of legal history, legal philosophy, and human rights. To have even a brief conversation with Brian was to understand instantly that he had a big brain and a big heart and loved to ask big questions. And the question he had explored in the work that we were pursuing at St. Andrews was a mighty big one indeed: "What is law?"

Will's magnificent—and magnificently complex—play *Measure for Measure* reflects a similar passion for big questions, including that one. Indeed, the play explores that question in multiple variations: Is law still law when it goes unenforced for a long time? When it's unfairly severe? When it becomes a tool for manipulation, abuse, and self-serving? Questions about law lie right at the center of this powerful, perplexing, and powerfully perplexing play.

Scholars believe Will wrote *Measure for Measure* around 1603 or 1604. It qualifies as a comedy for the same structural reasons *The Merchant of Venice* does: In the end, multiple couples overcome a series of daunting obstacles and a clutch of weddings follows. But, also like *The Merchant of Venice*, *Measure for Measure* qualifies as a problem play. Dark and malevolent forces drive much of the action. And, in the end, Will leaves us pondering just how happy those happy marriages are.

In writing the play, Will drew material from a variety of sources. Those include a tale by the Italian writer Cinthio, who, as you'll recall, served as a source for *Othello* as well. But Cinthio's story ends tragically, so Will borrowed subplots from other sources to leaven the narrative with humor. As always, the final product is distinctly his own.

Measure for Measure has not always received a warm reception. Samuel Johnson grumbled over its idiosyncrasies, remarking that there is "not one of Shakespeare's plays more darkened than this by the peculiarities of its author . . ." The early critic Charlotte Lennox excoriated Shakespeare for filling the play with endless contrivances in an effort to "torture it into a Comedy" and to bring about "three or four weddings." What we really want at its conclusion, Lennox suggests, is just "one good beheading." In researching this book I discovered a Master of Arts thesis written in 1953 by one Jacques Boettcher that began with this assessment: "[*Measure for Measure*] has probably suffered more abusive criticism than any other play by Shakespeare with the exception of *Hamlet* . . . [I]t is rare today that the play is considered worthy of production."

Johnson had a point about the peculiarities of the play, and Lennox was right to question its unsatisfying conclusion, and Boettcher's perspective was probably spot on in 1953. But in recent years the play has enjoyed a remarkable revival in interest and performance. No less discerning a critic than Harold Bloom pronounced it one of his two favorite Shakespeare plays, praising its murkiness and describing it as a "masterpiece of nihilism."

Some of the current enthusiasm for the play is occasioned by its eerily relevant portrayal of the power dynamics of sexual harassment and sexual assault. When Angelo dismisses Isabella's threat to reveal his advances and his hypocrisy with the words "Who will believe thee, Isabel?" it chills us with its familiarity. Except for the antique pronoun, the question could come out of the testimonial record of almost any twenty-first-century sex discrimination or rape case. And *Measure for Measure* isn't just a story about a villain; it's a story about the social—and even legal—structures that make this sort of villainy possible.

This is not to say that the play comes to us unburdened of difficulties. As Bloom noted, *Measure for Measure* is "as great as it is finally opaque" and even enthusiastic modern audiences may struggle with its knottier conundrums. For example, it's hard to divine the Duke's motivations for doing many of the things he does; Isabella is a puzzle unto herself; and the play famously concludes with a conspicuous ambiguity as to how the Duke's proposals of marriage fare with her. We may scratch our heads over the moral of this fable, if it has a moral, and we may sensibly wonder who, if anyone, we're supposed to find likable in this story. For our purposes, however, all that fuzziness just makes the conversation more interesting.

Summon the innkeeper. The Tabard may need to stay open late. We have a lot to discuss.

What Is Law, Anyway?

The Duke of Vienna has a problem—of his own making. His city has more than enough harsh laws in place, but he's been lax about enforcing them, and as a result things have gotten out of hand. Because the fault lies with him, he worries that a crackdown on his watch won't sit well with his subjects. So, he comes up with a plan: He'll announce that he's headed out of town; he'll put his deputy Angelo in charge; he'll give Angelo free rein to restore order; and he'll disguise himself as a friar so he can keep an eye on Angelo and the cleanup effort. What could go wrong?

Let's pause here to note that in the course of the play the Duke has lots of ideas and most of them are quite bad. Take this one, for example. Why doesn't the Duke ask himself why the laws have gone unenforced? Is it possible they're not worth enforcing? Does the Duke really think that having his deputy do the dirty work will save him from blame for whatever goes wrong? Isn't the Duke's delegation of this unpopular and unenviable task to Angelo an utterly gutless move? Why does the Duke give Angelo unbridled power if he also feels the need to spy on him and watch for trouble?

Throughout the play, the Duke never seems to know what he's doing. That adds to the comic sensibility of the action, and it may help explain his failure to mete out perfect justice in its final scene. But, for reasons I'll explain much later, I think the weirdness of this plan actually tells us something important about the world of *Measure for Measure*—and about our own world as well. Still, let's not get ahead of ourselves: Let's start where the play does, with Angelo's efforts at legal reform.

Once at the helm, Angelo enthusiastically revives laws that have long lain dormant. How long? Well, it depends on who you ask. The Duke puts it at 14 years and Claudio puts it at 19 and it's hard to tell what to make of the discrepancy. Neither of these may strike us as especially lengthy periods, but it is helpful to remember that during the Elizabethan era 19 years was a good chunk of human lifespan. It seems clear that Will wanted us to think of it as a dormancy of sufficient length that reasonable people could come to view these laws as dead letters.

Such circumstances invite a host of intriguing questions: Are long-neglected laws really "law" at all? If not, then why not? Weren't those laws valid and enforceable at some point in the past? If so, then when did they stop having the force of law? If unenforced laws do still qualify as law, then why is that so? At some point, don't long-neglected laws lose their place in the public consciousness and their authority? And isn't it unjust to blindside people with the enforcement of neglected laws that they understandably—and through no fault of their own—have come to view as inoperative and irrelevant?

The story of Claudio and Juliet perfectly embodies the dilemma. No one denies that a law against fornication—sex outside of marriage—has remained on the books in Vienna. But the law has gone unenforced for years and it's not clear that anyone has ever been executed for violating it. Furthermore, Claudio and Juliet have pledged to marry and their commitment has proceeded to an advanced stage; they hardly seem like the kind of reckless sexual miscreants the law has in mind. More on that later.

For now, note that the scenario sets up the conflict nicely.

Angelo sees things in stark terms: Claudio must die. The law is the law.

Will asks: Or is it?

Different legal systems address the problem of dormant laws in different ways, including through the doctrine of desuetude, which comes from a Latin root that means "disuse." Briefly summarized, the doctrine of desuetude treats obsolete laws as a nullity if enforcing them would violate basic notions of fairness and due process. In the United States, you could receive a very fine legal education and never hear the word "desuetude" uttered in the classroom, because the doctrine hasn't attracted much attention or favor in our courts.

A few exceptional cases exist, however, including the 1992 West Virginia decision in *Committee on Legal Ethics v. Printz*, which has a somewhat labyrinthine procedural history. The case began with the misconduct of one Larry Kesecker, the manager of Kable Oil. Attorneys for Kable, including one Charles Printz, Jr., discovered that Kesecker had been stealing money from the company. Rather than pursue criminal charges, Printz negotiated a deal with Kesecker by which he'd repay the embezzled funds to Kable.

When it was revealed that Kesecker had actually misappropriated almost twice as much as originally thought, negotiations were reopened. Those discussions fell apart, criminal charges were filed against Kesecker, and he pled guilty, agreed to pay restitution, and was put on probation.

Lawyer disciplinary charges were filed against attorney Printz based on his conduct in the matter. The charges relied on a 1923 West Virginia statute that made it a crime to offer not to prosecute someone in exchange for a return of misappropriated funds. If this statute was valid then Printz was in trouble, because that's exactly what he'd done.

But was this law still law? The statute had grown dusty with neglect. And someone could be forgiven for not anticipating that it was unlawful to allow a repentant wrongdoer to avoid a criminal prosecution by making the injured party whole. In light of these considerations, the West Virginia Supreme Court of Appeals concluded that it needed to examine the law under the doctrine of desuetude. In the course of discussing the doctrine, the court made a passing reference to a literary exemplar of the problem: William Shakespeare's *Measure for Measure.*

The court explained that, at its core, the doctrine of desuetude asks whether the defendant had fair notice that he or she might be prosecuted under the statute at issue. The court held that answering this question required consideration of three factors: First, whether the crime in question was *malum in se* (that is, intrinsically wrong in itself) or *malum in prohibitum* (that is, deemed wrong only because the law says it is); second, whether there have been longstanding and open violations of the statute; and, third, whether there has been a conspicuous policy of nonenforcement of the law. Applying these factors, the court found that the West Virginia statute was null and void, at least "to the extent it prevents a victim or his agent from seeking restitution in lieu of a criminal prosecution."

If we consider the circumstances presented in *Measure for Measure* through the lens of the doctrine of desuetude we arrive at an interesting place. Under this collection of considerations, it seems clear that Claudio had a powerful argument that he shouldn't have been prosecuted under the anti-fornication law. Or, at least, he had two-thirds of a powerful argument.

Taking the second two factors first, enforcement of the anti-fornication law had indeed grown conspicuously nonexistent and violations of it had indeed become commonplace. The Duke admits as much: He acknowledges that the "rod" of these laws has become "more mocked than feared" and that his decrees are now "dead to infliction." In contemporary parlance, we lawyers would call these uncontested facts.

That leaves us with the first factor—whether fornication is *malum in se* or just *malum in prohibitum.* Now, notice that—in its own way—this first factor also has to do with ideas of fairness. Consider: If a law addresses conduct that is *malum in se*, then every reasonable person understands that they may be prosecuted for doing it. No one expects to get a pass simply because no recent occasion for enforcement had arisen. The *Printz* court offered up this memorable example: "[I]f no one had been prosecuted under an obscure statute prohibiting ax murders since Lizzie Borden was acquitted, we would still allow prosecutions under that statute today." Agreed: If you're killing someone with an ax, you should know you shouldn't be doing it.

Printz also gives us a useful example of conduct that is *malum in prohibitum.* Unlike your average garden-variety ax murder, it wasn't at all obvious that the conduct engaged in by Printz was intrinsically wrong. Why shouldn't we allow a repentant wrongdoer to repay the victim rather than suffer prosecution? Doesn't doing so achieve justice much more cooperatively and efficiently than a long drawn-out trial? Would someone in Printz's position have any reason to think he might be prosecuted for showing an offender a little grace and giving them the chance to set things right? To the contrary, doesn't Portia suggest in *The Merchant of Venice* that we have a moral obligation to let mercy "droppeth as the gentle rain from heaven"—especially if someone is willing to repay their debt?

The first factor in the desuetude analysis therefore leaves us with a fascinating question as to the anti-fornication law at issue in *Measure for Measure*: Is fornication more like (a) the obviously wrong ax murder or (b) the not-obviously-wrong gesture of allowing someone to pay restitution and avoid prosecution? And that legal question leads us, in turn, to questions of personal morality and political philosophy: What kind of sexual behavior is morally acceptable? What power, if any, should the state have to enforce those sexual norms?

As I said, this is a play about big questions.

Measure for Measure takes its title from the seventh chapter of the Gospel of Matthew: "Judge not, that ye be not judged. For with what judgment ye judge, ye shall be judged; and with what measure ye mete, it shall be measured to you again." Still, the line comes from the Duke, who is not the world's crispest thinker, and who seems here to conflate the New Testament message of non-judgment (as found in the gospels) with the Old Testament message of proportional judgment (as found in the books of Exodus and Leviticus: an eye for an eye).

In any event, in the biblically saturated world of this play fornication would seem easily to qualify as *malum in se*. Numerous Old and New Testament passages expressly and unqualifiedly condemn fornication. Leviticus 20:1 says those who commit fornication must die; and various letters attributed to Paul, such as Romans 1:29, include fornication in their inventories of sinful and forbidden conduct.

Isabella, who we first meet as she prepares to enter a convent and who has the truest moral compass of any character in the play, certainly sees fornication as *malum in se*. She entertains no doubt whatsoever about the wrongfulness of her brother Claudio's conduct. "There is a vice that most I do abhor," she says in her initial meeting with Angelo, "and most desire should meet the blow of justice." Even Claudio admits he did something wrong; when he encounters his friend Lucio he laments that he has exercised "too much liberty" and succumbed to "a thirsty evil."

But, Will says, not so fast. If fornication is so obviously wrong, then why did the Duke let it go unchecked for so many years? Doesn't the fact that he allowed enforcement to "slip" suggest that we have ambivalent feelings about this conduct? Can we imagine the Duke indulging a similar lapse with respect to the law against murder? "Well, for nineteen years now we've allowed people to kill whoever they wanted, and it didn't work out so we really need to do something about that now."

Furthermore, although Isabella plainly sees fornication as *malum in se*, she doesn't abhor the vice so much that she thinks it a capital offense. Having been told of the charges against Claudio, Isabella proposes a seemingly sensible remedy: "O, let him marry her!" The suggestion has a lot in common with lawyer Printz's view that Mr. Kesecker should have an opportunity to make amends by paying back the money he stole.

Angelo certainly views fornication as *malum in se*, but that sends its own kind of mixed signal. After all, Angelo stands strictly against fornication right up to the point where he feels tempted to force Isabella do it. At that juncture, his perspective changes. His attraction to Isabella transforms fornication from *malum in se* to *malum con exceptionibus*—an evil, but subject to exceptions.

An element of biography comes irresistibly into play here. As I've noted earlier, connecting the dots of Shakespeare's life to Shakespeare's work makes for a risky undertaking. But it can hardly be a coincidence that Will—who himself married a woman who, like Juliet, would have been visibly pregnant—assigns the most stridently judgmental position to the most odiously hypocritical figure we find in any of his works.

Is fornication *malum in se*? Perhaps.

But you're going to need a more persuasive witness than the detestable Angelo to make it so.

❖ ❖ ❖ ❖ ❖

As we've seen, the doctrine of desuetude largely focuses on the fairness and notice problems that long-dormant laws present. It helps to understand the concern if we imagine Angelo proceeding differently. Assume that, on the Duke's departure, Angelo had announced that—going forward—any *future* conduct in violation of the anti-fornication law would be prosecuted and punished. We might still question the wisdom of the law. But at least everyone would understand the risks entailed in engaging in the prohibited behavior.

Commentators and courts have pointed out, however, that the enforcement of long-neglected laws raises concerns beyond fairness and notice. For example, they argue that such enforcement is prone to be arbitrary and capricious. We get some sense of this in Angelo's selection of Claudio as a target. After all, it's not like Claudio was some priapic rake bagging as many sexual partners as he could score and spreading diseases around Vienna in the process. He had sexual intercourse with a woman whom he loved and who he intended to marry—if Angelo would only get out of the way and let him do it. He seems like the last guy you'd prosecute, not the first.

A sudden reinvigoration of a long-neglected law also creates the opposite risk—that the prosecution isn't arbitrary, but is instead selective and malicious. It doesn't appear that Angelo initially charged Claudio out of personal hostility. But, once Angelo got Isabella in his sights, things changed and an instrumental spitefulness set in. When Isabella resists Angelo's advances, he makes clear that he will not just kill Claudio—he will torture him in the process: "Or else he must not only die the death, / But thy unkindness shall his death draw out / To ling'ring sufferance." It's the kind of threat you can make with a long-dormant law, when no one knows what ordinary enforcement looks like.

Finally, the revival of an unenforced law creates risks of inequitable enforcement. The play suggests that some of this has taken place on Angelo's watch as well. The clownish pimp Pompey tells the brothel owner Mistress Overdone that they have closed all of the houses of ill repute in the suburbs, but that those in the city continue to do business because of the intervention of an influential burgher. Pompey doesn't provide details—such as whether money changed hands or whether Angelo was personally involved. But it's hard to imagine that so punctilious an overseer as Angelo would miss the fact that multiple brothels were continuing to operate despite his scorched-earth crusade against them.

Let's assume, for the sake of argument, that fornication qualifies as *malum in se* and that everyone in Vienna understood that the pause in prosecution could end at any moment and the law could be enforced against them. And let's put aside any concerns we have about arbitrariness, malice, or inequity in the enforcement of the anti-fornication law. We might still wonder whether this law qualifies as "law" in light of the extraordinary severity of its penalty.

The Eighth Amendment of the United States Constitution, which prohibits "cruel and unusual" punishments, embodies as much a moral principle as a legal one, and the penalty here would certainly seem to fit its terms. Let us stipulate that beheading is cruel—especially if seasoned with a dash of pre-execution torture, as Angelo proposes. And let us agree that execution for fornication has always been a rarity, regardless of the stern and absolute command of Leviticus.

Indeed, it turns out that even Leviticus didn't strictly follow Leviticus. Biblical scholars have observed that the complex procedural rules put in place by the Talmud made it extraordinarily difficult to execute anyone for an infraction of Levitical law. As a result, the command wasn't taken literally and the law was more severe in theory than in application. In contrast, the wooden literalism embraced by Angelo made executions for fornication in Vienna easy and straightforward propositions.

In earlier chapters, we saw that Shakespeare was intrigued by the idea that when a law is too literally and too severely enforced it may lose its authority and its standing as law. Indeed, he seems to go further. He appears to have believed that law so enforced may actually violate some higher concept of law—natural law, if you like—that defines a society as a fair and just one. He pokes at all these themes in both *Henry VI, Part 2* and *The Merchant of Venice*. But it is in *Measure for Measure* that Will really rolls up his sleeves and gets his arms around them.

In *Measure for Measure*, no one seems to doubt that the law Angelo is enforcing is, in fact, the law. No one, that is, except William Shakespeare. In the play, Will shows us all of the reasons why long-dormant laws and excessively punitive laws should not be viewed as law at all—reasons that align with our concepts of desuetude, due process, and cruel and unusual punishment.

I imagine sitting down with Will at the Tabard Inn and asking him that big question of which Brian Simpson was so fond: "What is law, anyway?"

Will smiles faintly. "Watch me do a magical trick," he says.

"I will show you something that for all the world looks like law."

He leans in and adds:

"But it isn't."

Shameful

The great trial lawyer Edward Bennett Williams represented a wide array of notorious figures in the course of his long and storied career—mob bosses, corrupt politicians, suspected spies, corporate raiders, the list goes on and on. From time to time, some indignant nonlawyer would corner him at a cocktail party and ask how he could in good conscience defend such people. Williams had a stock reply: "In the law there is a presumption of innocence. It is a legal concept, not a moral one. I defend my clients from legal guilt. Moral judgments I leave to the majestic vengeance of God."

Many of Will's plays convey the sense that he similarly wanted us to leave moral judgments to a higher and better-informed power. The villains he gives us often have redeeming characteristics, just as his heroes often suffer from deep and destructive imperfections. Even the well-intentioned Brutus went astray in his thinking; and even the malignant Aaron had the virtue of loving his son.

When we get to Angelo in *Measure for Measure*, however, we may struggle to find qualities that make him even remotely sympathetic. Granted, he does show some initial hesitancy about accepting the assignment the Duke gives him—but he gets past that pretty quickly. And maybe Mariana, to whom he was once engaged, sees things in him that we don't—but it's difficult to imagine what they are. Indeed, when, at the end of the play, the Duke commands Angelo to wed Mariana we can't feel anything like excitement for her. Putting aside his mistreatment of Isabella, it's hard to forget (although she appears willing to forget it) that Angelo terminated his prior marriage arrangement with Mariana because her dowry fell through—and then he justified his decision by publicly slandering her virtue.

Angelo shows the most dreadful dimensions of his character in his interactions with Isabella and we'll get to those in a moment. But, before we do, it's important to think a bit about Isabella apart from his baleful influence. We need to resist the gravitational pull of making this into a story about Angelo and reducing Isabella to the object of his abuses. After all, that's exactly what Angelo does. We must start with Isabella on her own.

We may find that easier said than done, however, because Isabella presents as something of a mystery and, well, we have questions. For example, why is she joining the famously ascetic Order of St. Clare? Is it out of deep religious conviction? If so, then why would she abandon that commitment to marry someone? And, more particularly, why would she abandon it to marry the Duke, whose closest connection to matters of faith appears to be his almost vaudevillian impersonation of a friar?

Some critics have suggested that Isabella joins the order primarily to escape the male-dominated society in which she lives and to claim some agency over her life. But why would a woman who valued such things then change her plans to marry someone like the Duke? Nothing in his behavior reflects any great respect for the autonomy of women—to the contrary, he moves them around like chess pieces to reward or punish men as he sees fit. And in the concluding scene he treats Isabella herself horribly, initially leading her to believe that he doesn't credit her accusations against Angelo and allowing her to think her brother had been executed. His marriage proposals come hard on the heels of these abuses. Why on earth would she consent?

Then there's the question of whether she in fact does consent. The final scene gives her two opportunities to accept—clearly and unambiguously—the Duke's offer of marriage. But the play is loudly silent about how she responds. Different productions have filled the void with everything from the enthusiastic offering of her hand to the dismissive ridicule of her laughter. Some have kept the void a void, leaving everyone on stage staring at each other.

For our purposes, what matters is that we understand Isabella to be a person of great strength, character, and purpose, who has—for whatever reason—decided to dedicate her life to her faith. It's a decision that Angelo takes it upon himself to destroy, which in itself makes him a villain of the first order. Everyone in Shakespeare's audience would likely have known the passage in the eighteenth chapter of the Gospel of Matthew where Jesus says: "Whoever causes one of these little ones who believes in me to sin, it would be better for him if a millstone were hung around his neck, and he were drowned in the depth of the sea."

That's precisely Angelo's game plan: not just to engage in fornication, which would be outrage enough given the hypocrisy, but to force someone else into fornication in violation of their faith. It's a horrific breach of an injunction that comes from the lips of Christ himself.

That's how bad Angelo is.

Well, not quite.

He's actually worse.

When I say that Angelo is worse, what I mean is that Shakespeare quietly—but in my view unmistakably—shows us in the course of the play that Angelo's abuse of Isabella isn't the isolated lapse of an otherwise noble soul. It instead arises from something that is missing within Angelo: a critical component of character. Angelo's abuse of Isabella is the outward and visible sign of an inward and invisible darkness—a darkness so deep that it makes any crime possible.

To see how Will conveys this idea to us, we need to follow a narrative thread that runs throughout the play and that becomes particularly pronounced in the final act. I refer here to the sequence of opportunities that Angelo receives to acknowledge his own weakness and his failings and to take a different path. Time after time these off-ramps become available to him; time after time he turns a blind eye to them and races past.

The first of these opportunities comes at the very beginning of Act II, before Angelo has even met Isabella. In that scene, Escalus (the Duke's wise old advisor) comes to Angelo and tries to persuade him to show mercy to Claudio. In essence, he invites Angelo to consider whether even he—"one most strait in virtue"—might not have made the same mistake as Claudio did if he'd had the chance. To say the least, the argument doesn't play well. Angelo huffily proclaims that there's a difference between being tempted and acting on the temptation. He then summarily declares: "Sir, he must die."

The scene brings to mind the New Testament story about the men who take to Jesus a woman who they claim to have caught in an act of adultery, an offence ostensibly punishable by death. Jesus calmly writes in the dirt with his finger and then says: "Let he who is without sin among you cast the first stone." Reflecting on their own imperfections, the men depart.

I have the sense that Angelo would have responded differently. I can imagine him sticking around, grabbing a bunch of rocks, and enthusiastically getting the stoning underway. That this seems perfectly plausible says a lot about Angelo. Hold on to that idea—I'll return to it later.

The point here is that Escalus gave Angelo an opportunity to think differently about the wisdom of charging Claudio in the first instance, and Angelo took a hard pass. At this juncture, so early in the play, we might chalk that mistake up to pride or arrogance on Angelo's part, and he may well have some of both. But, as I'll try to show, I think something else is going on here.

The next opportunity for Angelo to rethink things comes in the second scene of the second act. The counsel he receives echoes that which was given by Escalus, but this time it comes from Isabella. Like Escalus, she pleads for Angelo to look into his own heart. "How would you be," she asks, "if He which is the top of judgment should but judge you as you are?" Angelo shrugs off the question and sticks to his guns: "He must die tomorrow."

Isabella continues to press the argument. "Go to your bosom," she says, "knock there, and ask your heart what it doth know that's like my brother's fault." She makes progress; in an aside, Angelo acknowledges that he's starting to buckle. But his choice of language signals that he's being moved by something other than the force of her logic and decency: "She speaks, and 'tis such sense, that my sense *breeds* with it." After she leaves, he confesses his lust for her—confirming that Escalus and Isabella had things exactly right.

In the last scene of the second act, Angelo proposes his terrible bargain: he will have mercy on Claudio if Isabella will sleep with him. Appalled at the idea, Isabella threatens to "tell the world aloud" with "outstretched throat." The vigor of her rejection might have slapped Angelo into a different consciousness, but it doesn't. Instead, Angelo makes clear that he knows how the world works: "Who will believe thee, Isabel?" And she admits that she knows, too: "To whom should I complain? Did I tell this, / Who would believe me?"

In the final scene of the play, Angelo receives in quick succession a series of opportunities to make a different choice and to confess his wrongdoing. They have something in common: At each of these moments, it must seem to us that anyone with any sense of decency would at long last own up to their error. But Angelo does no such thing.

The first of these opportunities arrives when Isabella—despite her understanding of how the world works—musters her courage, comes before the Duke, and discloses what Angelo has done. Angelo knows she's right—indeed, at this point he believes that she has slept with him to fulfill the bargain. But he does nothing to intervene when the Duke responds to her with astonished hostility, rebukes her, and orders her to prison. As the guards lead her offstage, Angelo passively stands and watches, allowing the injustice to take its course.

At this point, Mariana steps forward and reveals that Angelo actually slept with her when he thought he was sleeping with Isabella. The trap now fully revealed, we might expect Angelo to come clean and admit his crime. But, enraged rather than chastened, Angelo instead goes on the offense and begs the Duke's permission to examine the two women who have offered testimony against him. The Duke grants the request, along with an allowance to "punish them to [his] height of pleasure." When Escalus disappointingly injects himself into the proceedings and waxes over his eagerness to browbeat Isabella—"You shall see how I'll handle her . . . I will go darkly to work with her"—Angelo says nothing to dissuade him.

That planned interrogation stalls, however, when the Duke appears in the costume of the friar. He casts off the disguise and reveals everything, including his knowledge of Angelo's treachery. Finally cornered with no escape, Angelo admits his guilt: "O my dread lord, / I should be guiltier than my guiltiness / To think I can be undiscernible, / When I perceive your Grace, like power divine / Hath looked upon my [tres]passes. Then, good prince, / No longer session hold upon my shame, / But let my trial be mine own confession. Immediate sentence then and sequent death / Is all the grace I beg."

In this passage, we hear a word that we don't tend to associate with Angelo. It pertains to the trait that seems to me wholly absent from Angelo's character.

The word is: "shame."

In a number of his plays, Will builds dramatic tension—and conveys a moral lesson—by giving someone multiple chances to avoid an unfolding and increasingly imminent disaster. Think of how many opportunities Shylock has to retreat from his demand for a pound of flesh. Or how many opportunities Othello has to give Desdemona the benefit of a doubt. Or how many opportunities Richard II has to act justly and like a true king. But some flaw in their character prevents them from thinking differently and compels them to stay their ill-advised course. As I mentioned in the chapter on *Othello*, if you practice law long enough you'll have at least one client who fits this description.

In my view, Angelo is a special case: He doesn't seize on any of the chances at redemption that come his way because he lacks the capacity to feel shame. Granted, other shortcomings probably contributed to his troubles. As I noted earlier, his arrogance and pride made him blind to his own weaknesses. But, whatever imperfections helped get him into these difficulties, it was his inability to experience shame that kept him there.

Think back to my discussion of the biblical story of the woman taken in adultery. Her accusers leave because Jesus makes them face their hypocrisy. The exercise shames them away from judgment and into retreat. This is why we can imagine Angelo looking around for the first stone to throw—because, throughout the play, he shows himself to lack a quality that the men who took the woman in adultery possessed: a capacity for shame.

That's more than a little ironic.

After all, as zealots who were prepared to kill someone in cold blood for an act of infidelity, those men were Angelo's religious forebears.

In recent years, shame—like revenge—has gotten a bad rap. A variety of factors have probably contributed to this development. We have become increasingly sensitive to the value of individual human dignity, which shaming undermines. And, once guilt has been established and a penalty imposed, exacting shame from the wrongdoer may feel like piling on.

Within a legal system, shaming conjures up images of Puritan magistrates forcing Hester Prynne to wear a scarlet "A" on her gown to confess her adultery. Some contemporary courts apparently think the Puritans were on to something. In recent years, judges in several states have ordered convicted drunk drivers to display bumper stickers on their cars reading "convicted DUI," and at least one judge has ordered a man convicted of larceny to wear a T-shirt stating that he's on probation for theft.

Legal scholars and philosophers have vigorously debated whether shame—and its consequent stigmatization, degradation, and embarrassment—has any proper place within a just and appropriately restrained legal system. In her book *Hiding from Humanity: Disgust, Shame, and the Law*, Martha Nussbaum argues that it generally does not. But even Nussbaum acknowledges that in some instances shame has its constructive uses.

Nussbaum primarily sees value in shame when it is the result of critical self-examination. She offers this example: Americans who seriously consider the problem of working class poverty may feel shame at our collective failure to acknowledge and work toward solving the problem. Such shame is an appropriate response to the thoughtful recognition of our failures and may help promote reform.

We might see shame as a sort of returning to oneself. To stay with the biblical themes for a moment, we see such an event in the gospel story of the Prodigal Son. The young man, who sought his inheritance early from his father and who has squandered his resources, returns home only after he arrives at the lowest point in his life, looks around, and comes back to who he once was.

Isabella has it right when she tells Angelo to knock first at his own heart.

For that strategy to work, however, someone has to be at home.

Shame has an important role in the world of *Measure for Measure* and in the lives of its characters. Claudio and Juliet may have committed no great offense by having sex in the context of a committed relationship. But Angelo wants to shame Claudio, making an example of him and having him led through town on a perp walk. And both Claudio and Juliet talk about the shame they bear as a result of their mistake.

Angelo, however, seems utterly incapable of the sort of critical self-examination that would lead to a productive sense of shame and move him onto a different and better course. It's not even clear that he experiences shame when his evil and duplicity are fully revealed in the final scene. Granted, he acknowledges that he must die for his wrongdoing, but there's no great honor in admitting you've committed a capital offence after your guilt has been proved beyond any reasonable doubt.

The patriarchal social structure in Vienna favors Angelo. So does the legal system, set up to allow Escalus to destroy Isabella on Angelo's behalf. In the end, things go right—to the extent they do—solely because of an intricate and utterly implausible scheme concocted by a Duke who doesn't know what he's doing. It's a thin reed for justice to stand upon.

In such a context, the most dangerous man in the world is the one with no shame.

For he will say nothing against himself.

And he will sit back and allow the machinery of the law to do his work for him.

9

"Horrible Imaginings"

Macbeth

Backdrop

Macbeth has everything: compelling characters, a storyline that moves at a brisk pace, witches and apparitions, political intrigue, multiple plot twists, murders and more murders, a sword fight that culminates in a stunning revelation, and some of Will's most memorable, quotable, and magnificent poetry. It even has its own legend: Theater tradition holds that speaking the play's name conjures up bad juju; we should call it The Scottish Play and hope for the best.

The one thing no one has ever called *Macbeth* is a "feel-good play." And, yet, *Macbeth* tells a story about the relentless and ultimately irresistible forces of moral order and justice. Macbeth's interactions with the witches—or the Weird Sisters, if you prefer—leave him convinced that he is destined for greatness and that no man can kill him. But the universe has other plans. It figures out ways to destroy Macbeth, even if to do so it has to put a forest on the march and put a weapon in the hand of someone who was born by cesarean section. To borrow a well-known image from Dr. King, the arc of *Macbeth*'s moral universe is long but it bends toward justice.

Will wrote *Macbeth* around 1606, just a few years after James VI of Scotland succeeded Elizabeth, ascended the throne, and became James I of England. In 1603, James had granted a charter to Shakespeare's company, the King's Men, and *Macbeth* was among the plays that the troop performed before him. In writing the play, Will once again drew heavily on Raphael Holinshed's *Chronicles* for source material, just as he did in writing his histories.

Will had a number of reasons to think the king would like the play. James had a deep and abiding interest in the occult. He believed witches had sent storms to frustrate his efforts to retrieve his bride from Denmark. He became personally involved in the infamous North Berwick witch trials, which lasted for years and resulted in large numbers of executions. He wrote a short book on demonology. And, apart from all its witchy stuff, *Macbeth* portrays Banquo, from whom James was descended, as a noble figure destined to initiate a line of monarchs.

As a number of Shakespeare scholars have observed, however, the most important aspect of *Macbeth* for James may have been its thematic connection to the Gunpowder Plot of November 5, 1605. In brief, the Gunpowder Plot was a conspiracy between a collection of Catholic activists to blow up Parliament along with King James, his queen, and their eldest son. The conspirators apparently hoped that the chaos resulting from the event would occasion the return of Catholic rule to England. The plot was foiled when a loyalist to the king received a tip and authorities commenced a search of the cellars underneath the Houses of Parliament.

There they found Guy Fawkes, one of the conspirators, in the company of a box of matches and 36 barrels of gunpowder. It's hard to come up with a benign explanation for keeping company with 36 barrels of gunpowder in the cellars underneath a government building, so Fawkes was arrested and interrogated until he confessed the plan and identified the other conspirators. The British still celebrate these events on Guy Fawkes Day with bonfires, fireworks, effigies of Fawkes, and nursery rhymes—"Remember, remember the fifth of November, gunpowder, treason, and plot."

British nurseries are evidently grim and politically charged places.

The Gunpowder Plot had come perilously close to succeeding. In a pedestrian sense, its failure was attributable to simple mistakes: a leak of information to the wrong person, and a decision by the conspirators to persist in their scheme even after they suspected it had been discovered. And so it goes; the annals of criminal law include far more bunglers than masterminds. As a criminal defense lawyer friend of mine likes to say, "Professor Moriarty exists only in fiction."

But the dramatic failure of the plot was a signal moment in English history and suggested a cause greater than fortunate accident. It gets people's attention when the line between stable society and violent anarchy consists in a single match. And the foiling of the conspiracy seemed to testify to the influence of those same forces of moral order and justice that we find at work in *Macbeth*. The story of the Gunpowder Plot is a feel-good story in the same odd way that *Macbeth* is.

Regardless of how James I greeted the play, critics and audiences have admired it for centuries. Harold Bloom identifies it as one of his two favorite Shakespeare plays and I'm on board: It's the play to which I return most often and it always seems to bring me something new.

It remains immensely popular and is frequently staged. Multiple film versions have been made of the play, some quite good, and its supernatural elements, creepy aesthetic, and graphic violence make it particularly adaptable to the screen. Plus, its legend tantalizes: For the superstitious, every stage production brings with it the added excitement of potential misfortunes large or small.

All of this makes *Macbeth* powerful and engaging theater, but none of it makes the play an obvious candidate for consideration through the lens of law. In my view, however, *Macbeth* explores two issues that continue to be critically relevant to legal institutions and legal theory. As with *Julius Caesar*, we experience some of this play's key themes as our own.

The first issue concerns the sturdiness of the political structures that make law and social order possible. Because those structures shape so much of our existence and experience, and because they grow familiar and define business as usual, we may come to think of them as stable and durable—perhaps even as inevitable. But *Macbeth* shows us how frail and assailable they really are and how quickly things can change.

The play reveals a basic truth about human society—that we should never assume that any political or legal system comes with assurances of permanence. To the contrary, all such systems are desperately more fragile than we tend to believe. And, as I'll discuss, the play conveys these ideas as much through its structure as through its substance.

The second issue concerns the nature of conscience. The idea of conscience has historically had an important place in United States law, especially constitutional law. The Supreme Court has described freedom of conscience as the only absolute right, and the First Amendment exists largely to protect expressions of conscience—like speech, religion, and assembly—from government interference. We think of conscience as essential to our liberty and to our understanding of our responsibilities as human beings and citizens.

But conscience turns out to be more complicated than we might at first think. Do we know what it is and where it comes from? Do we understand how it works—or why sometimes it doesn't? Our friend Will has lots of questions about conscience, and he uses *Macbeth* to pose and explore them.

Let's draw a chair up to his table and start the conversation. Will has things to tell us. They may help explain why we love *Macbeth*—and why it haunts us, and leaves us deliciously uneasy.

Bleed, Bleed Poor Country

Many of Shakespeare's plays work toward the resolution of a rebellion. In *Henry VI, Part 2* the rebellion lead by Jack Cade finally fails. In *Richard II*, the rebellion of Bolingbroke ultimately succeeds. In *Julius Caesar*, the rebellion driven by Brutus and Cassius meets an inglorious end—as do Brutus and Cassius themselves. *Macbeth*, too, tells the story of a usurper of royal power and follows his treachery to its ineluctable conclusion.

Interestingly, however, *Macbeth* also *begins* with a rebellion and its resolution. Early in the first act, we learn that the Thane of Cawdor tried to unseat Duncan but "brave Macbeth" laid his forces to waste. The King of Norway raised troops in support of Cawdor's rebellion, but Macbeth put them down as well. We must imagine Scotland strewn with the corpses of its enemies and its people much relieved.

Modern audiences know the play well. So, we understand that the body count has only started, that Duncan's rule remains under a grave and imminent threat, and that Macbeth will in short order initiate one of history's most famous criminal conspiracies. But that familiarity makes it easy for us to miss something important about Will's decision to start the play here. Pause for a moment to notice that, at this point in the story, the people of Scotland would not have grasped or expected any of these things. Quite the contrary.

Think of these circumstances through their eyes: Not one but two serious threats to the kingdom have materialized and have been decisively extinguished. The danger averted, Duncan's rule must have appeared safe and secure, at least for the foreseeable future. And, ironically, knowing that the fearsome Macbeth stood ready to defend Scotland would have contributed to this sensibility.

In other words, Will begins the play with Scotland in a place of apparent safety, security, and stability—the same place England may have seemed before the discovery of the Gunpowder Plot. And that's exactly where Will needs to begin his story if he wants to show us how quickly all of those seemingly sturdy things can vaporize.

And so they do.

In quick succession, the witches forecast Macbeth's rise, Duncan alienates Macbeth by naming Malcolm as Prince of Cumberland and successor to the throne, and Macbeth confesses to us his "black and deep desires." The play begins with Duncan's rule settled and stable. Within four scenes, that same rule has grown fraught and fragile.

The breakneck pace continues. By the sixth scene, Duncan has arrived at Inverness. By the seventh scene, the Macbeths have put firmly in place their plot to murder the king. By the second scene of the second act, Duncan is dead. By the end of the second act, Macbeth is king. *Macbeth* may be Shakespeare's shortest tragedy, but some productions nevertheless struggle to sustain this level of energy and eventfulness through all five acts. It's not unusual for a director to pluck out some optional middle bits to help sustain the play's momentum.

In my view, the speed at which things change in the first two acts is precisely the point. The structure conveys the message. Many of Will's plays, especially the histories, show us a gradual dismantling of power. In *Macbeth*, Will shows us something else altogether: that social and legal order can vanish in a heartbeat—literally. And the play invites us to think about how and why that can happen.

❁ ❁ ❁ ❁ ❁

As a useful starting point, we might identify some of the factors that tend to keep such sudden ruptures from occurring. One of these, of course, is the deterrent influence of the law and its corresponding threat of punishment. In short, we count on law to preserve the order that makes law possible.

Macbeth certainly understands the legal prohibitions in place and the risks presented by violating them. He could hardly miss the possible consequences of his actions: The former Thane of Cawdor has just been executed for attempting precisely what he, the new Thane of Cawdor, now conspires to achieve. Macbeth even exhibits some anxiety about it. "If we should fail—" he says to Lady Macbeth, who does not let him finish the sentence because they both know exactly what failure would mean under the law.

Strong social norms also help to preserve order, and the circumstances presented by the play implicate several of those: Duncan is Macbeth's king; he is also Macbeth's kin; and he is a guest in Macbeth's home. This combination of factors puts Duncan in Macbeth's care in the strongest possible sense. Indeed, the opportunity to commit the murder arises precisely because Duncan thinks himself safe and has no reason to suspect danger. Again, Macbeth understands: "He's here in double trust: First, as I am his kinsman and his subject, / Strong both against the deed; then, as his host, / Who should against his murderer shut the door, / Not bear the knife myself."

Lady Macbeth overcomes these objections with relatively modest effort. In the last chapter, we explored the uses and abuses of shaming—and here Lady Macbeth mobilizes a ruthless shaming strategy to her advantage. She plays on Macbeth's masculine ego, suggesting that a failure to go through with the murder of Duncan would imply a kind of impotence. When he expresses misgivings over the plan, she pushes him back toward his most sinister impulses: "When you durst do it, *then* you were a man," she snarls.

Earlier, when Macbeth was still turning things over in his thoughts, he mused: "If it were done when 'tis done, then 'twere well it were done quickly." And, indeed, pace matters here. Duncan is so quickly murdered precisely because the Macbeths so quickly manage to move themselves beyond law and social norms—two of the restraints that would ordinarily prevent, or at least delay, the extraordinary project they undertake. 'Tis done quickly because 'tis quickly resolved—although, as we will discuss, not without second thoughts.

We might think that social and legal order would soon return after the cataclysmic change in rule takes place and things settle down, but the play disabuses us of any such optimistic notions. Once he has power, Macbeth can keep it only through perpetual offenses against such laws and norms. He must murder his friend and confidant, Banquo. He must murder Banquo's son, Fleance (or at least try to do so). He must murder Macduff's wife and children.

Murder becomes eerily normalized. In the film version of the play starring Patrick Stewart, Macbeth casually makes sandwiches for two mercenary killers as he explains their grisly job assignment. In such a world, the strange becomes commonplace: as the play proceeds, Macbeth checks in with the Weird Sisters as if he were a business executive monitoring the progress of a strategic plan.

The play shows us something else as well. We sometimes think of dramatic political change as entailing a wholesale restructuring of the order, the sort of thorough and emphatic transformation reflected in the American, French, Russian, or Chinese revolutions. But *Macbeth* involves no political structural change at all: monarchy one day, monarchy the next, a simple shift from one king to another. The upheaval entailed only a change in personnel. But, of course, that sufficed to change everything.

In this sense, *Macbeth* offers a powerful cautionary tale for our own time, in which we have seen governments suddenly but fundamentally change. Those changes have sometimes come in ways that have tested the limits of law and social norms—or simply ridden roughshod over them. But they have taken place largely though changes in personnel, rather than through formal changes in political architecture. An authoritarian republic remains a republic, at least technically, even if it no longer does so in spirit or in lived experience.

Macbeth warns us that we shouldn't shrug off such change as a phase that will swiftly and quietly pass. Those who choose to step outside of the law and our strong shared social norms may find themselves very much at home there. Having won the spot so dearly, they may cling to it stubbornly.

We may wake up to discover that we have fallen under the thumb of their rule tomorrow, and tomorrow, and tomorrow.

'Till Birnam Wood Do come to Dunsinane.

Murdered Sleep

Law has a close but complicated relationship with conscience.

On one hand, we think of conscience as aligning with the law and even helping the law accomplish its goals. Like the law, conscience serves as yet another bulwark against anarchy and disorder. We don't engage in certain conduct—the murdering of kings, for example—not just because the law says we shouldn't do it but because doing it would offend our innate sense of right and wrong.

On the other hand, an individual's exercise of conscience may conflict with the law. Sometimes, when this happens, the law declares conscience the winner. So, for example, in the 1943 case of *West Virginia State Board of Education v. Barnette*, the Supreme Court struck down under the First Amendment a state statute that required public school students to recite the pledge of allegiance at the beginning of each school day—despite their religiously grounded objections to doing so.

Of course, conscience does not always prevail over law in our system. The civil rights protestors who marched in Birmingham, Alabama, in 1963 did so as an act of conscience. But, in the 1967 case of *Walker v. City of Birmingham*, the Supreme Court of the United States nevertheless upheld a judge's decision holding those protestors in contempt for violating a court order that prohibited the march. Their incarceration bore its own kind of fruit; it provided the occasion for Dr. King's famous *Letter from Birmingham Jail.*

Nevertheless, for the past half-century or so our law has generally been highly deferential to the individual human conscience. True, it has allowed constraints over some of its exercises. But, for the most part, it has treated conscience itself as off limits to legal interference.

The law has a lot to say about conscience.

And so does *Macbeth*.

Will uses *Macbeth* to explore just a few of the many mysteries that exist around conscience. The play reflects a particular interest in the connections between conscience, choice, and responsibility, in the myriad ways that conscience manifests to us, in why we depart from conscience, and in what happens when we do. Those questions have a central place in the plotline. Indeed, *Macbeth* wouldn't be *Macbeth* if we extracted from it all questions and concerns about conscience.

Let's start with Macbeth himself. Toward the beginning of the play, Macbeth has two competing ideas fighting for space in his head. They are conflicting ideas about who—or what—controls the course of human events.

The first idea makes free will the prime mover in such matters. In this understanding, what happens next depends on the decisions that Macbeth makes. The question he faces is whether in making those decisions he will honor the constraints of conscience.

Those constraints are formidable. As noted earlier, Macbeth recognizes that he has responsibilities to Duncan not just as his king, but also as his kin and as a guest in his home. Allowing any harm to come to Duncan—let alone serving as the instrument of such harm—would gravely offend the moral order. Macbeth faces a fearsome choice: conscience or ambition.

The second idea floating around in his head makes fate—or as Macbeth calls it, "chance"—the prime mover. In this understanding, what happens next depends not on Macbeth but on destiny. The Weird Sisters have divined his fate, and it is fixed and immutable.

If that's right, then Macbeth doesn't have to worry about choice and conscience; he can just sit back and let fate work everything out. "If chance will have me king," Macbeth says after learning he has become both Glamis and Thane of Cawdor, "why, chance may crown me without my stir." It's a simple formula: No free choice, no exercise of conscience; no exercise of conscience, no moral dilemma; problem solved.

But Will likes problems much more than solutions, so he gives us a twist: Unfortunately for Macbeth, fate doesn't cooperate. Instead of further elevating Macbeth, Duncan appoints his eldest son Malcolm as Prince of Cumberland and successor to the throne. At this point, Macbeth reveals his true colors: Leaving it all to fate sounded pretty good until fate took an unwelcome detour, but now he needs a different plan.

In an aside immediately following the appointment of the prince, Macbeth shifts his thinking. No longer satisfied with passively sitting by and letting fate figure things out, he gives himself the lead role in fulfilling his destiny: "The Prince of Cumberland! That is a step / On which I must fall down or else o'erleap, / For in my way it lies."

Macbeth's language betrays him. His words make clear that he chooses his fate every bit as much as his fate chooses him. *He* decides to "o'erleap" the obstacle presented by the appointment of the prince; and that appointment stands in *his* way—not in the way of destiny. Fate is a stalking horse. Behind it lurks Macbeth and his agendas, his choices, and his conscience—or lack thereof.

Macbeth doesn't even fool himself. All of his talk about fate notwithstanding, his conscience continues to dog him. The perceptive Lady Macbeth spots the problem and worries. She frets aloud that he has a nature "too full o' th' milk of human kindness" to fulfill his destiny in "the nearest way."

By "the nearest way" she means murdering Duncan, and there's the rub. The nearest way to achieving his ambition runs head-on into the very problem of conscience with which he's struggling. And she obviously can't suggest that he solve this moral obstacle through the simple expedient of slashing his way straight through it.

So what does she do? She carefully avoids any explicit talk of murder and she pledges to help him secure "that golden round" that "fate and metaphysical aid" have promised to him. In other words, she pulls the same trick that he does: She tries to avoid the problem of conscience by invoking the irresistible power of fate. The argument doesn't work any better for her than it worked for Macbeth, and it's not too hard to see why.

In one of his most famous essays, the French existentialist philosopher Jean-Paul Sartre tells a story about a young man who came to him for advice about a difficult moral decision he had to make. We have to sympathize with the impulse, which strikes me as charmingly opportunistic. Hey, if you have a challenging ethical quandary on your hands, why not check in with one of the great thinkers of the twentieth century and see what they have to say?

But Sartre's response may have left the young man disappointed. In essence, he said: You are free; you have to choose for yourself; so, choose. Sartre suggests that even if he had told him exactly what to do, the young man would still have to decide whether to follow the advice. Little wonder Sartre called the human condition one of "terrible freedom"; precisely because we are free, we have responsibilities that we cannot escape.

I think Will wants us to see something similar with respect to all of this talk of fate. Macbeth and Lady Macbeth invoke fate because they believe that doing so insulates them from the claims of conscience. But they fail to acknowledge—at least openly—that treating the predictions of the Weird Sisters as authoritative and dispositive is also a choice.

And the facts presented in the play make clear that it *is* a choice: After all, the Macbeths could have chosen to let events unfold without interference. But they instead embrace "fate" to the extent that it aligns with their ambitions. So, when the evidence suggests that the moral arc of the universe has bent away from them, they do everything they can to bend it back. We can accuse the Macbeths of many things, but we can't accuse them of letting "chance" run its natural course.

Will shows us that we cannot escape the demands of conscience through hollow invocations of fate.

Perhaps we cannot escape them at all.

Macbeth and Lady Macbeth have a powerful connection. It has been said, only half-jokingly, that theirs may be the only truly happy marriage depicted in any of Shakespeare's plays. But Lady Macbeth has her own relationship with conscience. And it is very different from Macbeth's.

When Lady Macbeth reads her husband's letter about his meeting with the Weird Sisters, her thoughts immediately turn to her conscience—and her need to dispense with it:

> Come, you spirits
> That tend on mortal thoughts, unsex me here
> And fill me from the crown to the toe top-full
> Of direst cruelty. Make thick my blood.
> Stop up th' access and passage to remorse,
> That not compunctious visitings of nature

> Shake my fell purpose, nor keep peace between
> Th' effect and it . . .
> Come, thick night,
> And pall thee in the dunnest smoke of hell,
> That my keen knife see not the wound it makes,
> Nor heaven peep through the blanket of the dark
> To cry "Hold, hold!" (I:5:47–61)

When Macbeth arrives and informs her of Duncan's imminent arrival, she makes her intentions clear. Macbeth dodges her: "We will speak further."

Indeed, it soon becomes plain that Macbeth harbors doubts. When next we hear from him, all of Lady Macbeth's worries have materialized. His conscience has upended his resolve.

He acknowledges his duties to Duncan. He worries that any evil he does will return to plague him. He reflects on the goodness and blamelessness of the king. He confesses that he has no reason even to consider the act except his lust for power: "I have no spur / To prick the sides of my intent, but only / Vaulting ambition, which o'erleaps itself / And falls on th' other—." Finally, he declares to Lady Macbeth: "We will proceed no further in this business."

At this point, Will has situated Macbeth and Lady Macbeth at opposing points on the continuum of conscience: Macbeth continues to grapple with his, whereas Lady Macbeth has disentangled herself from hers. The tension persists and they argue. As noted earlier, she shames him by questioning his manhood, and when he raises the risk of failure she shrugs it off: "We fail? / But screw your courage to the sticking place / And we'll not fail." Finally, he relents under the weight of her bravura: "I am settled."

It's bold of him to say so, but a plan of this nature can only leave a person of conscience unsettled, and it immediately unsettles Macbeth. Before he has even taken what the law calls "an overt act in furtherance of the conspiracy," a vision of a dagger comes before him. He puzzles over the source of the vision and asks: "Art thou not, fatal vision, sensible / To feeling as to sight? Or art thou but / A dagger of the mind, a false creation / Proceeding from the heat oppressed brain?"

Conscience continues to harass Macbeth after he has done the deed and murdered Duncan and his servants. He recounts to Lady Macbeth the screams from the men as he slay them. She presses him to overcome conscience by ignoring it, just as she does: "Consider it not so deeply . . . These deeds must not be thought / After these ways." Then she adds, presciently: "it will make us mad."

But Macbeth persists. Conscience has now also come to him as a voice: "Methought I heard a voice cry 'Sleep no more! / Macbeth does murder sleep'—the innocent sleep, / Sleep that knits up the raveled sleave of care, / The death of each day's life, sore labor's bath. / Balm of hurt minds, great nature's second course, / Chief nourisher in life's feast . . . Macbeth shall sleep no more."

The voice has affected him so deeply that he has brought the daggers with him from the slaughter. When an astonished Lady Macbeth tells him to return them, he refuses. She declares him "infirm of purpose" and does it herself. He seems traumatized, and the presence of trauma—like the presence of the visions and the voices—suggests the presence of conscience.

Indeed, it suggests something stronger: the brutal doggedness with which conscience pursues us.

More on that shortly.

If we did not know the story so well, we would expect Macbeth to be the one driven mad by conscience and Lady Macbeth to be the one who ruthlessly soldiers on. All the evidence we have toward the beginning of the play suggests things will unfold this way. But, of course, almost the exact opposite happens.

Lady Macbeth had only an incidental physical role in the murders—she returned the daggers and smeared the servants with blood, bloodying her own hands in the process. But she cannot rid herself of her guilt, or of the bloodstains she imagines on her hands. "Out, damned spot, out I say" she cries as she furiously scrubs, all to no avail, because her unwelcome conscience will not let her unsee what she has seen. "What's done cannot be undone," she says in her ranting. She fulfills her own prophecy; her conscience drives her mad unto death.

Macbeth, in contrast, proves surprisingly resilient, resolute, and remorseless. Having chosen the path of murder and mayhem that he rationalizes fate requires of him, he contents himself to remain on it. He does not compulsively wash his hands of anything, although from this point on he will mostly use the hands of others to get his dirty work done.

Still, Macbeth's unflagging persistence in treachery doesn't mean his conscience leaves him alone. To the contrary, the ghost of the murdered Banquo appears to him, although not to Lady Macbeth, who again tries to steel her husband by shaming his masculinity: "Are you a man? . . . What, quite unmanned in folly?" When he can't control his outbursts, she urges him to seek comfort in (ironically) the very place that he has murdered: sleep.

By time we get to the last few scenes, we cannot tell what (if anything) remains of Macbeth's conscience. He certainly has not lost all capacity for feeling—the news of Lady Macbeth's death draws from him one of the most powerful meditations on the brevity and meaninglessness of life in the English language: "Out, out, brief candle / Life's but a walking shadow . . . a tale told by an idiot, full of sound and fury / signifying nothing."

But we may wonder whether any of the final pangs Macbeth experiences are pangs of conscience. He sees no more floating daggers, hears no more voices, sees no more ghosts. And when at the end of the play Macduff confronts him, Macbeth retreats to the comfort of destiny: No man of woman born can kill him. Alas, the argument proves misplaced: Macduff "was from his mother's womb untimely ripped."

It turns out that fate loves a good loophole.

In everyday language, we use a vast array of metaphors and symbols to try to get at the idea of conscience. We compare it to a compass, an anchor, a straight path, an inner light, a clean heart, an open book, a still small voice, and so on and so on. Those images emphasize the ways in which conscience directs, steadies, brightens, and counsels our lives. We think of conscience as the good, white-robed angel sitting on our shoulder.

But the world of *Macbeth* is a dark and foreboding one, so here Will gives us a collection of images that depict conscience as more shadow than light. A floating dagger. A despairing voice sobbing over the death of sleep. A bloodied ghost come back to torture the living. No welcoming and brightly lit path here; Will gives us the full chiaroscuro of our inner moral landscape. Conscience can look this way, too, Will says to us. In fact, it often does.

Francis Thompson's great poem *The Hound of Heaven* describes God's loving pursuit of a hesitant believer. The poem begins: "I fled Him, down the nights and down the days, / I fled Him, down the arches of the years. / I fled Him, down the labyrinthine ways / Of my own mind, and in the mist of tears / I hid from him."

In this play, something is with equal zeal pursuing Macbeth and Lady Macbeth. It is something very different from the force at work in Thompson's poem. It is something that has nothing to do with grace and mercy and forgiveness. It is something with teeth. It is something terrible.

Perhaps it is their terrible freedom, and the responsibility that goes with it.

Whatever it is, it drives Lady Macbeth mad. And it murders Macbeth's sleep—and then stands sentry over the grave.

As I said at the beginning of this chapter, our country's legal system has historically given a wide berth to the individual human conscience. In a law journal article, Supreme Court Justice Harlan Fiske Stone wrote:

> [B]oth morals and sound policy require that the state should not violate the conscience of the individual. All our history gives confirmation to the view that liberty of conscience has a moral and social value which makes it worthy of preservation at the hands of the state . . . [N]othing short of the self-preservation of the state should warrant its violation; and it may well be questioned whether the state which preserves its life by a settled policy of violation of the conscience of the individual will not in fact ultimately lose it by the process.

In the same spirit, the Supreme Court has on a number of occasions described conscience as inviolable and the freedom to believe as absolute. "Courts, no more than constitutions," it had declared, "can intrude into the consciences of men or compel them to believe contrary to their faith or think contrary to their convictions."

We tend to think of this approach as a way to protect conscience, to keep the law from interfering with our freedom to believe as we will. But *Macbeth* suggests a different way to think about it. Maybe this approach also helps protect law.

Macbeth shows us a universe that has a relentless and hounding moral order to it. It's an order that forces foul deeds to rise, that demands the allegiance of our conscience, and that in the end will prevail—in ways we do not expect and at whatever cost. It's an order that follows its own slow, strong, steady march toward a destination so fixed that it can feel like fate.

And maybe it is.

In any event, law would be well advised to get the hell out of its way.

10

"Darkness and Devils"

King Lear

Backdrop

Many critics, poets, and playwrights count *King Lear* not just as one of Will's greatest works, but as one of the greatest works in the history of the English language. Percy Bysshe Shelley celebrated it as "the most perfect specimen of the dramatic art existing in the world." And George Bernard Shaw gushed (uncharacteristically) that "no man will ever write a better tragedy than *Lear.*" Marjorie Garber observes that the play "has often, and rightly, been regarded as a sublime account of the human condition."

Lear may deserve all this adulation (I join with those who think it does), but it is also a play full of "darkness and devils." Emma Smith describes it as "perhaps Shakespeare's most desolate tragedy," and she has a point. Indeed, its horrors unfold in such quantity and variety—and at such a relentless pace—as to lead us to believe that, surely, a favorable turn of events must wait at the end.

Alas, no.

In this sense, *Lear* presents us with a serious challenge. How should we experience and think about a play that is so profoundly and unceasingly grim? Literary history has offered three possible answers. Change it. Admire it. Or embrace it.

As Emma Smith observes, over the course of the past few centuries critics have dealt with *Lear* in all of those three ways. In the late seventeenth and eighteenth centuries, they deemed the play artistically wanting, particularly in its dreadful conclusion, prompting reworkings to give it an improbably happy ending. In the nineteenth century, they respected the play as holding a mirror up to the awesome, if unforgiving, forces of nature and life. And, in the post-war twentieth century, they celebrated its emptiness and nihilism, seeing it as a hauntingly modern work. And so it is, rather like *Measure for Measure*, if for different reasons and in different ways.

Scholars generally agree that Will wrote *King Lear* around 1605. The Quarto and Folio versions of the play differ. Among other things, the Quarto includes a pretend "trial" of the king's claims against his offending daughters. It's a scene that has been examined closely in some books and articles on Shakespeare and the law, but we will focus our attention elsewhere.

In writing *Lear*, Will once again drew from a wide variety of sources. They almost certainly included familiar myths and legends, Ralph Holinshed's *Chronicles*, and some earlier plays. Stephen Greenblatt suggests that Shakespeare may also have taken inspiration from a well-publicized 1603 lawsuit in which some calculating daughters attempted to get their father declared insane.

Lear was apparently performed before the king in 1606 at the Feast of St. Stephen, the day after Christmas. The play might seem an odd choice for a holiday season hootenanny, but it wasn't entirely off theme. The Feast of Stephen marks the death of the first Christian martyr, and by the end of the play Lear may strike us as the embodiment of a tortured but illuminated soul.

Indeed, *Lear* is thick with influences from the Hebrew Bible and New Testament. Many literary scholars have pointed out the symbols and allusions that associate Cordelia with Christ. For example, when in the final scene Cordelia lies dead draped over Lear's arms it's hard to miss the iconography of a pietà—even if the genders are reversed.

Echoes of the book of Job are similarly strong. After all, Job is, at least in part, a story about God's complete authority to do as He chooses. *Lear* similarly gives us a bracing sermon on our helplessness in the face of powers beyond our control.

The comparison to Job underscores just how very dark this play is. It's a remarkable thing to claim that you had it worse than Job, but Lear has a plausible argument to that effect. Consider: In the end, Job enjoys redemption and restoration that Lear does not. Indeed, Lear's return to power has a terrible cause: He gets his kingdom back because the daughters among whom he divided it are all dead.

If *Lear* makes for hard reading, then it makes for even harder watching. The blinding of Gloucester (Cornwall bellowing "Out, vile jelly!" as he stomps his victim's eyeball with his boot) has turned more than a few stomachs. And Lear's cries of despair at the end ("Howl! Howl! Howl! Howl!") remind us of every moment when we have stood dumb in the face of inexpressible grief. As Marjorie Garber observes, one of the themes of the play is that some things are so dreadful they cannot even be spoken.

A few years ago, my wife and I had a last-minute opportunity to attend a high-level well-cast production of *King Lear*, but I demurred. Given my passion for seeing as much Shakespeare as I can, she was surprised and asked why. I told her that I hadn't had adequate time to train for it. Like *Hamlet*, *Lear* asks a lot of us, and sometimes it asks more than we can at that moment give.

Lear's literary greatness notwithstanding, it was at first not clear to me why I should subject my students to all the agony that goes along with a close study of it. Law school offers more than enough stress and suffering on its own. Plus, much of the literature about the connection between *Lear* and the law focuses on a kind of estate planning problem: How can you make a living gift of property to your children while still exercising control over what they do with it? Sorting that question makes for a fun legal puzzle, but I hoped to find a different and perhaps subtler connection between *Lear* and the law.

I found one.

Indeed, I found two.

And, to my astonishment, *King Lear* turned out to be among my students' favorite plays.

❂ ❂ ❂ ❂ ❂

One reason so many of my students warm to *Lear* has nothing to do with the law but everything to do with the stage of life at which most people find themselves in law school. In part, *Lear* resonates with my students because they have started to experience personally some of the problems presented by the play: How do we deal with an aging and increasingly infirm parent? What do our loved ones want and need of us as they near the last stage of life? How do we manage the financial and emotional complexities that accompany the transfer of property within a family?

The problems of *Lear* are their problems writ large. And, because my students are often the "lawyer in the family," navigating those problems disproportionately falls to them. They take *Lear* personally, as I suppose we all do. At my stage of life, it feels like a terrifying warning against voluntary retirement.

But *Lear* also touches on two issues of keen interest to the law and lawyers more generally. And, with all due respect to estate planning problems, I found them vastly more interesting.

One of those issues relates to the matter of compromise. Compromise has a central place in the practice of law. It shapes the transactions that lawyers shepherd to completion; it resolves most criminal charges; it drives the outcome of the vast majority of civil lawsuits. One aspect of competent representation includes advising clients about compromise, and the failure to do so can amount to an ethical breach or even malpractice.

Paradoxically, however, a law school education typically provides very few opportunities to explore the dynamics of compromise. In law school, we teach doctrine as if every legal dispute ended in a United States Supreme Court opinion. In reality, however, most legal disputes end in a brokered deal, and most students leave law school with very little understanding of how that happens and what might get in the way of getting it done. Looking at *Lear* through the lens of the law allows us to think about compromise—and all the things that can prevent it from happening.

To be clear: It would be wild overstatement to claim that *King Lear* is a play "about" compromise. I don't contend that Will saw it as one of the central themes of the play, in the way that I think he saw conscience as a central theme in *Macbeth*. And yet, at several points in *King Lear* a refusal to compromise has a key role in determining the trajectory of events. As I'll discuss, a critical one comes early in the play in connection with the so-called love trial. And it is not too much to say that *King Lear* is just one sensible compromise away from an averted disaster.

So, although *King Lear* is not a play "about" compromise, it provides us with excellent fodder for thinking about how compromise works—and why sometimes it doesn't. And, precisely because *Lear* is such a "desolate tragedy," it powerfully conveys the risks involved in our failures to resolve our differences. When we do not compromise, we lose control over the course of events. And those events can take us to places far beyond our worst imaginings.

The other issue in *Lear* that I think benefits from a viewing through the lens of the law is that of legitimacy. The events of *Lear* are strongly influenced by the machinations of Edmund, Gloucester's bastard son. And Edmund finds much of his motivation in his status as a social outcast.

We could, of course, think narrowly about this issue, focusing on the prevailing view of bastardry in Jacobean England. But, in my view, *Lear* ushers us into a broader consideration of the power of law to determine who does—and does not—count as a "legitimate" human being. It is a determination that arises in a variety of legal contexts, from family law to immigration law to constitutional law. We can learn a lot from viewing the issue of legitimacy through the wide-angle lens the law has to offer us.

The tavern door is open. Will summons us to enter into the terrible and storm-tossed world of *King Lear.* Let's take a deep breath, gird our loins, and seek out the meaning in all this "darkness and devils."

Will has more than enough of it waiting for us.

That Glib and Oily Art

King Lear starts with an exercise that scholars sometimes call his "love trial." The king—advanced in years and weary of rule—has concocted a ritual for his own amusement and flattery. He has decided to divide his kingdom between his three daughters: Goneril, Regan, and Cordelia. Apparently two of the three parts of his kingdom are of similar bounty, the final third somewhat greater. Each daughter will, in turn, argue that she loves her father most. The king will bestow the most valuable third of his fortune on the winner. It's a bizarre indulgence.

As trials go, it's also a farce. Lear, the decision maker, will hear from three witnesses. Each witness has a direct stake in the outcome of the proceeding. It's hard to imagine more biased and self-interested testimony. Indeed, for hundreds of years at the Common Law parties could not testify in civil cases precisely because of concerns over the unreliability of this kind of evidence. Such a prohibition obviously goes too far: in many cases, the parties have the best knowledge of the facts, and the opposing lawyer can explore the issue of bias through cross-examination. But the fundamental idea—that self-interested testimony tends to be less trustworthy—remains a sound one.

The evidence presented in Lear's love trial is also of dubious value because it relates to a subjective interior state of mind. The witnesses can gush all they like, but flattery hardly serves as objective proof of anything. Of course, his daughters could buttress their claims by providing specific examples of instances in which they have through their actions exhibited their great love for their father. But, tellingly, neither Goneril nor Regan has much to say in that regard.

Instead, the testimony offered by both of them feels embarrassingly abstract and empty. Goneril begins: She loves Lear "more than words can wield the matter" and so on and so on, yadda yadda yadda. Regan continues: Okay, well, everything my sister said but oh so much more, and so on and so on, yadda yadda yadda. The love trial is heavy on speeches but light on facts.

Furthermore, the trial is rigged, or at least Lear thinks it is. Again, remember that Lear has set himself up as the decision maker. He favors Cordelia and he intends to give her the richest part of his kingdom. So, he has Goneril and Regan go first, saving the best for last. Of course, Goneril and Regan—being who they are—play along and lavish adoring platitudes on their father.

That part of the ceremony goes just as he expected. But, when Lear asks what Cordelia has to say, she replies: "Nothing." Boom. It's a show-stopper of a response.

A stunned Lear asks for an explanation and Cordelia gives him two. First, she will not lie. Yes, she loves her father, but surely a time will come when she will have a husband she loves more, and she won't make grandiose and disingenuous statements pretending otherwise. Second, she has not cultivated the "glib and oily art" of shameless flattery, as her sisters have done. The virtues of honesty and dignity leave her unpracticed in such matters; she is who she is; she'll take the consequences.

We might have a variety of possible reactions to what Cordelia says here. On one hand, we might see it as an exercise of conscience—the virtue we discussed at length in the last chapter. The civil rights activist Father Daniel Berrigan famously said: "Know where you stand and stand there." Cordelia does just that, even to the wild outrage of her father and to her economic and familial calamity.

But, alternatively, we might wonder about the unyielding absolutism of Cordelia's stance. An old man has asked for a show of affection. Would it really entail any great sacrifice of principle on her part to give him one? Know where you stand and stand there, yes, but doesn't this seem an odd and unnecessary place to draw a line in the sand? Truth unbending to affection would yield cruel and curious results: "Do you like my new dress?" grandma asks. "My conscience compels me to declare it ugly," you boldly reply, chest and jaw jutting out in righteous defiance.

Some critics, like Marjorie Garber, see a straightforward enough explanation: "she, like her sisters, is her father's daughter, stubborn and proud."

Perhaps, but I'm not sure this gives Cordelia enough credit or Lear enough blame. Things seem more complicated to me.

I hesitate to lay all the responsibility here at Cordelia's feet. Granted, Lear gives her multiple chances to reverse course, but we have no reason to believe he would accept anything short of her complete and unqualified capitulation to his whims. It's not really a compromise if Cordelia has to give him everything he wants.

Besides, in a sense she does offer him a compromise. She acknowledges that she will obey him, honor him, and "most love" him. She just won't join her sisters in slobbering all over him. But Lear finds this unacceptable; it doesn't meet his demand for unqualified rhapsodic hyperbole.

Of course, dire consequences follow from the failure of Lear and Cordelia to find anything resembling middle ground. A settlement of differences between them would have swiftly provided the happy ending that those eighteenth-century critics wanted, but father and daughter couldn't get there. Indeed, they didn't even seriously try to do so.

An adage among litigators holds that every trial is a failed settlement. The subsequent tribulations that unfold in *King Lear* all result from the failure of the king and Cordelia to figure out how to resolve the love trial on terms acceptable to everyone. So it sometimes goes with compromises: That which shouldn't be difficult, especially given the stakes, proves utterly impossible.

Every experienced litigator can give you a list of the various dynamics that get in the way of compromise. Here are a familiar few: Greed. Anger. Resentment. Envy. Arrogance. Ignorance. Write up an inventory of every possible human foible and you'll have your catalog of the reasons parties fail to resolve their differences.

Those foibles can blind disputants to the straightforward realities of self-interest. Years ago, I served as a mediator in a contract lawsuit involving a very substantial sum of money. We made solid progress over the course of a long and tiresome day, me shuffling back and forth between the two rooms holding the parties.

But when we arrived at a difference of just a few hundred dollars we got stuck. Both parties dug in their heels and vowed they would not budge another inch. It took almost three additional hours for us to close the deal, even though at my hourly rate this ended up costing both parties more than they would have paid if they'd simply split the difference—as I kept encouraging them to do, and as they ultimately did. Why was it so hard to get them there? Who knows? I suspect it had something to do with pride and with wanting to make the other side bend to their will, even if that bend involved a trivial amount of money.

In the opening scene of the play, Cordelia and Lear similarly dig in their heels. She will not lavish even one additional word of affection on him. What more does she have to offer? "Nothing." And he will bend in nothing as well. He will accept only Cordelia's fulsome effort to outdo her sisters in praise. Getting stuck in these places serves neither of their respective self-interest, but they either can't calculate the costs and benefits or don't care about them. Something blinds them to the straightforward realities of the situation.

What is it? What gets in the way? Shakespeare doesn't tell us directly, but I believe he gives us abundant hints.

In the opening scene, Will paints a telling picture of Lear's personality. He shows us the king's vanity and sense of entitlement; indeed, who but a crazily vain and entitled person would concoct an exercise like the love trial? He also shows us the king's immaturity and rashness: Lear makes a series of impetuous and ill-advised decisions, casting Cordelia from his sight, dividing his kingdom between his two serpentine daughters, and depriving his favorite child of her dowry—leaving her to an uncertain fate. And Will shows us that Lear cannot listen to reason: When the noble and loyal Kent tries to derail Lear's disastrous juggernaut, the king rebukes and threatens him.

If Lear's behavior in the first scene were out of character, if it signaled a recent departure from how he had generally conducted himself in the course of his life, then we might write it off to the vagaries of an aging and increasingly mercurial temperament. Regan and Goneril debate the possibility, but reject it:

> **Regan:** 'Tis the infirmity of his age. Yet he hath ever but slenderly known himself.
>
> **Goneril:** The best and soundest of his time hath been but rash. Then must we look from his age to receive not alone the imperfections of long-engraffed condition, but therewithal the unruly waywardness that infirm and choleric years bring with them. (I:1:339–346)

In short, Lear has always been a narcissistic hothead. His blowup after the failed love trial is entirely predictable.

In my view, this insight helps us understand why Lear can't compromise his demands: He lacks the self-knowledge that makes compromise possible. To reach an effective compromise, we need to know enough about ourselves—including our weaknesses—to recognize the qualities that may get in the way of acting in our self-interest. To draw an example from another play that we've discussed: If I don't realize that my hatred has perversely distorted my decision-making, then I will insist on collecting my pound of flesh—even if by doing so I unwittingly ensure my own downfall.

Lear can't see himself for who he is. He doesn't recognize his outburst as nothing more than a silly tantrum. He can't grasp the spoiled and petty nature of his behavior. Instead, he casts himself as a fearsome "dragon" who will have his way, period, full stop. He has no idea how quickly this dragon will lose its teeth and claws.

His blind spots also keep Lear from seeing *others* as *they* are. He accepts the bloated flatteries of Goneril and Regan as sincere expressions of love but dismisses the wise counsel of Kent as unwelcome interference. He tags Cordelia as the traitor among his children when it is of course exactly the other way around.

He can't even see *things* as they are. A plan to surrender all of your property and power—while also traipsing around the country doing as you please with a retinue of one hundred knights traipsing along with you—borders on the delusional. Goneril puts it this way: "Idle old man / That would still manage those authorities / That he hath given away."

Kent foresees the obvious unworkability of the plan and the vulnerable position in which it will leave the king, but Lear won't listen to him. Ironically, the only leverage Lear would have retained under his ill-conceived scheme lay in his relationship with Cordelia and her ability to protect him if things went wrong. But he cast that leverage aside.

Critics have noted that *King Lear* relies heavily on images of sight and blindness. Some of those images are literal, like the blinding of Gloucester. Many are figurative, as when in the fourth scene of the first act Lear expresses his grief at Goneril's disobedience by exclaiming that if his eyes cry again he will pluck them out.

In this very first scene, however, Lear shows himself already blind—blind to his own foibles, blind to the character of others, blind to the realities of life, blind to all the things that drive sensible people to resolve differences when the stakes are high. In any context, the involvement of someone possessed of Lear's foibles would make compromise hard to achieve. But this is a context of unique complexity: This is, after all, a play about a family.

Where else would you find anything resembling a love trial?

Will wrote all his plays as if the action begins *in medias res*, in the middle of things as they existed before the first player speaks the first line. The characters share a history that predates the play and that they bring into it. Think, for example, of *The Merchant of Venice* and all that has taken place between Shylock and Antonio before the curtain rises—and that sets the arc of the entire story.

But, again, *Lear* is a play about a family, and every family interaction comes with its own customized set of checked and carry-on baggage. Ask any lawyer who practices family law, or who works with family-owned businesses, or who has handled litigation between family members. They will tell you that the involvement of families makes everything more difficult, including compromise, perhaps especially compromise. Here, reason and logic and self-interest may find themselves trumped by dusty grievances, durable jealousies, and festering wounds.

In the course of the first scene, Will gives us a peek inside some of the baggage of this family. Cordelia clearly comes into the play with little regard for her sisters. She makes her feelings plain when she distinguishes her candor from the "glib and oily art" of Goneril and Regan.

Of course, it seems unlikely they hold much affection for her, either. After all, Goneril and Regan have spent their entire lives listening to Lear tell them that Cordelia is his favorite. Little wonder they approach their relationship with him as if they have a score to settle.

Remembering that *King Lear* is a play about a family helps us understand why Cordelia doesn't do more to appease her father. She has lived all her days under her father's thumb, contending with his imperious and impetuous mood swings. Her grievances have accumulated. She's had enough. She won't bend.

Sure, all things being equal, she would happily take a third of Lear's kingdom. But she wants something else even more: She wants her father to see her as a person in her own right and not just as a pawn in his ridiculous love trial. Tragically, he confirms her suspicion that he can't do it—or at least he can't do it until it's much too late.

To be clear: None of this means that Cordelia doesn't love her father. To the contrary, it is precisely because she loves Lear that she can't commoditize her affection, play along, and give the old man what he wants. Because she loves deeply she must also love sincerely. Goneril and Regan suffer under no such constraints.

Lear feels the full brunt of his lack of self-knowledge and his inability to bend. Hard on the heels of taking an uncompromising position Lear finds himself in an uncompromising universe. The two daughters between whom he has divided his kingdom tell him he does not need one hundred knights. Or, for that matter, fifty. Or, for that matter, one. His contingent becomes a fool. His kingdom becomes the heath, where nature holds its brutal and unforgiving sway.

Their inability to compromise traps both Lear and Cordelia. The failure sets things in motion. And, following a law of emotional physics, such things put in motion tend to remain in motion until something stops them.

In *King Lear*, nothing does.

I don't want to overstate the case in favor of compromise. Most disputes don't threaten tragic consequences if the parties can't amicably resolve them. Yes, in the end someone may regret not having settled things when they had the chance. But the odds that those regrets will include a stack of bodies like we find at the end of *King Lear* are, to say the least, extremely remote.

Furthermore, compromise isn't always a good thing. Indeed, sometimes a refusal to compromise reflects virtues that we celebrate, like conscience and courage. When the old spiritual says, "Like a tree planted by the water, I shall not be moved," it forecloses the possibility of compromise. As with most other human activities, whether compromise qualifies as commendable depends on a wide array of factors and considerations.

Nevertheless, *Lear* offers us a powerful cautionary tale about the refusal to bend. A firm and unwavering stand may serve us well in certain circumstances. But, particularly in the context of familial relations, some things once said are hard to unsay and some things once done are hard to undo. It is paradoxical but true that we can be broken in half by the very rigidity of our own spines.

Lear counsels us to work toward peace and resolution when and while we can. If we see little risk in digging in our heels, well, the play tells us, so did Cordelia and King Lear. And if it is hard to find the words to compromise, well, the play tells us, it is harder still to find the words adequate to grief.

As *Lear* painfully displays, it is a bad bargain to trade the sometime clumsy language of reconciliation for the raw and ragged protest of the howl.

Fine Word, "Legitimate"

Lear starts with a story about a family, but not the king's. Our introduction to delicate family matters comes in the opening lines of the play, in which

Gloucester acknowledges the illegitimacy of his son, Edmund. Gloucester treats the subject with anything but delicacy:

> **Kent:** Is not this your son, my lord?
>
> **Gloucester:** His breeding, sir, hath been at my charge. I have so often blushed to acknowledge him that now I am brazed to 't.
>
> **Kent:** I cannot conceive you.
>
> **Gloucester:** Sir, this young fellow's mother could, whereupon she grew round-wombed and had indeed, sir, a son for her cradle ere she had a husband for a bed. Do you smell a fault?
>
> **Kent:** I cannot wish the fault undone, the issue of it being so proper.
>
> **Gloucester:** But I have a son, sir, by order of law, some years elder than this, who yet is no dearer in my account. Though this knave came something saucily to the world before he was sent for, yet was his mother fair, there was good sport at his making, and the whoreson must be acknowledged. (I:1:8–24)

We don't know whether Edmund overhears this particular exchange, but it scarcely matters. Edmund understands his place in the order of things and his father plainly makes no effort to conceal his embarrassment. That Gloucester leavens the embarrassment with fondness for Edmund doesn't change matters. These are just the facts: Edmund's older brother, Edgar, is legitimate "by order of law"; under the same law, Edmund is less than invisible.

Law does this, and not just a little of it. For many purposes and in many contexts, it determines who counts as a human being and who doesn't. In the process, it allocates property, liberty, power—all the things that determine futures and fortunes and freedom.

These efforts to define who counts as a human being have led to some of the law's gravest and most embarrassing blunders. An infamous example comes in the Supreme Court's *Dred Scott* decision of 1857. In that case, Dred Scott and his wife Harriet, both of whom had been enslaved people, sued in federal court for their freedom. The case wound its way to the Supreme Court of the United States, where Chief Justice Roger Taney—a member of the Southern aristocracy—wrote the opinion.

Taney's notorious screed hit the odiousness trifecta. He found that people of African descent were not United States citizens and so could not sue in federal court. He found that the Constitution protected the owners of enslaved people (but not the enslaved themselves) because the enslaved were their property. And he found that the Missouri Compromise statute passed by Congress, which prohibited slavery in certain territories, was unconstitutional. According to Taney, under the law Dred and Harriet Scott did not count as human beings; they were objects to own and to sell or buy; and, like any other object, they had no rights to enforce or vindicate.

In addition to yielding dreadful precedents, the law's efforts to determine who counts as a human being have generated an abundance of controversy and confusion. For example, in its 2010 decision in *Citizens United v. Federal Election Commission*, the Supreme Court of the United States held that a federal statute limiting independent expenditures on political campaigns by legal entities like corporations and labor unions ran afoul of the First Amendment. In this context, the Court gave corporations all the humanity that it denied to Dred and Harriet Scott: they could sue in federal court; the Constitution protected them as if they were people; and a statute that burdened their rights was held invalid.

Full disclosure: I happen to agree with some parts of the Court's decision in *Citizens United*. Given the underlying theory and goals of the First Amendment, it makes sense to me to afford speech rights to legal entities like corporations and unions. But many people found the outcome deeply counterintuitive and the idea that corporations are people lends itself to easy ridicule. One popular dissenting bumper sticker declares: "I'll believe that corporations are people when Texas executes one."

But perhaps no legal effort to determine who counts as a human being has created as much confusion and controversy as the Supreme Court's abortion jurisprudence. Even an abbreviated outline of that case law, from the recognition of a woman's constitutional right to terminate her pregnancy in *Roe v. Wade* (1973) to the rejection of such a right in *Dobbs v. Jackson Women's Health Organization* (2022), would take us far afield from our subject and mire us in complexities from which we might never escape.

For present purposes, it suffices to note that the abortion issue is very much a debate over who counts as a human being. One side argues that a fetus qualifies as a person who deserves our protection. The other side argues that a woman must have the authority to make decisions related to her body, health, and reproduction. To compel a woman to carry a pregnancy to term, that side argues, is to reduce her to an object, to enslave her in the service of another just as the Scotts were enslaved.

In recent years, a debate has also raged about how we should view and treat immigrants who are within the United States without full documentation.

Again, even a truncated exploration of so complex an issue lies well beyond the scope of this book. Suffice it to say that a contingent exists within our society who equate humanity with citizenship. The now largely abandoned phrase "illegal immigrant" reflects this sensibility, labeling someone as not just inadequately credentialed but as having unlawfulness as their essence.

All this brings us back to Edmund and the law's declaration of him as "illegitimate." The word "illegitimate" comes from a Latin root literally meaning "not lawful," that is, a person defined by their standing outside of the law. In the England of Shakespeare's time, the question of legitimacy could be a bit complicated—for example, a child born illegitimate could become legitimate (at least in the eyes of the church) if their parents married. But, as Will makes plain here and in other plays, illegitimacy carried with it an unmistakable and significant stigma and, under both common law and canon law, bastards had no automatic right to inherit anything. The law decides who counts as a human being and who doesn't, and it tells Edmund that he doesn't count at all.

Edmund has other ideas. He sees himself as fully his brother's equal (and then some) and rejects the label of illegitimate as random and irrational. Indeed, he makes the case for the innate superiority of bastards, conceived as they are in the heat of passion rather than in the sleepy offices of marital duty. He honors only one law, the law of nature and not the law of man:

Thou, Nature, art my goddess, to thy law
My services are bound. Wherefore should I
Stand in the plague of custom, and permit
The curiosity of nations to deprive me,
For that I am some twelve or fourteen moonshines
Lag of a brother? Why bastard? Wherefore base?
When my dimensions are as well compact,
My mind as generous, and my shape as true,
As honest madam's issue? Why brand they us
With base? with baseness? bastardy? base, base?
Who, in the lusty stealth of nature, take
More composition, and fierce quality,
Than doth, within a dull, stale, tired bed
Go to the creating a whole tribe of fops,
Got 'tween sleep and wake? Well, then,

Legitimate Edgar, I must have your land.
Our father's love is to the bastard Edmund
As to the legitimate: fine word, "legitimate!"
Well, my legitimate, if this letter speed
And my invention thrive, Edmund the base
Shall top th' legitimate. I grow, I prosper:
Now, gods, stand up for bastards! (I:2:1–23)

Edmund does not just rebuff the hierarchy created by law; he inverts it. And, in most performances, he does this not just in substance but in tone, the word "legitimate" dripping with derision.

If we view Edmund as a Machiavellian schemer who imagines himself above the law, then he may remind us of many characters we've met in earlier chapters: Aaron in *Titus Andronicus*; Gloucester in *Henry VI, Part 2*; Iago in *Othello*; Macbeth. But something distinguishes Edmund from all of those figures. In Edmund's case, it is the law that rejects him, that declares him illegitimate, that labels him "not lawful" from the moment of his birth. The theology that proclaims us all born *into* sin has nothing on the law of bastardy, which proclaims Edmund born *as* a sin.

Edmund has no difficulty identifying the fundamental contradiction that exists within his social status. The law says that he counts for nothing but then also demands his allegiance. Little wonder he turns away from the law of society and embraces the law of Nature.

Edmund's invocation of Nature is important. To some extent, it's a play on words. As Garber observes, in the old sense a "natural" child was one born outside of the social structures of marriage. Where would a natural child go for guidance but to Nature itself?

But the Nature to which Edmund alludes here is of a particular sort. For example, it bears little resemblance to our understanding of natural law theory—a conviction that the universe has embedded within it a discernable moral order that determines right from wrong. Edmund finds his inspiration in a Nature in which only the strongest survive and prevail, the Nature "red in tooth and claw" described by Tennyson. The Christian God of natural law would not stand up for a murderous bastard, but the pagan gods of Nature would do so—so that's who Edmund invokes.

King Lear is a play of many parallels and, in some respects, Cordelia finds herself in a position not so different from that of Edmund: placed outside the line of succession. Indeed, her position may even be worse, insofar as Lear rejects all relations with her while Gloucester makes no secret of his affection for Edmund. But for our purposes the critical point is that society does not declare Cordelia unlawful; it just gives Lear the power to decide whether she should receive part of his kingdom. Lear casts out Cordelia; the law itself casts out Edmund.

Some critics have suggested that Edmund's status as a bastard doesn't do much work in the plot of *Lear*, but I strongly disagree. In my view, Edmund takes that status as a license to do whatever he deems necessary to advance. And much of the evil that gets done in the play gets done precisely because Edmund views himself as standing outside legal and social constraints. He betrays his father; he orchestrates events against his brother; he plays Goneril and Regan against each other.

Declare me unlawful? I will show you unlawful, Edmund says.

In the final scene, Edmund confronts the full implications of his lawlessness when they bring the bodies of Goneril and Regan before him. He has a sudden change of heart: "Some good I mean to do." He tries to call off the executions of Lear and Cordelia that he has ordered, but the news comes too late to save the king's favorite child.

Edmund says he does this good "Despite of mine own nature," effectively equating his personal nature with the ruthless and unfeeling Nature he invoked at the beginning. We might take this as an act of repentance, as the kind of dramatic reversal we find in the story of the Prodigal Son. But, to use the words of the King James Version, the Prodigal Son "came to himself"—that is, he returned to the person he had been. In his attempt at redemption, Edmund tries to become someone else altogether.

In that moment, the unlawful Edmund seeks to relocate himself within the law: within natural law; within moral law; within society's law. It may strike us as way too little way too late. And I doubt that anyone has ever left a performance of *King Lear* full of warm and fuzzy feelings for the remorseful Edmund.

But I think that Will wanted us to recognize that Edmund is not the one who put himself outside of the law in the first instance. The law itself did that. And Edmund seeks to relocate himself within the law not because of the law but in spite of it.

Go cautiously, *King Lear* tells us, in declaring that certain people do not count as human beings under the law. They may take the declaration as an engraved invitation to lawlessness. And we may find ourselves at the mercy of their decision to show a greater humanity than we claim they possess.

11

"Flower of Warriors"

Coriolanus

Backdrop

Most of us come to *Coriolanus* for the first time not knowing what to expect. It's certainly not among Shakespeare's best-known plays. It may even qualify as relatively obscure, at least among general readers. When I teach it in my Shakespeare & the Law seminar, the vast majority of my students have never heard of it. They're not even sure how to pronounce it.

Once we get into the play it may strike us as, well, not very Shakespearean. At first blush, we may think it lacks the complex grandeur that we tend to associate with Will's greatest works. We do not find here the elaborate parallel structures of *King Lear* or the rich digressions of *Hamlet*. Even the byzantine subplots of some of the early plays, like *Henry VI, Part 2*, are missing in action.

Coriolanus instead follows a mercilessly direct line straight to its tragic conclusion. In one of his many delightfully over-the-top poems, Robert Service wrote of the Yukon: "Some say God was tired when He made it." An unimpressed reader might wonder if the same could be said of Will when he made *Coriolanus*, the last and least ornamented of his tragedies.

Indeed, the play's plotline may strike us as downright spare. A celebrated military hero finds that his personality and skill set do not translate well into the political sphere. He has a falling out with his countrymen. He changes sides and joins the enemy. But, in the end, his mother persuades him to return to the fold and he gives his life for his homeland.

The play's protagonist may strike us as similarly straightforward. In many of his works Will gives us characters who struggle mightily with deep inner conflicts about who they are. Hamlet is the obvious example, but (as we explored in an earlier chapter) even the blood-soaked Macbeth grapples with his conscience. Will offers up complicated personalities about whom we develop complicated feelings. We find ourselves sympathizing with the unsympathetic, liking the unlikable, and having something less than admiration for the presumptively admirable.

But Caius Martius Coriolanus is different. He knows exactly who he is—a "flower of warriors," as Cominius says, hardened from birth for battle. And he has all the qualities we would expect to find in such a person, or more accurately, in a machine with such hardwiring. He is courageous, relentless, honorable, violent, decisive, inflexible, quick to fight, and coldly intolerant of anything and anyone he perceives as weak or performative.

We may have complicated feelings about Coriolanus—indeed, I'll suggest that we should. But they don't arise because he's a particularly complicated human being. To the contrary, they arise precisely because of his uncompromising purity of character.

Compared with the plays we have considered in previous chapters, *Coriolanus* may initially seem like a fairly simple, even ordinary, bit of theater. But *Coriolanus* can surprise you. In its very simplicity, many distinguished critics and poets have found greatness.

❂ ❂ ❂ ❂ ❂

As I noted earlier, scholars generally identify *Coriolanus* as Shakespeare's last tragedy, probably written somewhere between 1606 and 1608. In crafting it, Will returned to a reliable and well-worn source: Sir Thomas North's 1579 translation of Plutarch's *Lives*. Parts of the play follow North very closely, other parts do not, and as usual Will restructures events and fleshes out characters for his own dramatic purposes. Will probably wrote another Roman tragedy, *Antony and Cleopatra*, again drawing heavily on North, at roughly the same time.

Fans of the play have included T. S. Eliot, who in a 1919 essay famously bypassed all other contenders to declare *Coriolanus* Shakespeare's greatest tragedy—easily better than *Hamlet*, which Eliot thought a miserable failure. As Marjorie Garber observes, other enthusiastic champions of the play have included everyone from Bertolt Brecht to Edmund Burke.

And what's not to love? *Coriolanus* may not tidily align with what we have come to expect from Shakespeare. But it has abundant virtues.

It is short, punchy, and pointed. It's a very good story very well told. It lends itself to imaginative and powerful staging. Many directors have capitalized on the dramatic potential that lies within that early moment when the blood-drenched Caius Martius emerges from his single-handed victory over the Volscian city of Corioles, earning him his new title. Many years ago, I saw a Royal Shakespeare Company production of the play that left him red from head to toe, showing only the whites of his eyes.

We may not find here Shakespeare's most lyrical poetry or most sublime explorations of the human condition. But *Coriolanus* does give us (among many other things) one of Will's most powerful political documents. As Garber points out, the play is "a brilliant primer on the grooming of a candidate for high public office—complete with handlers, coaches, strategists, and the stage mother to end all stage mothers." Furthermore, the political issues it explores have an unsettling timelessness to them. *Coriolanus* feels as fully modern as *Measure for Measure* or *King Lear.* And, as we'll discuss, therein lies a cause for concern.

But what does the play have to do with the law? Quite a lot, in my estimation. In this chapter, I'll focus on two connections that seem to me particularly intriguing.

The first has to do with the idea of role morality. Caius Martius Coriolanus possesses all of the qualities that make for an effective and virtuous military leader. But those same qualities betray him when he moves into the political arena.

The play invites us to ask: What does that mean? That Coriolanus is a morally flawed human being? That the things he takes for virtues aren't virtues at all? That politics is an inherently corrupt undertaking?

In attempting to answer these sorts of questions in analogous contexts, many ethicists have relied on a theory of role morality. Distilled to its essence, this theory maintains that moral standards vary depending on the role that an individual plays within a society. Specialized roles, the argument goes, yield specialized responsibilities. Under this reasoning, we don't condemn the executioner as a murderer because the executioner's job is to execute people. That's what we hire him to do.

The idea of role morality has strongly influenced the field of professional ethics, including legal ethics. Indeed, it's not too much to say that the rules of legal ethics, which prescribe the baseline responsibilities of lawyers, wouldn't make any sense without such a theory. After all, under the provisions of the ethics rules, lawyers are allowed—or even required—to do many things that would be condemned as unethical if done by a non-lawyer.

We need an explanation for why that outcome makes sense. The theory of role morality provides it—or so the argument goes.

It turns out that the easy solution role morality provides to our ethical dilemma may be a bit too easy. *Coriolanus* puts the strengths and weaknesses of the concept on full display. The play should therefore interest anyone who relies on the concept of role morality to justify their conduct. And that happens to include every single person who engages in the practice of law—and many people from other professions as well.

The second theme of interest here can be stated more succinctly and has to do with this question: When does a political leader threaten to become a danger to the people's civil liberties? Some of Coriolanus's political opponents believe he poses such a risk. Do they have a point? Should they be concerned? What does this play tell us about when *we* should become concerned with respect to *our* political leaders? We earlier encountered these sorts of questions in connection with *Julius Caesar*—but Will wrote that play toward the beginning of his career. Does *Coriolanus* send the same messages?

Will is older now. He will not stay up quite so late with us at the tavern. He may say less and ask us to figure out more on our own. But he is still quite wonderful company.

And so is *Coriolanus*.

The Butterfly Eater

Consistent with the play's overall spareness and efficiency, its first fifty lines put squarely before us the moral puzzle that is presented by the person of Caius Martius. Rome has acquired a supply of grain to address an emergency shortage, but, under Martius's orders, little of it is finding its way to the people. Rome's political leaders will decide what the people get and when they get it, and the plebians are restless.

Two competing views of Martius immediately find voice in the characters of First Citizen and Second Citizen. First Citizen sees Martius as "chief enemy to the people . . . a very dog to the commonalty." Nor does First Citizen credit Martius for any of his military triumphs. First Citizen says Martius did those celebrated deeds in service of his own pride and to make his mother happy. Nothing worth admiring there.

Second Citizen sees things differently. He thinks Martius has acted out of a sense of duty. "Consider you what services he has done for his country?" he demands of First Citizen. Furthermore, Second Citizen thinks

Martius has conducted himself in a manner consistent not only with what he is but with who he is. "What he cannot help in his nature you account a vice in him," he says to First Citizen.

Enter Menenius, respected as an honest broker by both First Citizen and Second Citizen. He counsels against an uprising, using an elaborate and unfortunate metaphor about how the Senate (the "good belly" of Rome) will help ensure that nutrition (the grain) will reach the plebians ("the great toe" of the assembly). It sounds a lot like current theories of trickle-down economics, about which we still have First Citizen and Second Citizen opinions.

At this point, Martius comes onstage and two things quickly become clear. First, he has no regard for the masses. In rapid succession he calls them "dissentious rogues," "curs," and "fragments." Second, he holds them in contempt for a very specific reason. He thinks that the commoners do not share his martial virtues, that they are weak and changeable, and that they do not know what's good for them. "They'll sit by th' fire and presume to know / What's done i' th' Capitol," he rages.

Indeed, Martius has much more respect for the principal enemy of Rome—the Volscian leader Tullus Aufidius—than he has for the Roman citizens themselves. "I sin in envying his nobility, / And, were I anything but what I am, / I would wish me only he." Martius and Aufidius share a set of values, and it is to those values that Martius's loyalty attaches. This allegiance helps explain why later, when Rome banishes Coriolanus, he has so little difficulty returning the favor by "banishing" Rome and joining up with its chief enemy.

Up to this point, Martius may strike us as pretty insufferable. He seems proud, arrogant, and elitist—and his little speech about how he would be Aufidius if he didn't get to be himself only confirms the impression. He seems utterly indifferent to the hunger and suffering of the people of Rome. And he seems willfully disrespectful of any opinion but his own.

But then something happens—the Volscians attack. And that event instantly transforms Martius from the man that Rome can't stand to the man that Rome can't spare. They urgently need him. And Martius delivers.

Cominius leads the charge against the Volscians, but he and his troops end up in retreat. It is a concept alien to Caius Martius. When the Volscians emerge through the city gates of Corioles to attack the Romans, Martius and his troops force them back. Martius advances so aggressively that he ends up inside the battlements, alone and grossly outnumbered. Everyone assumes Martius has met a gruesome fate, but then he emerges, victorious, covered from head to toe in the blood of the enemy.

And he's not done. He has more fight in him and he wants to take it to Aufidius. "My work hath not yet warmed me," he growls, and it's no idle boast. He pursues and confronts Aufidius, who manages to escape only because his men intervene. Aufidius flees, embarrassed by his rescue, and Martius wins the day.

When Cominius offers Martius one-tenth of the spoils as tribute to his valor, Martius declines. "I thank you, general, / But cannot make my heart consent to take / A bribe to pay my sword. I do refuse it / And stand upon my common part with those / That have beheld the doing." In this response, Martius shows himself a warrior not just of unflinching bravery but of uncompromising honor, and we may find our hearts moving right along with those of the Romans. Yes, Martius may be a ruthless brute, but he's *our* ruthless brute, and he comes in mighty handy when there are enemies at the gate.

In an earlier scene, his mother Volumnia—surely one of Shakespeare's most outsized and magnificent creations—explains how she molded him for just such purposes. In his youth, she sent him off to "a cruel war." On his return, she greeted his many scars not as objects of horror but as badges of honor and sources of pride and delight. The worse the wound the better.

Her friend Valeria comments that she sees the same qualities in Martius's own child. She describes how she recently watched the boy chase down a lovely butterfly—and then viciously tear it asunder . . . with his teeth. Really? A butterfly eater? What kind of society wants and needs such a monster in its service? Up go the hands of Volumnia and Valeria. And maybe our hands go up as well, even if uncomfortably.

In the 1992 film *A Few Good Men*, a military lawyer has taken on the defense of two United States Marines charged with killing a fellow Marine named Santiago during a hazing exercise. The lawyer (played by Tom Cruise) suspects that the men were following the orders of a Marine Colonel (played by Jack Nicholson). In a famous scene, the lawyer cross-examines the Colonel at trial.

The Colonel proves evasive in responding to questions so the lawyer presses him, insisting that he's entitled to answers. Finally the lawyer cries: "I want the truth!" The Colonel responds: "You can't handle the truth!" He goes on:

> Son, we live in a world that has walls, and those walls have to be guarded by men with guns. Who's gonna do it? You? You, Lieutenant Weinberg? I have greater responsibility than you can possibly fathom. You weep for

> Santiago, and you curse the Marines. You have that luxury. You have the luxury of not knowing what I know—that Santiago's death, while tragic, probably saved lives; and my existence, while grotesque and incomprehensible to you, saves lives. You don't want the truth because deep down in places you don't talk about at parties, you want me on that wall—you need me on that wall. We use words like "honor," "code," "loyalty." We use these words as the backbone of a life spent defending something. You use them as a punch line. I have neither the time nor the inclination to explain myself to a man who rises and sleeps under the blanket of the very freedom that I provide and then questions the manner in which I provide it. I would rather that you just said "thank you" and went on your way. Otherwise I suggest that you pick up a weapon and stand the post. Either way, I don't give a damn what you think you're entitled to.

In a violent world we need violent men in our service, the theory goes. Butterfly eaters. And we can't expect those men to follow the same rules that the rest of us do. They live in accordance with their own principles of honor and loyalty, their own code, their own role morality. The people can't handle the truth, the Colonel declares, and Coriolanus heartily agrees.

❁ ❁ ❁ ❁ ❁

Coriolanus's great military victory provides an opportunity for his political advancement to consul. But he faces hurdles. He is proud and remains unpopular with the people. And military glory tends to fade. It is indeed not the kind of thing we talk about at parties.

Still, his handlers have a chance at making sure the people remember his heroics, at least for a while. Coriolanus carries with him constant and conspicuous evidence of his deeds: the many wounds that he has earned in battle. On previous occasions, he has sworn never to use those honorable scars for dishonorable purposes of self-promotion. But his advocates, including the iron-willed Volumnia, pressure him to do so now.

He loathes the very thought of it and resists: "Your Honors, pardon. / I had rather have my wounds to heal again / Than hear say how I got them." Menenius badgers him: The Senate wants to make him consul; consistent with custom, he must plead the support of the people; why not let them see what he has suffered on their behalf? Coriolanus bristles at the notion. "I do beseech you, / Let me o'erleap that custom, for I cannot / Put on the gown, stand naked, and entreat them / For my wounds' sake to give their suffrage."

They prevail upon him to give it a try. So he dresses up (or, perhaps, down) in a humble gown and heads out to meet with the people. Some citizens remain skeptical. "You have been a scourge to [Rome's] enemies; you have been a rod to her friends. You have not indeed loved the common people," one charges, and Coriolanus can barely endure what he sees as impertinence. Eventually, however, more voices weigh in and the people grudgingly grant their endorsement.

Only the approval of the Senate remains. Coriolanus has two immediate questions: Will this process take place at the Senate House? (Yes.) And can I get out of these ridiculous humble clothes now? (Yes, again.) That he can tolerate the company and the costume of the people for only so brief a period of time tells us a lot about how committed he is to one identity and how unhappily he wears the other.

As soon as Coriolanus has left the scene, the tribunes Sicinius and Brutus stir up discontent among the people: Did you not see how he mocked you? Have you forgotten the malice he showed you? Shouldn't you have tested him and extracted assurances from him? The citizens have buyer's remorse: "Almost all / Repent in their election."

They head off to the Capitol in mutinous unity, seeking to undo that which they have just done. Coriolanus's political fortunes have changed in an instant. And his insistence on clinging to a role that doesn't align with his newfound political aspirations has had no small part in the debacle.

Coriolanus's downward spiral continues in the third act. After he learns that the plebians have withdrawn their support, he rants against the people and their tribunes. Brutus and Sicinius accuse him of treason, reiterate their role as "the people's magistrates," and then—serving as prosecutor, jury, and judge—pronounce him guilty and sentence him to death. Coriolanus draws his sword to resist arrest but, before blood gets drawn, Cominius and Menenius intervene and send him home.

The patricians try to talk sense into Coriolanus, and Volumnia joins the chorus. But Coriolanus has an argument with his mother: She made him the man he is and trained him to remain true to his nature. Would she now have him betray all that?

Volumnia's answer touches on a theme we explored in *Lear*: compromise. In essence, she says, well, you could have been a less strident version of yourself *and* remained true to who you are *and* held onto the role of consul. "You are too absolute," she declares. It's roughly the same advice he got earlier in the play from Menenius, and we all know how that went.

The next round goes no better. The tribunes (again) call Coriolanus a traitor; he (again) launches into a volley of insults; and they (again) find him guilty of treason and order his death. They commute his sentence to banishment but he replies: "I banish you!"

Then he makes sure they understand the consequences of their decision. To borrow from *A Few Good Men*, they want and need him on that wall, but they will no longer have him there. He rages:

> I banish you!
> And here remain with your uncertainty;
> Let every feeble rumor shake your hearts;
> Your enemies, with nodding of their plumes,
> Fan you into despair! Have the power still
> To banish your defenders, till at length
> Your ignorance—which finds not till it feels,
> Making but reservation of yourselves,
> Still your own foes—deliver you
> As most abated captives to some nation
> That won you without blows! Despising
> For you the city, thus I turn my back.
> There is a world elsewhere. (III:3:153–165)

He departs and the people cheer their victory. But they soon have fresh reasons for regret. In short order, word reaches Rome that Coriolanus has joined forces with Aufidius and an invasion is underway.

The people of Rome are worried, and they have reasons. Cominius tells the tribunes exactly what's coming their way:

> He is their god; he leads them like a thing
> Made by some other deity than Nature,
> That shapes man better; and they follow him
> Against us brats with no less confidence
> Than boys pursuing summer butterflies . . . (IV:6:115–119)

The butterfly eater, who their society fashioned, is coming home. And they are the butterflies.

The fickle citizens beat a hasty retreat: "For mine own part, / When I said banish him, I sat 'twas pity." "And so did I." "And so did I. And, to say the truth, so did very many of us . . . and though we willingly consented to his banishment, yet it was against our will." We can't help but wonder whether maybe Coriolanus's harsh judgment of them was spot on.

In the final act of the play, former allies line up to try to persuade Coriolanus to spare Rome. They all fail except Volumnia, and she succeeds only because she appeals to the very virtues that he has been unwilling to compromise, particularly his sense of honor. Her speech moves Coriolanus—indeed, it even manages to move Aufidius. Coriolanus relents.

Rome celebrates. The Volscians conspire to kill him and then, once dead, they celebrate his purity as a warrior: "Bear from hence his body, / And mourn you for him. Let him be regarded / As the most noble corse that ever herald / Did follow to his turn." Coriolanus clung to his role to the last. The very last. He will be buried wearing its mantle.

❂ ❂ ❂ ❂ ❂

In my view, *Coriolanus* tells us a lot about role morality, and particularly about where our reliance on it might lead us astray. The point here is not that role morality has nothing to contribute to our thinking. To the contrary, it is indeed useful in helping us to understand how context might shape our ethical reasoning. But we need to approach role morality with our eyes wide open to its limitations.

Let's start here. In a sense, the theory of role morality doesn't so much solve our ethical dilemma as redirect it. Rome may indeed have had need for a brutal and uncompromising warrior like Coriolanus—a butterfly eater, if you will. But notice how that argument works: It really just shifts the inquiry from one about Coriolanus to one about Rome. In short, it invites us to ask whether Rome is a morally just society.

An analogy may help here. We don't say of the Nazis who ran gas chambers: "Oh, well, running gas chambers was their role in society, so they weren't murderers." We think they were murderers. And we think they were murderers because we think that the society that put them in the role of executioner was a profoundly evil and unjust one. In other words: Our conviction that role morality provides a satisfactory validation for conduct is only as strong as our conviction that the role is itself morally defensible.

This insight has profound implications for legal ethics. Let's take a simple example. Say that at trial a lawyer has to cross-examine Adverse Witness

A. The lawyer is absolutely convinced that Adverse Witness A is telling the truth. But, through aggressive questioning, the lawyer could easily imply to the jury that Adverse Witness A is lying. Oh and by the way: This is not some law professor's exotic hypothetical; it happens all the time.

Now, outside of the context of legal practice, we would say that it's misleading, deceptive, and ethically improper to suggest that someone is lying when you are firmly convinced that they are telling the truth. But, inside of the context of the practice of law, we get a different outcome. Indeed, we get the exact opposite outcome.

Lawyers have a duty of competent, diligent, and zealous advocacy on behalf of their clients. That includes an obligation to cross-examine effectively any adverse witness that the other side calls. The ethics rules therefore don't just allow the lawyer to conduct such a cross-examination; they (at least arguably) command it, provided that the lawyer honor certain guardrails like not making any knowingly false statements in the process.

This outcome follows only because we have an adversary system of justice. A different kind of system could easily dictate a different kind of result. In this sense, every defense of what lawyers do—at least when our conduct departs from generally applicable ethical standards—requires a defense of the system that allows or requires us to do it.

If we had complete confidence in the moral efficacy of the adversary system, then this move would pose no great challenge. But do we?

The adversary system has many qualities that make it less than ideal: It places a premium on representation by a lawyer. It gives a decided advantage to the well-resourced. It creates barriers to justice to those of modest or no means. It elevates winning over reconciliation. To circle back to the very first chapter of this book: In an adversary system, law can look a lot like revenge. Saying "It is ethical for me to do this because of my role" is easy; explaining why the role itself is ethical can be considerably tougher.

I do not come to bury the adversary system, or to praise it. My point is simply that when we lawyers justify our conduct by invoking our role within that system, we haven't put the ethical question to bed. We've simply changed the question that we're asking. Now, we're asking what we think of a social structure that says it's okay to make an honest person look like a liar.

It's just like asking what we think of a social structure that celebrates butterfly eaters.

A second problem with role morality is that we may come to conflate our societal or professional role with our personal identity. Caius Martius Coriolanus clearly does so. He doesn't treat his role in the way that a stage actor would treat theirs, as something to take on and off as circumstances dictate. For Coriolanus, his role as a military leader is self-definitional. It is who he is—down to his very essence—and he abhors any suggestion that he depart from it.

We may admire Coriolanus's purity—many people in the play do—but we may also find him maddeningly frustrating—many people in the play do that, too. With all respect, we may feel that Coriolanus has rather missed the point. The martial virtues that he embraces serve him well in the role of military commander. But different roles require different sets of skills and entail different ethical expectations. And, when he seeks to become consul, he implicitly signs on to the idea that he will have to adopt the qualities that are relevant to that role. But he just. Can't. Do it.

We lawyers similarly get ourselves into trouble when we can't move beyond our roles as zealous advocates. Even within our professional activities, the job description sometimes entails things other than partisanship and table-pounding. In the course of our careers we may take on a different kind of role that requires a different kind of ethical framework.

For example, in our legal system we view prosecutors as having special obligations toward fairness and justice. Yes, we want effective prosecutors, but (as the legal ethics rules say) we also want them less focused on their win-loss record and more focused on ensuring that only the guilty are charged and convicted. A lawyer who becomes a prosecutor—but who clings to a litigator's "pure" ethic of winning at all costs—has, like Coriolanus, missed the point.

By the same token, lawyers who carry their professional role into their private lives can run into serious problems. The qualities that make for an effective attorney occasionally have their place in interpersonal relationships. When our then eight-year-old son would ask me to second-guess a decision his mother made, I would summarily declare: "Appeal denied!"

But, in general, the ethical code that governs professional participants in an adversary system fits poorly when we take on roles like spouse, parent, neighbor, and friend. The practice of law often demands an ethos of combat. The practice of life often does not.

In Oscar Wilde's play *Lady Windemere's Fan*, Lord Darlington says: "It is a good thing to have all the virtues, but a better thing to know when to put them to sleep." Lord Darlington makes the statement in the spirit of moral flexibility, and we might hesitate to subscribe to his libertine philosophy. But it is true that Coriolanus may have been well served to know when to put his martial virtues to bed and turn off the light. And it is similarly true that lawyers sometimes do well to put aside their adversarial virtues in favor of the virtues of other roles.

Alas, some of us, like Coriolanus, Just. Can't. Do it.

Hang 'Em

After the people put their fragile support behind Coriolanus, Brutus and Sicinius work to shatter it. Brutus says:

> Get you hence instantly, and tell those friends
> They have chosen a consul that will from them take
> Their liberties, make them of no more voice
> Than dogs that are as often beat for barking
> As therefore kept to do so. (II:3:237–241)

Staying with the dog metaphor for a moment, Brutus has one in this fight. He is a tribune and therefore a representative of the people; he knows that Coriolanus thinks the aristocracy committed a terrible blunder in allowing the people to have tribunes; and he's worried about his job. He's hardly an unbiased witness against Coriolanus.

Nevertheless, we may have reason to think his concerns are sincere and we may share in them. Coriolanus has shown himself perfectly willing to take other oppressive measures against the common people; when he is told about the people's demands for grain he says: "Hang 'em." He is by nature and vocation a hammer, so everything looks to him like a nail that needs a good whack with full military force. And the people may be playing into an imposition of martial law by engaging in violent unrest. The play sets things up with this memorable opening stage direction: "Enter a company of mutinous Citizens with staves, clubs, and other weapons."

We might hear in this play's Brutus an echo of the Brutus of *Julius Caesar*, who worried about his country's slow descent into tyranny. But this Brutus clearly thinks he has the stronger case. That Brutus speculated about who Julius Caesar might become if allowed to follow his vaunting ambition. This Brutus talks about who Coriolanus already is, what he has already done, and what he undoubtedly will do.

As we discussed in an earlier chapter, the Brutus of *Julius Caesar* may have made a good decision or a bad one. To some degree, the greatness of that play derives from the moral complexity of the choice Brutus faces. If we think he made the right choice, then that's probably because we think he rightly concluded that Caesar was a very dangerous man.

If Coriolanus is also very dangerous man, then it is in different ways and for different reasons. He doesn't share Caesar's vaulting political ambition. To the contrary, it seems pretty clear that his handlers keep setting him up for a job he doesn't particularly want. The amassing of personal political power doesn't motivate him.

It underscores the different natures of the two men that Caesar couldn't wait to get to the Senate because he wanted to be crowned, while Coriolanus couldn't wait to get to the Senate because he wanted to escape from the common folk. Caesar wanted to be among his fawning admirers. Coriolanus wanted to be among his aristocratic pals.

If Coriolanus is, indeed, a very dangerous man, then it is that deep affection for and commitment to the traditional order that makes him so. That traditional order tells him that a natural structure governs things. And it creates a world that makes sense to him.

It is a world where the aristocrats decide what's best. It is a world where defending the realm is the highest and best use of a man's life. It is a world in which the commoners shut up and do what they're told. For Coriolanus, these things follow like the irresistible logic of a syllogism.

These convictions make him very dangerous because they override all other considerations. The people point to their stomachs and say they are starving. Coriolanus points to the social order and tells them to remember their place. Would such a man really deprive the people of their liberties? In a heartbeat, we must conclude. In a heartbeat.

And, yet, in the end, Will taunts us with the possibility that Coriolanus might be both dangerous and right. When Rome faces an existential threat, the common folk have no idea what to do about it. They need Coriolanus on that wall. He gives his life for a country that has betrayed him because he clings to an ideal of honor and loyalty that the rest of us treat like a punch line. His is the noblest corpse of all.

With all that said, I don't join with those who see *Coriolanus* as some sort of personal endorsement of aristocratic attitudes on Will's part. On that reading, Will uses the play to tell us something. And, as I've said before, I think Will uses his plays not to tell but to ask. The question he leaves us with here is a particularly knotty one.

A famous quotation attributed to Ben Franklin says: "Those who would give up essential liberty, to purchase a little temporary safety, deserve neither liberty nor safety." Like many of Franklin's quotations, it's a pretty one. But, in *Coriolanus*, I think Will asks us whether we really believe it's true.

And he asks us to ponder how we will feel about it when the Volscians are at the gates.

Closing Time

"To the Elements Be Free"

The Tempest

Backdrop

Scholars generally agree that Shakespeare wrote *The Tempest* in 1610–1611 and that it's probably the last play he wrote alone. A traditional reading sees it as a valedictory play that draws a connection between Prospero's resignation of his magical powers and Will's departure from the creative wizardry of playwriting. When we encounter Shakespeare at the bar at this point in his career, the argument goes, we join someone in semi-retirement. He keenly feels his mortality. He will pass from the earthly stage to the celestial one in 1616.

The play certainly has moments that could reinforce such an understanding. Prospero's most famous speech makes the interpretation hard to resist:

> Our revels now are ended. These our actors,
> As I foretold you, were all spirits and
> Are melted into air, into thin air;
> And like the baseless fabric of this vision.
> The cloud-capped towers, the gorgeous palaces,
> The solemn temples, the great globe itself,
> Yea, all which it inherit, shall dissolve,
> And, like this insubstantial pageant faded,

> Leave not a rack behind. We are such stuff
> As dreams are made on, and our little life
> Is rounded with a sleep. (IV:1:165–175)

It sure sounds like we find Will stepping away from "the great [G]lobe itself," perhaps even (to borrow from *King Lear*) crawling toward death.

But is any of that right? Harold Bloom dismisses the interpretation as romantic nonsense. He notes that in 1611 Shakespeare was only forty-seven; he went on to write substantial parts of at least three more plays. And it makes no more sense to see Prospero as a thinly disguised portrait of Will than it makes to see Dr. Faustus as a thinly disguised portrait of Christopher Marlowe.

I said in the last chapter that a misjudgment of *Coriolanus* would conclude that Will "was tired when he made it." In the same vein, I don't think that we find in *The Tempest* any of the weariness of enterprise that might characterize an exhausted playwright's final push through the creative grind. To the contrary, *The Tempest* seems to me a play full of fresh ideas and energy.

Its opening event is "ripped from the headlines"—shipwrecks on exotic islands were in the news in Will's time. And *The Tempest* is one of his few plays where Will did not rework an existing historical or literary source; instead, we get here the product of his own wild and wonderful imagination. The play that most closely resembles it in this sense is *A Midsummer Night's Dream*, a relatively early work that scholars generally date to 1595. In sum, *The Tempest* may show us an artist at full maturity, but it hardly shows us a haggard and hoary one.

These days, readings and productions of the play don't just strive to keep Will young; they seek to make him our contemporary and give him a modern perspective on the issue of colonialism. A substantial body of modern criticism explores the theme, specifically in Prospero's seizure of the island from Caliban, the lone indigenous figure, who claims title to it through his mother, the witch Sycorax. This take on things invites a sympathetic view of Caliban, whom Prospero has put under the yoke of his unwelcome rule.

Again, Harold Bloom takes a contrarian view, dismissing any such reading as politically correct drivel. If Will wanted to portray Caliban sympathetically, then he did a very poor job of it, Bloom argues. After all, the play casts him as foul, bestial, crude, and an aspiring rapist. No noble savage here, Bloom contends; just plain savage.

In this brief concluding chapter, I'm going to shift our attention in a slightly different direction. I want to focus us instead on an issue that I believe Will quite plainly wanted us to ponder in our engagement with *The Tempest.* It's an issue that benefits from a viewing through the lens of the law.

It's the issue of freedom.

And it's the question of whether true freedom is something we can know within this mortal coil.

Dilemmas of Freedom

In a short essay published by the Folger Shakespeare Library in 2022, Professor Judith Spicksley noted that a close study of Will's poems and plays reveals some 163 references to slaves. Although Shakespeare uses the term both literally and figuratively, and in a variety of contexts, Spicksley observes that he consistently employs it to invoke notions of arbitrary and absolute power over someone who has no capacity to change their circumstance. In this sense, she adds, Shakespeare's use of the term "prefigures the eighteenth-century rhetoric that would drive abolition."

The Tempest is one of Will's plays most rich in the language of slavery. The spirit Ariel's first words on appearing before Prospero are "All hail, great master!" and Prospero addresses him as "Thou, my slave." The bestial Caliban is more truculent, but he too understands his position and Prospero repeatedly refers to him as his slave both in and outside of his presence. That both Ariel and Caliban are unwillingly and unhappily enslaved to Prospero is entirely unambiguous.

The matter of how Prospero came to enslave both Ariel and Caliban seems equally unambiguous. He wanted them in his service. He had the power to enslave them. So he did.

In both relationships, Prospero casts himself as a benign master, apparently insensitive to the oxymoron. When Ariel tells Prospero that he longs for his liberty, Prospero reminds him of his prior condition. Sailors transported the witch Sycorax and her son, Caliban, to the island; Sycorax brought Ariel as her servant, but he proved too "delicate" to perform her dreadful commands; so Sycorax imprisoned Ariel in the cleft of a pine tree, where he suffered until the witch died and Prospero released him. In short, Prospero says: You owe me.

Ariel does not argue the point—he is, after all, a delicate spirit averse to conflict. But, to the extent that Prospero sees his release of Ariel as an act of liberation, he is deeply confused. True, he has relieved Ariel from the agonies of being trapped inside the pine tree, but Ariel knows nothing like freedom. And Prospero's relationship with Ariel lacks the grace we associate with liberation. It is instead transactional: Ariel has a debt to pay and Prospero holds him to it.

Prospero's argument with respect to Caliban is different. In Caliban's case, the slavery is punitive. Everyone agrees on the basic facts: When Prospero first arrived on the island, he and his daughter Miranda treated Caliban very well, even inviting him into their home. But then Caliban tried to rape Miranda—an offense for which he shows no contrition—and Prospero cast him out into the rocks and into hard physical labor.

Like Ariel, Caliban seems to go from one form of bondage to another. Enslaved by Prospero, he becomes infatuated with the shipwrecked Stephano and pledges his loyalty to him. That Caliban is also deeply confused about the nature of liberation is reflected in his celebration of these developments. In one breath, he calls out: "Freedom, high-day! High-day, freedom! Freedom, high-day, freedom!" In the next breath, he refers to Stephano as his "new master."

Will thus shows us a world in which both the enslaver and the enslaved have incoherent notions of what it means to be free. One way of reading *The Tempest* is that the narrative moves us from a place of slavery (and confusion over its meaning) to a place of freedom (and celebration of its fulfillment). After all, by the end of the play both Caliban and Ariel have been turned loose from their bonds. But, as in every story Will has to tell us, things are not quite so tidy.

It is true that, when the play concludes, Caliban no longer lives under the heel of Prospero. But that has less to do with Prospero granting Caliban his freedom and more to do with Prospero deciding to abandon the island. Caliban achieves such freedom as he has only because his master has lost interest in enslaving him. And he has lost interest in enslaving him only because he has no further use of the man or the place.

Still, we might think of Caliban as receiving something very close to complete and perfect freedom. After all, the lone source of restraint upon him—Prospero—has departed and has left him to his own devices. Caliban can now install his own rules or, if he prefers, no rules at all.

And, indeed, what need does Caliban have of law? After all, law governs humans in relationship with each other. The play suggests that Caliban now occupies the island alone, the restored monarch of his kingdom of one. He has become a law unto himself.

But is Caliban truly free? As a corporeal being (unlike Ariel), he remains subject to the burdens of physical survival. So, while Prospero's departure saves Caliban from gathering wood for his master, it does not save him from gathering wood. And it might seem to us that Prospero leaves Caliban enslaved to the most terrible master of all: loneliness.

Only Ariel, who is pure spirit, knows complete and perfect freedom on his release. "To the elements be free," Prospero commands him at last. We might think of Ariel as dispersing and dissolving into a thousand different places, unbound, servant to no one and nothing, not even to the vagaries of flesh.

In the law, we worry a great deal about freedom. We worry about how to protect it from infringements by the state. We worry about how to shield it from violations by other people. We worry about how to cabin it so it doesn't encroach on the freedom of others. We worry about how to define it, how to dispense it, and how to defend it.

If we understand *The Tempest* as a play that is at least in part about freedom—which I think we must, given the arc of its narrative and how it concludes—then we need to ask what it has to say to us on the matter. Or, more properly, because (again) Shakespeare prefers questions to declarations, we need to discern what it *asks* us about freedom. My own view is that it poses some deeply provocative questions, especially about what it might mean for us to be free.

Can we achieve the freedom that Caliban finally knows? Would we want to? It is true that in the end Caliban answers to no man and to no law, but surely we have to wince at the cost. The wild expansiveness of Caliban's freedom derives from the total absence of other people. His liberty looks horrifically like solitary confinement.

Can we achieve the freedom that Ariel knows? Would we want to? It is true that Ariel knows perfect and complete freedom, but only because he is pure spirit. So long as we remain physical, mortal beings, perfect and complete freedom will elude us. Some form of bondage goes with the territory of human existence.

One of Robert Frost's poems includes the memorable line: "For this is love and nothing else is love." We might think of Ariel's release in the same way: For this is freedom and nothing else is freedom—or at least nothing else is freedom in the perfect and complete sense. We gain that sort of freedom only at the cost of becoming pure unbounded spirit, released to the elements.

In short: Unalloyed freedom comes only in the company of death. In all other contexts, the content of freedom gets negotiated. And some negotiations come out better than others.

The freedom we can know in this life doesn't get sorted in a romantic fantasy. It gets sorted in tragedies and histories and dark comedies, where the ways in which we use our limited freedom turn out to be an endless source of problems, puzzles, and predicaments. We can make Ariel completely and perfectly free in an extravagant exercise of imagination, precisely because it works nothing like that in real life.

In real life, freedom gets left to the rough machinery of human decision-making.

It gets left to accident and circumstance.

It gets left to politics and to the uses and abuses of power.

It gets left to law. Such as it is.

They're extinguishing the candles at the Tabard Inn. It's been a lovely conversation, but it's time to head home. There is so much more to say, so much more to discuss, so much more to ask.

Still, we don't need to mourn the absence of Will's company.

He will go with us.

He always does.

Bibliography

General

For texts of the plays, I relied on the updated editions published by the Folger Shakespeare Library, Washington, DC. For dating and source information about the plays, I relied primarily on the websites of the Folger Shakespeare Library and the Royal Shakespeare Company and the biographical and critical texts cited below. For background biographical information about William Shakespeare and historical information about Elizabethan and Jacobean England, I relied primarily on Jonathan Bate, *Soul of the Age: A Biography of the Mind of William Shakespeare* (New York, NY: Random House, 2010); Bill Bryson, *Shakespeare: The World as Stage* (New York, NY: HarperCollins, 2007); Stephen Greenblatt, *Will in the World: How Shakespeare Became Shakespeare* (New York, NY: Norton, 2016); and Michael Wood, *Shakespeare* (New York, NY: Basic Books, 2003).

For background critical analysis of the plays, I relied primarily on Harold Bloom, *Shakespeare: The Invention of the Human* (New York, NY: Penguin, 1998); Marjorie Garber, *Shakespeare after All* (New York, NY: Pantheon 2004); and Emma Smith, *This Is Shakespeare* (New York, NY: Pantheon, 2019). For other analyses of connections between Shakespeare and the law, I also consulted Daniel Kornstein, *Kill All the Lawyers? Shakespeare's Legal Appeal* (Princeton, NJ: Princeton University Press, 2005); Kenji Yoshino, *A Thousand Times More Fair: What Shakespeare's Plays Teach Us about Justice* (New York, NY: HarperCollins, 2012); and Bradin Cormack, Martha C. Nussbaum, and Richard Strier, eds, *Shakespeare and the Law: A Conversation among Disciplines and Professions* (Chicago, IL: University of Chicago Press, 2016).

Introduction

Books, Articles, and Podcast

"Barry Edelstein on the Old Globe's Henry 6," *Shakespeare Unlimited* podcast 242 (August 12, 2024), https://www.folger.edu/podcasts/shakespeare-unlimited/completing-the-canon-barry-edelstein-old-globe-henry-six.

Martha Carlin, "The Bard at the Tabard," *Times Literary Supplement* (September 24, 2014).

Martha Carlin, "Shakespeare the Roisterer at the Tabard Inn," *Shakespeare Documented*, https://shakespearedocumented.folger.edu/resource/document/shakespeare-roisterer-tabard-inn (last updated January 25, 2020).

Neville Coghill, ed. and trans., Geoffrey Chaucer, *The Canterbury Tales* (2003).

"Shakespeare, Chaucer, and the Tabard Inn," *Shakespeare Unlimited* podcast 28 (July 15, 2015), https://www.folger.edu/podcasts/shakespeare-unlimited/shakespeare-unlimited-episode-28.

Chapter 1

Book

William Ian Miller, "In Defense of Revenge," in *Medieval Crime and Social Control*, ed. Barbara A. Hanawalt (Minneapolis, MN: University of Minnesota Press, 1999).

Case

Brown v. Entertainment Merchants Association, 564 U.S. 786 (2011).

Chapter 2

Books and Articles

Russell Fraser, *Young Shakespeare* (New York, NY: Columbia University Press, 1988).

Stephen Greenblatt, *Tyrant: Shakespeare on Politics* (New York, NY: Norton, 2018).

John Julius Norwich, *Shakespeare's Kings* (New York, NY: Touchstone, 1999).

Peter Westen, "The Empty Idea of Equality," 95 *Harv. L. Rev.* 537 (1982).

Case

Walters v. Radiation Survivors, 473 U.S. 305 (1985).

Chapter 3

Books and Articles

Kwame Anthony Appiah, *Experiments in Ethics* (Cambridge, MA: Harvard University Press, 2008).
Don Herzog, *Sovereignty RIP* (New Haven, CT: Yale University Press, 2020).
Len Niehoff and Shannon Hickey, "A Law at War with Itself: Character Evidence and the Doctrine of Chances," 50:4 *Litigation* (September 2024).
Len Niehoff, *Evidence Law: Concepts and Insights* (St. Paul, MN: West Academic, 2016).
John Julius Norwich, *Shakespeare's Kings* (New York, NY: Touchstone, 1999).

Rule

Fed. R. Civ. P. 404.

Chapter 4

Books and Articles

Frederick S. Boas, *Shakespeare and his Predecessors*, (London, England: John Murray, 1896).
D. M. Cohen, "The Jew and Shylock," 31 *Shakespeare Quarterly* 53 (Spring, 1980).
Christopher Marlowe, "The Jew of Malta," in *The Complete Plays*, eds. Frank Romany and Robert Lindsey (London, England: Penguin, 2003).
Richard Posner, "Law and Commerce in *The Merchant of Venice*," in *Shakespeare and the Law: A Conversation among Disciplines and Professions* (Chicago, IL: University of Chicago Press, 2016).

Chapter 5

Books and Articles

Coppelia Kahn, "*Julius Caesar*: A Modern Perspective," in William Shakespeare, *The Tragedy of Julius Caesar* (Washington, DC: Folger Shakespeare Library, 2011).
"The Robben Island Shakespeare," *Shakespeare Unlimited* podcast 1 (June 26, 2013), https://www.folger.edu/podcasts/shakespeare-unlimited/robben-island-shakespeare.
Thomas Jefferson, letter to William Stephens Smith (November 13, 1787), https://www.monticello.org/research-education/thomas-jefferson-encyclopedia/tree-liberty-quotation.

Kate Tummarello, "Debunking the Patriot Act as It Turns 15," *Electronic Frontier Foundation* (October 26, 2016), https://www.eff.org/deeplinks/2016/10/debunking-patriot-act-it-turns-15.

Case

Terminiello v. City of Chicago, 337 U.S. 1 (1949).

Chapter 6

Books and Articles

Nancy Ehrenreich, "Attempt, Merger, and Transferred Intent," 82 *Brook. L. Rev.* 49 (2016).
T. S. Eliot, "Hamlet and His Problems," in *The Sacred Wood: Essays in Poetry and Criticism* (London, England: Methuen, 1920).
"Shakespeare's Laws: A Justice, A Judge, A Philosopher, and an English Professor," in *Shakespeare and the Law: A Conversation among Disciplines and Professions* (Chicago, IL: University of Chicago Press, 2016).
Robert Traver, *Anatomy of a Murder* (New York, NY: St. Martin's, 1958).
Jeffrey R. Wilson and Henry F. Fradella, "The Hamlet Syndrome," 1:16 *Law, Culture & the Humanities* 82 (2020).

Case

Commonwealth v. Carter, 481 Mass. 352 (2019).

Chapter 7

Book

Charles T. McCormick, *Handbook of the Law of Evidence* (Indianapolis, IN: Bobbs-Merrill, 1954).

Cases and Rules

Bell Atlantic Corp. v. Twombly, 550 U.S. 544 (2007).
Commonwealth v. Almeida, 433 Mass. 717 (2001).
Snyder v. Phelps, 562 U.S. 443 (2011).
Fed. R. Evid. 401.

Chapter 8

Books and Articles

Jacques Boettcher, MA thesis, "A History of the Criticism of Shakespeare's *Measure for Measure*" (1953), https://archive.udmercy.edu/handle/10429/460.
Martha C. Nussbaum, *Hiding from Humanity: Disgust, Shame, and the Law* (Princeton, NJ: Princeton University Press, 2006).
Evan Thomas, *The Man to See* (New York, NY: Simon & Schuster, 1992).

Case

Committee on Legal Ethics v. Printz, 416 S.E.2d 720 (W. Va. 1992).

Chapter 9

Books and Articles

Jean-Paul Sartre, *Existentialism Is a Humanism*, trans. Annie Cohen-Solal (New Haven, CT: Yale University Press, 2007).
Harlan Fiske Stone, "The Conscientious Objector," 21 *Col. Univ. Q.* 253 (1919).

Cases

Cantwell v. Connecticut, 310 U.S. 296 (1940).
Jones v. Opelika, 316 U.S. 584 (1942).
Walker v. City of Birmingham, 388 U.S. 307 (1967).
West Virginia State Bd. of Educ. v. Barnette, 319 U.S. 624 (1943).

Chapter 10

Cases

Citizens United v. Federal Election Commission, 558 U.S. 310 (2010).
Dobbs v. Jackson Women's Health Organization, 597 U.S. 215 (2022).
Dred Scott v. Sandford, 60 U.S. 393 (1857).
Roe v. Wade, 410 U.S. 113 (1973).

Chapter 11

Book

T. S. Eliot, "Hamlet and His Problems," in *The Sacred Wood: Essays in Poetry and Criticism* (London, England: Methuen, 1920).

Rules

ABA Model Rules of Prof'l Conduct 1.1, 1.2. 1.3, 3.3, 3.8.

Closing Time

Article

Judith Spicksley, "Shakespeare and the Language of Slavery," Folger Shakespeare Library Fellow essay (June 14, 2022), https://www.folger.edu/blogs/shakespeare-and-beyond/shakespeare-language-of-slavery.